FootprintItalia

Rome

Julius Honnor
Marina Spironetti
Charlotte Vaudrey

Introducing the city

About the city

The ancient city

Centro Storico

Vatican City & Prati

Trastevere & around

Contents

Villa Borghese & Tridente

Trevi, Quirinale, Monti & Esquiline

Day trips from Rome

Practicalities

About the authors

Julius

Charlotte

Marina

Writer and photographer **Julius Honnor** has written and photographed for books on Naples, Verona, Tuscany, Umbria and the Marche, Bologna and Turin. He rented a flat in the heart of Trastevere to help write this book and didn't want to leave.

Milan-born photojournalist and writer **Marina Spironetti** learnt to love Rome during her university days and has been a regular visitor ever since. She is now London based, although she spends most of her time travelling. Her reportages are regularly featured on Italian and English newspapers and magazines. She is currently working on a photographic book about Italy's less-known traditions and festivals.

Charlotte Vaudrey first felt the compelling need to live in Rome while working in Amsterdam on the staff of an interior architecture and design magazine. Deciding to trade in everything she had for everything she missed, she gave up racing round after architects and artists in Tokyo, St Petersburg and beyond to find herself inundated with freelance commissions, and sunlight-seeking friends. Crediting her Jamaican-Argentian genes for her taste for travel, Charlotte lived in New York, Paris and Delft before hitting Italy.

Acknowledgements

Julius Thanks to everyone who helped with suggestions, especially for all those bars and restaurants; thanks to Chiara for making us feel so at home; thanks to short lets for being great; thanks to Marina and Charlotte for sharing the joys and the pains; thanks to Olivia, Paul, David, Nerea, Melger and Juanna for paying us restorative visits. And thanks to Clair for all her sacrifices, help, enthusiasm and an unceasing love of Rome and Romans.

Marina Special thanks to Stefania Gatta and Alessandra Smith from ENIT for their kind assistance; Alessandra Neri and Carla Ceccarelli from Colline Romane for their precious help while touring the Castelli Romani; Cinzia Saccardo for her much-appreciated tips on nightspots; my dear friends Stefano and Giorgio for their hospitality during my stay in Rome; Tim Allen and Stefania Lippolis for introducing me to the culinary delights of the Prati area; my dear mum for her priceless support.

Charlotte Thanks to the following individuals for their valuable assistance: Elyssa Bernard, Gianfranco D'Angelo, Luisa Berio, Raffaella Cappella, Johnny Serra Caraciolo, Luciano Chisini, Flavia Corteggiani, Angela Dialetto, Cinzia Farias, Mario Gammino, Mimmo Laganà, Chiara Mammì, Cory Natale, Massimo Natale, Roberto Pucci, Leighton Rees, Barbara Ricci, Franco Severino, Maurizio Taliano, Massimo Valentini.

About the book

The guide is divided into five sections: Introducing the city; About the city; Around the city; Day trips from Rome and Practicalities.

Introducing the city comprises: **At a glance**, which explains how the city fits together by giving the reader a snapshot of what to look out for and what it distinct from other parts of the country; **Best of Rome** (top 20 highlights); **A year in Rome**, which is a month-by-month guide to pros and cons of visiting at certain times of year; and **Rome on screen & page**, which is a list of suggested books and films.

About the city comprises: **History**; **Art & architecture**; **Rome today**, which present different aspects of life in the city today; **Nature & environment** (an overview of the landscape and wildlife); **Festivals & events**; **Sleeping** (an overview of accommodation options); **Eating & drinking** (an overview of the city's cuisine, as well as advice on eating out); **Entertainment** (an overview of the city's cultural credentials, explaining what entertainment is on offer); **Shopping** (what are the city's specialities and recommendations for the best buys); and **Activities & tours**.

Around the city is then broken down into six areas, each with its own chapter. Here you'll find all the main sights and at the end of each chapter is a listings section with all the best sleeping, eating & drinking, entertainment, shopping and activities & tours options plus a brief overview of public transport.

Map symbols

Informazioni / Information		Monumento / Monument	
Luogo d'interesse / Place of Interest		Stazione Ferroviaria / Railway Station	
Museo/Galleria / Museum/Gallery		Escursioni a piedi / Hiking	
Teatro / Theatre		Metropolitana / Metro Station	
Negozi / Shopping		Mercato / Market	
Ufficio postale / Post Office		Funicolare / Funicular Railway	
Chiesa Storica / Historic Church		Aeroporto / Airport	
Giardini / Gardens		Universita / University	
Percorsi raccomandati / Recommended walk			

Picture credits

Marina Spironetti pages 1, 2, 3, 6, 9, 10, 20, 58, 61, 81, 83, 132, 140, 145, 146, 154, 155, 156, 157, 161, 190, 198, 201, 205, 207, 209, 217, 248, 261, 262, 263, 270, 271, 272, 273, 274, 277, 281.
Julius Honnor pages 2, 9, 11, 13, 14, 15, 17, 26, 33, 36, 38, 44, 45, 52, 54, 56, 62, 64, 67, 68, 69, 70, 72, 77, 78, 86, 88, 90, 91, 99, 101, 103, 105, 114, 131, 143, 144, 152, 157, 164, 166, 168, 170, 173, 174, 175, 176, 178, 179, 180, 181, 183, 185, 186, 187, 188, 189, 204, 225, 226, 228, 250, 253, 254, 255, 256, 257, 258, 259, 268, 282, 283.
Charlotte Vaudrey pages 2, 9, 16, 92, 100, 104, 110, 111, 118, 124, 126, 231.
tips pages 47: foodanddrinkphotos.com;
page 200: Donnata Pizzi; pages 202, 210, 237:
Andrea Pistolesi; page 264: Aris Mihich.
Shutterstock pages 3, 9, 220, 221: 4745052183;
page 11: Denis Babenko; page 12: tkachuk;
pages 12, 34: markrhiggins; pages 15, 31, 42: Luciano
Mortula; page 21: Christian Noval; pages 28, 39, 139:
javarman; page 29: StijntS; pages 30, 107: Andre Nantel;
page 31: page 32: GJP Holdings, LLC; page 40: lexan;
page 43: Kirill Trifonov; pages 41, 74, 106, 125: Eugene
Mogilnikov; page 73: iofoto; page 94: Massimo Merlini;
pages 95, 116: Vicente Barcelo Varona; page 109: sokolovsky;
page 127: Konovalikov Audrey; page 134: Konstanttin;
pages 148, 233: Francesco Dazzi; page 149: Vit Kovalcik;
page 151: Martijn Smeets; page 152: Bryan Busovicki;
pages 159, 222, 227: pippa west; page 162: Shutterschock;
page 163: Pål Espen Olsen; pages 123, 172, 206: Ackab
Photography; page 192: Dino; pages 195, 197: Mauritius;
page 224: Joerg Humpe; page 264: Khirman Vladimir.
Superstock pages 36, 79, 232, 236: age fotostock;
page 41: Bridgeman art library; pages 120, 158: Superstock inc.
Kami Spa page 247.
David Tepper for The Beehive pages 50, 240, 243.
Pado Frisina for The House of Love & Dissent page 244.
Dominique Bollinger for Daphne Inn page 238.
The Rocco Forte Collection pages 212, 213.
Landmark Trust page 214.
Pineider page 219.
Andrea Kim Mariani/AltaRoma page 18.
P.Tauro,Romaeuropa Festival 2008 page 49.
Wikipedia page 112.
Penguin Press page 24.
**Steerforth Press of Hanover,
New Hampshire, USA** page 24.

Veer Front cover.
Veer; Javerman/Shutterstock Back cover.

Contents

A bright mural on Via Fra' Albenzio,
near the Vatican Museums.

Introducing the city

The past seems more recent in Rome. With history oozing out of every deep-fried rice ball, the world's one-time *caput mundi*, the capital of the world, still lives among its ancient stones and their accompanying ghosts.

Rome's Baroque splendours and over-the-top ornamentation give it romantic cinematic backdrops. Anita Ekberg striking dripping-fountain poses might seem like silliness in another city but here the weighty seriousness of centuries of importance gives Rome an unmatchable substance; an operatic sense of glamour.

Whether you are walking Roman roads, worshipping at the shrines of the Renaissance, spending euro millions in fashion palaces or sipping *aperitivi* on pretty piazzas, it is a city that wears its history proudly on its flaking sleeve. And though many of its extraordinary ruins are worryingly dilapidated, the openness of its stones to the weather, the traffic fumes and the tourists is also democratizing, bringing the ancient world to the door of every café, bar and cheese shop.

Cleaned and opened up for the millennium, and daring to be new, Rome has shaken off some of its conservative skin and increasingly rivals Milan for stylishness. But while the city's bars, hotels and restaurants become slowly hip, the city's inward-looking traditions mean that local identities are retained, and chain stores and corporations largely resisted. Among the gleaming new museums and arts showcases there are still places closed for stagnant "renovation". There is a sense that Rome is a city beginning to look to the future, while, of course, living with the past.

At a glance
A whistle-stop tour of Rome

View of St Peter's dome from the terrace of the orange tree garden near Santa Sabina all'Aventino.

Famously built on seven hills, Rome sits on either side of the Tevere – the river Tiber – with the main city centre on the east bank, Trastevere and San Pietro to the west.

Rome was founded on the Capitoline and Palatine Hills: these, together with the Roman Forum between them, make up the heart of the city's ancient remains. To the north and west is the centro storico, the heart of modern Rome, partly enclosed in a bend of the river. To the north and east, the Tridente, so-called because of the three main roads that stretch out from piazza del Popolo, includes many of the city's shopping hotspots, and down to it slopes the centre's biggest park, the gardens of the Villa Borghese. Across the river to the west, St Peter's Basilica is the focal point of the Vatican, home of the Pope and the huge Vatican museums. Still on the west bank of the river, to the south, Trastevere is a pretty area of cobbled streets filled with bars and restaurants. To the east of the historic centre, in the Quirinale, Monti and Esquilino, the sights are slightly less densely packed, but it's easier to escape from the crowds and there are plenty of local shops and restaurants as well as some spectacular churches. To the south, the Aventino is a smart residential hill, whereas Testaccio, beyond, is a grittier area, being slowly gentrified, with some great eateries.

The lowdown

Money matters
B&Bs offer the best value for accommodation in the city. Staying in one of these out of high season, not going to too many sights and eating pizza by the slice you could get by on €100 per person per day. Eat out and see some more sights and that will quickly rise to €150, while €200 a day would allow a little more in the way of style.

Opening hours & holidays
Away from the main shopping streets, many shops still close for lunch, opening 0930-1300 and 1530-1930, and also close on Sundays. Much of the city empties out to the coast in August, leaving most smaller shops closed for at least a couple of weeks. Museums and archaeological sites often open on Sundays but close on Mondays instead.

Tourist passes
There is no single card or ticket for Rome's many museums and sights, though various options group together a few attractions over a few days. None are great value, and they often don't even allow repeat visits. For €20, the Roma Archeologia Card is valid for a week and is worth considering if you want to see the Forum, the Colosseo, the Caracalla Baths and the Appian Way. The Roma Pass, €23, is valid for three days and covers public transport, free entrance to the first two museums or sites and discounts to subsequent ones. For an extra €2, Roma&Piú extends into the province of Rome. These cards can be purchased online or from tourist information offices, all participating museums and sites, and at Fiumicino (international arrivals, Terminal C) and Ciampino (international arrivals) airports.

Tourist information
Roma C'é (romace.it) is the best listings magazine. Available weekly from news stands for €1.50, it has a good English language section in the back. **Wanted in Rome** (wantedinrome.com) is an entirely English language magazine aimed at Anglophone ex-pats in the city with articles and adverts for language lessons and accommodation. **Enjoy Rome** provide a private alternative to the city-run tourist information at Via Marghera 8, T06-445 1843; enjoyrome.com. **In Rome Now** (inromenow.com) is a good online what's on site in English.

Above: A cyclist rests in piazza del Popolo. Below: Casina dell'Orologio.

Introducing the city

Forum & around

Rome's ancient core was the centre of the empire, where its emperors lived and erected their great buildings of state, temples and monuments. Bounded by the Colosseum to the east, the Circus Maximus to the south and the Imperial Fora to the north, the area is also home to the huge marble 19th- and 20th-century national monument, the Vittoriano, towering over the traffic chaos in piazza Venezia.

Michelangelo designed the piazza Campidoglio, also on the Capitoline Hill, where the wonderful Capitoline Museums hold some of the best finds from the Roman Forum. The Forum itself is a feast of triumphal arches, temples and basilicas, where the important business of empire was once carried out. Beyond is the Palatine Hill, where rich and powerful Romans built extravagant villas. The extraordinary Colosseum is at the bottom of Mussolini's busy via dei Fori Imperiali, connecting it to piazza Venezia.

Celio, just to the east of the Colosseum, is a newly hip area, with good cafés and wine bars as well as some ancient churches.

Aventine, Testaccio & Ostiense

Smart and surprisingly peaceful, the Aventine Hill rises just to the south of the Circus Maximus, with large houses and gardens, some notable churches and a famous view through the keyhole of the Priorato di Malta. In contrast, Testaccio, to the south, has a younger feel, with bars and restaurants dug into Monte Testaccio, a giant Roman rubbish tip, or set up in the city's ex-slaughterhouse. To the east, the enormous Baths of Caracalla continue to crumble slowly, while further south, beyond the Pyramid of Caius Cestius, working-class Ostiense has the fascinating juxtaposition of ancient statuary displayed in a disused power station.

Centro Storico

Since Roman times the focus of the city has moved north, and the area between via del Corso and the river is tightly packed with many of the city's essential sights. But there are further reminders of antiquity here: the Pantheon is a breathtaking well- preserved ancient Roman building. The smart Baroque Rome of piazza Navona is here too, complete with elaborately cascading fountains: Nearer the river, Campo di Fiori is a more earthy, vibrant space, with a market in the mornings and bars and cafés that spill out into the piazza in the evening. West of here, narrow streets are packed with small boutiques; to the south, the Ghetto area retains some of its Jewish roots. To the east are the parliament buildings and the via del Corso, the main shopping street, running north to south.

Vatican City & Prati

Across the river, the Vatican City is a separate state within the city. Dominated by the vast hulk of St Peter's, it has its own elaborately uniformed guards, postal service and huge museums, which incorporate two of the great works of Western

Piazza del Campidoglio at night.

Vatican museum.

Between the two hills, increasingly fashionable Monti is an attractive area of cobbled streets with plenty of low-key bars and restaurants.

Hanging the washing out in Vicolo del Cedro, Trastevere.

culture: the Sistine Chapel, painted by Michelangelo, and the Raphael Rooms. Nearby are two landmarks on the river: the Castle of Sant'Angelo and the Palazzo di Giustizia.

Trastevere & around

Once Rome's bohemian district, gentrification and high property prices have taken away some of Trastevere's edginess, but it remains wonderfully picturesque, with greenery growing across the cobbled streets, washing hanging out to dry, and cafés, bars and restaurants opening up on pretty piazzas that buzz with life late into the night. There are churches and a couple of museums to explore, botanical gardens, and, from the Gianicolo Hill, great views across the city.

In the middle of the river, Isola Tiberina is one of the reasons that Rome was founded here, as it made the crossing of the Tiber relatively easy. It has some of the oldest surviving Roman bridges and good views up and down the river.

Villa Borghese & around

From piazza del Popolo, running south, via di Ripetta, via del Corso and via Babuino make up the shopping area of the Tridente. Across them are smaller streets such as via Condotti, packed with arresting window displays and designer-label retail opportunities. To the east, the Spanish Steps are a favourite of wedding photographers and leg-weary tourists. Beyond, via Vittorio Veneto was once the centre of *la dolce vita* and is still home to expensive hotels. North of here rises the park of the Villa Borghese, with winding paths through the greenery and an excellent gallery.

Trevi, Quirinale, Monti & Esquilino

Once the home of popes, the area to the east of the city centre houses the Palazzo Quirinale, the palace of the president, and Palazzo delle Esposizione and the Scuderie del Quirinale. There are more grand buildings on the Esquiline Hill, as well as Santa Maria Maggiore, one of the city's most important churches. Between the two hills, increasingly fashionable Monti is an attractive area of cobbled streets with plenty of low-key bars and restaurants. The startling extravagance of the Trevi Fountain is almost always surrounded by crowds of visitors.

Day trips from Rome

Outside the city centre, via Appia Antica, the ancient Appian Way, was once Rome's most important road. It still has a plethora of ruins, tombs and catacombs along its route south, out into the countryside. EUR, a suburb built by Mussolini, has stark architectural attractions of a more modern kind, as well as a good museum of Roman civilization.

Near Rome, Ostia Antica, the ancient port, is a beautiful and remarkably well-preserved Roman city, bearing comparison with Pompeii. Nearby are the beaches of Rome's rather ugly modern coastline.

Roman emperors went to Tivoli for their holidays, and the enormous, sprawling complex of the Villa Adriano – the villa of Hadrian – can be visited just outside the town. In Tivoli itself are other ancient remains and the extraordinary fountain-soaked gardens of the Renaissance Villa d'Este.

The wine towns of the Castelli Romani, in the nearby hills, make cool escapes from the city. Further afield is Viterbo, one of Lazio's most attractive towns, with some good Etruscan sites close by.

Best of Rome

Top 20 things to see and do

❶ Colosseum & Roman Forum
The structure that for many is the icon of the whole of ancient Roman history is an extraordinary building, remarkably intact and strikingly large. A model for all modern stadiums, a new museum adds to its allure. In the nearby Forum are the evocative ruins of the ancient city centre. Page 66.

❷ Capitoline Museums
On one of the hills on which ancient Rome was founded, some of its best relics are preserved in a brace of museums, set either side of a stunning piazza designed by Michelangelo (see page 72). A much-photographed head, hand and foot, probably belonging to a huge statue of Constantine, are among the highlights. Page 73.

❸ San Clemente
The church of St Clement is not the grandest of the city's many religious buildings, but it may be the most fascinating. It's an exceptional archaeological microcosm of Rome's history: on two levels below the beautiful medieval church is a much earlier fourth-century church, and, further down, two ancient Roman buildings. Page 76.

7 View through the keyhole, Piazza Cavalieri di Malta.

❹ Pantheon

Marvelled at for 2,000 years, and almost completely unaffected by the passing of time, the Pantheon is awe-inspiring. Its design – complexity masked by simplicity – still staggers modern architects and sightseers alike. Page 114.

❺ Jewish Ghetto

In the heart of the city, the Ghetto area retains some of its Jewish businesses and atmosphere. It's also notably unspoilt, with narrow cobbled streets of artisan workshops and bookshops as well as some excellent restaurants. Page 98.

4 Inside the Pantheon.

❻ A concert at Auditorium

Among Rome's few contemporary buildings, this is a great spot to listen to classical music in one of the armadillo-like concert halls. Around Christmas there is the added attraction of an ice-skating rink in the middle of Renzo Piano's iconic space. Page 199.

❼ Through the keyhole

One of Rome's most famous views is through a small hole in the door of the Villa Malta, home to the Grand Priory of the Knights of Malta, on the Aventine Hill. Designed to line up perfectly along the garden, giving a perfect view of St Peter's at the end of an avenue of trees, it is one of the city's unexpected pleasures. Page 80.

❽ Pyramid of Cestius

In the traffic-heavy and rather unlikely setting of piazzale Ostiense, one of ancient Rome's most unusual structures is also one of the best preserved. The 36-m marble-clad pyramid, the tomb of Caius Cestius, sits at the corner of the Non-Catholic Cemetery, home to numerous cats and the bodily remains of Keats and Shelley. Page 81.

8 The Pyramid of Cestius.

Exuberant fans at a Rome derby.

⑨ Football match at the Olympic stadium
The rivalry between Rome's two teams, AS Roma
and Lazio, is intense, and both play at the city's
Stadio Olimpico. Nothing beats the high tension
and drama of a derby between the two, but
the ground sharing means that there is a home
game here every weekend through the season.
The Italian national team sometimes plays here
too. While you're here, have a look around the
Fascist-era statues of the Foro Italico.

⑩ Basilica di San Pietro
Centre of the Catholic Church, St Peter's is a grand
statement in the country-within-the-city of the
Vatican. Visit on a Wednesday to see the Pope give
a weekly public address in the colonnaded piazza
outside. Page 149.

⑪ Sistine Chapel & Raphael Rooms
Michelangelo supposedly lay on his back here for
four years to paint his astonishing *Creation* on the
ceiling. Goethe put it well when he said, "Without
having seen the Sistine Chapel one can form no
appreciable idea of what one man is capable of
achieving." The frescoes in the four Raphael Rooms
are only slightly less astounding. Pages 158 and 160.

⑫ A Roman pizza
Neapolitans will tell you that they're not the
genuine article, but Romans are very proud of their
wafer-thin, burnt-at-the-edge pizzas. The best
ones come with a noisy, chaotic atmosphere
thrown in at one of the city's traditional pizzerias

⑬ Aperitivi & a meal in Trastevere
The cobbled streets of the right bank of the Tiber
have long been some of Rome's most sociable

places, and though these days the area is hardly undiscovered, there are still plenty of spots to drink and eat among the city's young and fashionable. Bars spill out into the open air under washing hung across the streets around via della Scala and piazza Santa Maria in Trastevere, while the narrow back streets have some great traditional eateries and literary cafés. Page 180.

⑭ Shopping trip in the Tridente
Whether you're window shopping or splashing the cash, the smart shops of the Tridente are the place to be. Via Condotti and the surrounding streets are packed full of Italian fashion and smart homewares. Afterwards you may feel the need for a rest on the nearby Spanish Steps. Page 204.

⑮ Ara Pacis
One of Ancient Rome's most famous and beautiful monuments, the quality of the stone carving on Emperor Augustus's Altar of Peace is startling. And, though many in the city would not agree, Richard Meier's light and airy modern structure, which now houses it, provides both a counterpoint and a suitably striking setting. Page 122.

⑯ Galleria Borghese
One of the city's best museums and galleries, the Borghese has an excellent collection of Baroque and Renaissance art, including paintings by Titian and Caravaggio, plus the added advantage of being at the edge of the Villa Borghese, central Rome's best green space, with winding paths, bikes, boats and lovers. Page 196.

⑰ An ice cream from one of Rome's top gelaterias
Nobody should leave the Eternal City without having experienced a *gelato Romano* – some of the world's best ice cream. Even in winter the gelaterias do a good trade, but once the sun comes out in spring it's practically de rigueur to be seen with one. Fior di Luna in Trastevere and Gelato di San Crispino is the best: so precious about the purity of it's flavours that they don't do cones. Page 184.

⑱ Santa Maria Maggiore
Built on the Esquiline Hill in the fifth century, the most impressive of Rome's four papal basilicas has the tallest campanile in the city and a wealth of artistic and religious treasures, from 1500-year-old mosaics to the tombs of several popes. Page 233.

⑲ Trevi Fountain
An exaggerated Baroque cliché it may be, but the Trevi Fountain, despite the overbearing security guards and permanent crowds, is required viewing. Of all Rome's fountains (and there are many), nothing quite matches this for enormous, dramatic exuberance, or cinematic heritage. Page 225.

⑳ Ostia Antica
Though not half as famous as Pompeii, the ancient remains of Rome's one-time port are just as impressive. The huge site, protected for hundreds of years by the silt of the Tiber, includes a 3000-seater stadium, frescoes and countless mosaics and temples. Page 256.

15 Ara Pacis.

20 Roman bakery in Ostia Antica.

Month by month

A year in Rome

Rome fashion show.

January

Snow in Rome is rare, though it does sometimes happen. Cold crisp days are more common, though even in January (the coldest month of the year) the average maximum temperature is 11°C. Nights are colder, on average dropping to 5°C. At the end of the month, *AltaRomaAltaModa* (altaroma.it) is a short fashion season with events in Auditorium (see page 199) and other locations in the city. It also runs in July. Presents are given to children on the 6th to mark Epiphany.

February

Carnevale, the week before Lent, is celebrated with confetti and costumes and *frappe* (deep-fried, sugar-dusted biscuits). As in January, at night the temperature falls to around 5°C, but already, with the lengthening hours of daylight, it rises to around 13°C during the day. Italy play rugby matches in the Six Nations tournament at the Stadio Olimpico.

March

For the first time since October, the sun appears from behind the clouds for an average of six hours a day and the temperature climbs to a fairly pleasant 15°C. The *Maratona di Roma* (Rome Marathon, maratonadiroma.it) takes place around the middle of the month, with thousands of runners pounding the city streets in Italy's biggest participative sporting event. To celebrate the onset of spring, the *Mostra delle Azalee* involves adorning the Spanish Steps with around 3000 pots of azaleas. For one weekend, the FAI (Fondo per l'Ambiente Italiano, fondoambiente.it) organizes free tours of churches and monuments that are usually closed to the public.

Tip...

Rome is a year-round city with little in the way of a low season. January, February and November are probably the quietest months, though many locals also clear out in August and head for the coast.

April

On Good Friday the Pope leads a procession around the Colosseum. Then, on Easter Sunday, he leads prayers outside St Peter's. The first really warm days usually happen, with the average daily high temperature hitting 19°C. Restaurants set up their tables on the pavements and trade picks up in the city's gelaterias. It's prime season for Rome's most characteristic vegetable, the globe artichoke. The *Settimana dei Beni Culturali* is a week of free entrance and tours of museums and monuments, to celebrate the anniversary of the founding of Rome on the 21st. The day itself is celebrated with music and fireworks. *FotoGrafia* (fotografiafestival.it) is an international photography festival, which takes place in the Museo di Roma in Trastevere and various other locations around the city through to May.

May

Broad beans are traditionally eaten – especially on *il primo maggio* (1 May), which is a holiday – often with some *pecorino romano*, the most Roman of cheeses. The Rome Masters tennis championships (internazionalibnlditalia.it) are held on clay courts at the Foro Italico. For a short period, the rose gardens above the Circus Maximus on the Aventine Hill are open to the public. Rome's literary festival, *Letterature* (festivaldelleletterature. it), runs from May into June, with international writers and music.

Introducing the city

June

The first ripe figs start to appear in the markets, alongside melons, peppers, aubergines and courgettes. Evening jazz concerts begin in the gardens of Villa Celimontana (see page 78), and run until September. On the Isola Tiberina is an open-air cinema (isoladelcinema.com) set up in summer (take insect repellent), and a temporary restaurant. Other events around the city also begin as part of *Estate Romana* (estateromanacomune.roma.it). *Fiesta* (fiesta.it) is a celebration of Latin American music and dance. To mark the anniversary of the proclamation of the Italian Republic on 2 June, the Quirinale Gardens, part of the presidential palace, are open to the public for one day only.

July

Bars are set up alongside the river for Lungo Er Tevere, and are a cool, bustling place to hang out in the evenings. In Trastevere it's also time to party, at the annual *Festa de' Noantri* event. In the middle of the day it's often too hot to do very much – Romans take long siestas and plan their August escape to the beach. The temperature hits 30°C on the average day and doesn't sink below 20°C at night; it can get unpleasantly hot.

August

Much of Rome decamps to the hills or the coast, leaving the sweating city to the tourists. *Ferragosto*, the Feast of the Assumption, is the hub of the holiday month, when almost everything shuts down. If there are any Romans around then, you may find them eating the traditional meal of chicken and peppers. August continues to be hot and, as in July, it seldom rains, though when it does there are often thunderstorms.

A street vendor selling roasted chestnuts, aka *"caldarroste"* on fashionable via Condotti, near the Spanish Steps.

September

La Notte Bianca (lanottebianca.it) is a celebration of the official end of summer, with all-night entertainment and shopping. One of the most pleasant months to be in the city sees temperatures around 26°C by day and 17°C by night. There are, on average, 25 dry days in a Roman September. *RomaEuropa* (romaeuropa.net) is a festival of music and dance that runs until December.

October

Chestnuts gathered in the Italian hills are roasted in the streets, and markets – and restaurant menus – begin to fill with autumn fare such as porcini mushrooms. Stars of the screen descend on the city for Rome's international film festival (romacinemafest.org).

November

Usually the wettest month of the year, though there are often beautiful warm sunny days, and dry days outnumber wet ones by nearly two to one. *Vino* *novello*, wine from the current year's grapes and Italy's answer to *Beaujolais nouveau*, arrives, often from the nearby vineyards of Lazio. Look out for *fave dei morti* – traditional biscuits that mark the *Giornata dei Defunti*, the day of the dead, on the 2nd, when families traditionally visit the graves of their relatives. You'll find *broccolo romanesco* – a strange-looking conical cauliflower – in the markets, and the fresh pressing of the new olive harvest should become available. It's also the second season of the artichoke.

December

Another cool and sometimes wet month, even in December it's quite possible to have relatively warm days: the average high is 13°C, but 19°C has been known. An ice-rink is set up in the middle of Renzo Piano's Parco della Musica and continues right through January. On the Capitoline Hill, the Basilica di Santa Maria in Aracoeli is the scene of a popular Christmas ritual. The 124 steps up to the church from piazza Venezia are lit by candles, and bagpipers play seasonal music to the crowds; at midnight the *Gloria* is sung and a carving of the baby Jesus is paraded to a nativity in one of the side chapels. Other Christmas activities include a candlelit mass with Gregorian chant in the Pantheon and midnight mass in the Basilica di San Pietro, delivered by the Pope. There's a Christmas market in piazza Navona, with a carousel, stalls selling water features and woodcutters for your nativity scene, fresh doughnuts and lots of plastic tat.

Christmas market.

Screen & page

Rome in film & literature

Roma Città Aperta (Rome Open City)
Roberto Rossellini, 1945

A brutally honest account of wartime resistance and a masterpiece of neorealism. It was 1945, just months after the liberation from the Nazis, when Rossellini took to the streets of the working-class Prenestino quarter, shooting almost entirely on location, mainly with available light, and capturing the real devastation of war. The film took the world by storm and earned Rossellini the Grand Prix at the first Cannes Film Festival in 1946.

Ladri di Biciclette (Bicycle Thieves)
Vittorio de Sica, 1948

Another masterpiece of neorealism, set against the backdrop of a war-ravaged Rome. American Academy Awards introduced a tailor-made award for the film as, at the time, there wasn't a 'best foreign movie' category.

Roman Holiday
William Wyler, 1953

Audrey Hepburn plays a bored princess who manages to escape her guardians and falls in love with an American reporter (Gregory Peck). The sequence of the two riding a Vespa through the streets of Rome is an icon of American cinema.

Accattone
Pier Paolo Pasolini, 1961

An insight into Rome's poorest ghettoes and a merciless account of the lowest class of Roman society – those who live 'beyond the last stop'.

La Dolce Vita (The Sweet Life)
Federico Fellini, 1960

A superb portrait of a dreamlike Rome: an unforgettable image of the glamorous, paparazzi-fuelled life of the 1950s and a celebration of decadence. The movie became a worldwide sensation and elevated the iconic status of the city, continuing to inspire tourists to visit several decades later. The sensual image of Anita Ekberg in the Trevi Fountain, beckoning Marcello Mastroianni, is probably the film scene that first springs to mind when one thinks of Rome.

Mamma Roma
Pier Paolo Pasolini, 1962

Actress Anna Magnani (who had starred in *Roma Città Aperta*) plays an ex-prostitute determined to make a fresh start for herself and her son Ettore against the backdrop of Rome's seedy suburbs.

Caro Diario (Dear Diary)
Nanni Moretti, 1993

Three witty yet sad autobiographical vignettes by cult film director Nanni Moretti. The part that sees Moretti zooming around the deserted streets of the Garbatella district on his Vespa reflects his passion and loving devotion to his home town. The long panning shots of modern Roman architecture are among the most beautiful scenes of contemporary Italian cinema.

L'Ultimo Bacio (The Last Kiss)
Gabriele Muccino, 2001

A romantic drama about entering adulthood, which explores infidelity and fear of commitment. The sequel is due to be released in 2010.

Le Fate Ignoranti (The Ignorant Fairies)
Ferzan Özpetek, 2001

This is one of the few Italian movies with a gay theme. When a doctor is killed in a car crash, his wife discovers he's been cheating on her with a man.

Bright Star
Jane Campion, 2009

A drama that explores the love pains of Romantic poet John Keats during his romance with Fanny Brawne in the three years leading up to his death.

Introducing the city

Fiction

Il Piacere (The Pleasure)
Gabriele d'Annunzio, 1889

The debauched life of the Roman aesthete Andrea Sperelli provides a wonderful exploration of a sensual, decadent Rome.

The Girl on the Via Flaminia
Alfred Hayes, 1949

Robert, a young American soldier stationed in Rome, falls for a pretty Italian girl against the backdrop of post-war Italy, in a thoughtful tale of loneliness, love and redemption.

A Woman of Rome
Alberto Moravia, 1949

Moravia is one of the 20th century's most acclaimed writers. He creates a biting portrait of Fascist Italy in the story of Adriana, a Roman model and prostitute, and the men in her life.

That Awful Mess on the Via Merulana
Carlo Emilio Gadda, 1957

This beautifully written detective story set in fascist Rome is considered Gadda's masterpiece – a tale that shows how the demand for justice can crash into the complexity of fate and the elusiveness of truth.

Non-fiction

Commentarii de Bello Gallico (The Conquest of Gaul)
Julius Caesar, c 50 BC

Caesar's own vivid and exciting account of his campaigns through Europe from 58 to 51 BC, his military strategies and his encounters with locals.

The History of the Decline and Fall of the Roman Empire
Edward Gibbon, 1776-1788

A classic book, whose title is self-explanatory. If you think you won't get through its six volumes, there is always an abridged version.

Italian Journey
Johann Wolfgang von Goethe, 1817

One of the greatest writers of all times perfectly captures the greatness of ancient Rome and the vibrancy of his own time in his account of his Italian travels in the 1780s.

Daily Life in Ancient Rome
Jerome Carcopino, 1941

This extraordinarily detailed study gives an insight into the beliefs and customs of Imperial Rome. Carcopino focuses on the details of everyday life in the Eternal City to create a backcloth against which the social, political and cultural aspects of ancient Rome are presented.

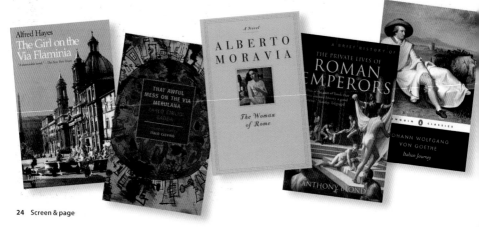

The Private Lives of the Roman Emperors
Anthony Blond, 2008
This is a revealing, scandalous exposé of the life of the Caesars: a must-read for those interested in understanding what was really going on in ancient Rome.

For children
The Ruthless Romans
Terry Deary, 2003
Part of the 'Horrible Histories' series, this book reveals all the terrible truths behind the greatest empire of all times. A great, funny read for kids and parents alike.

A Time in Rome
Elizabeth Bowen, 1960
An evocative account of the few months the Irish writer spent in Rome. What's best is the way Bowen manages to capture the atmosphere of the place. This is definitely not an ordinary guidebook, but an elegant yet amusing portrait of the city.

Hortus: The Roman Book of Gardening
John Henderson, 2004
A selection of texts on Roman horticulture, from Virgil to Pliny – beautifully translated by Henderson. Great for all gardening fanatics.

The Colosseum
Keith Hopkins and Mary Beard, 2005
A very special guidebook to Rome's most famous landmark, filled with interesting anecdotes.

Mussolini's Rome: Rebuilding the Eternal City
Borden W Painter Jr, 2007
Benito Mussolini, together with figures such as Augustus and Pope Sixtus V, was one of the great transformers of Rome. This book tells how one man managed to put his imprint on the city, from archaeological sites to public housing, in his drive to create a suitable backdrop for the new fascist empire.

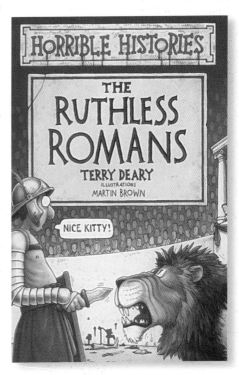

Contents

About the city

View from the Vittoriano.

History

Legends & beginnings

The story goes that Romulus and Remus were the twin sons of the Vestal Virgin Rea Silvia – the daughter of a local king, Numitor, a descendant of Aeneas – and the god Mars. Having broken her vows of celibacy, Rea Silvia was imprisoned, and orders were given that her children should be killed. A servant, however, took pity on the babies and instead laid them in a basket beside the Tiber. The waters rose and they were cast adrift on the river, from where they were rescued and raised by a she-wolf – the creature that remains the symbol of the city today.

The two brothers were later found and raised by a shepherd, and grew to be leaders of a tribe, which they decided to settle on the two hills above the river where they had been abandoned. But there were arguments between them about who should control and name the new city; eventually Romulus killed Remus, and the city was named after him.

Historians generally believe that Romulus was a mythical figure, created as the city's founder and named after it. Others, pointing to ancient walls uncovered on the Palatine Hill, which tie in with details of the myth, say that whether or not he was suckled by a wolf, he may indeed have existed in some form. More prosaic anthropological studies of the origins of the first Romans have suggested that they may have come from outside the Italian peninsula. Accounts from the time speak of a large percentage of fair-skinned and blonde-haired people, leading some to suggest that their origins may have been to the north.

Centred on two easily defended hills, the Palatine and the Capitoline, above a river crossing via an island in the Tiber, Rome was a natural site for habitation, about 30 km upstream from the sea. Legend dates the city's founding, very precisely, to 21 April 753 BC; archaeology backs up this timescale, at least approximately, confirming that in the eighth century BC there was indeed a settlement on the Palatine.

Rome began to grow, until it spread across the city's famous seven hills: the Palatine, Capitoline, Aventine, Caelian, Esquiline, Viminal and Quirinal. Its expansion was often at the expense of its neighbours. Inviting a local tribe, the Sabines, to a festival, the Romans proceeded to kidnap their women – this was the so-called rape of the Sabine

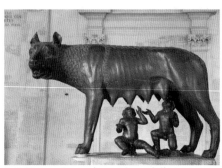

Capitoline she-wolf.

women, much featured in Roman art. A battle followed in which Rome gained the upper hand, setting the pattern for the following centuries.

Roman texts speak of seven ancient kings, ruling from 753 to 509 BC, starting with Romulus. At least two of these, Tarquinius Priscus and Tarquinius Superbus, were Etruscan, though historians disagree about the level of Etruscan influence over the city. In these early centuries the line between history and legend is blurred, but what can be said without doubt is that the Etruscans were the most powerful civilization on the Italian peninsula during the early days of Rome, and that the Romans adopted many of their innovations. They built the huge *Cloaca Maxima* (see page 68), Rome's first drain, making the lowland Forum area inhabitable, between the Palatine and Capitoline Hills. Many aspects of Roman culture were also taken from the Etruscans, who held chariot races, built thick walls around their towns and used the arch extensively in their architecture. Some even believe that the name 'Rome' itself may have come from the Etruscans. However, around 509 BC, the people of Rome rose up against the tyranny of the Etruscan king Tarquinius Superbus and overthrew him, setting up a republic in his place.

Republic

The Roman Republic set the scene for the world-conquering greatness of the empire that followed. It was a complex, clever and relatively democratic system, with balances designed to prevent any ruler achieving absolute power. During this period, Rome grew from a central Italian power to become the dominant force around the whole of the Mediterranean.

Under the unwritten constitution of the republic, the Senate had control of the coffers, directing both foreign affairs and civil administration. In theory it merely advised magistrates, but in practice its edicts were followed. *Senatus Populusque Romanus*, or SPQR ('the Senate and the Roman People'), symbolizes the

Manhole cover.

democratic balance of the republic and remains the motto of the city today: it can be seen inscribed everywhere, from buildings to manhole covers.

Councils and assemblies drawn from the Roman population enacted laws and elected magistrates. Society was divided into classes, but even the plebeians had their own council, and for centuries this system evolved and coped with competing powers. The heads of government were the consuls, elected in pairs for a fixed term of a year. Each consul had the power of veto over the other, preventing any one person from dominating political life. Despite such checks and balances, however, a number of powerful patrician families tended to control the political scene. Eventually, discord between this wealthy Roman aristocracy and the rest of the population brought about a constitutional crisis, and the system collapsed.

By the first century BC Rome had established its supremacy in the Mediterranean and was extending its empire across Europe. Julius Caesar, a ruthless and successful military leader, conquered Gaul and, in 55 BC, Britain. On his return to Rome he became one of the three dominant figures in Roman politics, part of a ruling triumvirate with Gnaeus Pompeius Magnus (Pompey) and Marcus Licinius Crassus. Crassus was killed in 53 BC, leaving Caesar and Pompey as heads of rival factions. In 49 BC the Senate ordered Caesar, who was once again in Gaul, to disband his army before returning to Rome for re-election as consul, but he famously broke Rome's treason laws by leading his troops

About the city

Above: Emperor Augustus. Opposite page: Trajan's Column.

across a small stream, the Rubicon, and south through Italy to Rome, sparking civil war. He defeated Pompey, who fled and was murdered in Egypt. Caesar became the lover of the Egyptian queen Cleopatra, and, after more military triumphs, returned to Rome a hero.

Elaborate celebrations followed, and Caesar invested in new building and restructuring of the Forum in the heart of the city. In some ways, his brief period as Rome's most powerful man was a successful one – he reduced poverty and, as well as erecting new buildings, he also reformed the Senate. He created the 365-day year, with a leap year every four years, and shifted the calendar to fit with the seasons. Naming his great-nephew Gaius Octavius (Octavian) as his successor, he changed the way the Roman world of the future would operate. His downfall, however, came as a result of the extent of his aggrandizement, having been declared first Imperator and then Dictator in perpetuity. In one of the most notorious episodes of Roman history, Caesar was murdered in the Senate by a group of conspirators, including his friend Brutus, who inflicted 23 stab wounds on him.

Instead of bringing peace and stability, as the conspirators had hoped, Caesar's murder brought chaos and civil war. The middle and lower classes had regarded him as a hero and were not well disposed towards his assassins. Marcus Antonius (Mark Antony), an ally of Caesar, took advantage of this and formed an alliance with the 19-year-old Octavian. Together with another of Caesar's loyal allies, Lepidus, they fought and defeated Brutus and Cassius and together formed a second ruling triumvirate. Julius Caesar was deified, celebrating his memory but also raising the status of his chosen successor. Once again, peace was not to last long, and after Mark Antony had married Caesar's ex-lover Cleopatra, war broke out between Octavian and Antony. Defeated, Antony and Cleopatra killed themselves in Alexandria; victory for Octavian resulted in him becoming the first Roman emperor, taking the name Augustus Caesar.

Empire

Augustus reigned from 27 BC until his death 41 years later. It was one of the longest and most successful reigns of all the Roman emperors. Wary of what had befallen his predecessors, Augustus ruled carefully and wisely, presiding over the so-called *pax romana*, the Roman peace. The Ara Pacis (see page 122), one of the great monuments of Rome, was built to celebrate this peace. Much of the city was rebuilt, taxation was reformed and an extensive road network spread across the Italian peninsula. For most of the Mediterranean region it was a time of stability and calm.

Careful leadership was not the way of all emperors, however, and the ruler's unprecedented powers meant that he could wield enormous influence, both benign and malign. Though this left the system open to misrule, it was also the time of Rome's greatest glories, as each emperor sought to leave his mark on history with ever grander buildings and monuments. By the second century AD, Rome had become a city of between one and two million inhabitants – a size unequalled anywhere in the world until the 19th century. The extent of the lands controlled from Rome was also at its maximum: it became, in effect, the world's first superpower.

Following Augustus were his stepson Tiberius and then Tiberius's great-nephew Caligula. Neither was without his achievements, but they are largely remembered for paranoia, persecution and insanity. After Caligula's murder, another relative, Claudius, succeeded him, a reluctant but thankfully low-key and sane leader. The same could not be said of the last of the Julio-Claudian dynasty, Nero. Though his reign was quite successful abroad, and he built up the city's cultural infrastructure, he is usually depicted as a tyrant who persecuted the early Christians and had his mother and adopted brother executed.

The Great Fire of Rome struck in July of AD 64. Starting in shops at the southern end of the Circus Maximus, it badly affected 11 of the city's 14 districts. The story of Nero fiddling while Rome burned is certainly apocryphal: some contemporary sources have him singing on stage, but others say that he was out of Rome at the time and rushed back to organize relief. In the aftermath of the fire, Rome was rebuilt on an even grander scale than before, with houses constructed of brick on wider roads to avoid a repeat of the disaster. The rebuilding included Nero's huge golden palace, the Domus Aurea (see page 237), which incorporated a 30-m statue known as the Colossus.

Whatever the real extent of Nero's cruelties, he was certainly not popular, and he eventually killed himself to avoid being murdered by his enemies. After a year of chaos between 68 and 69 AD, his eventual long-term successor was Vespasian, a military man and the first of the Flavian dynasty. Vespasian won over the Roman public by demolishing Nero's palace and building a huge public entertainment structure in its place, the Flavian Amphitheatre, commonly known today as the Colosseum (see page 70) after the huge statue that stood in front of it. Originally of Nero, the statue was adapted over time to portray subsequent emperors.

The short reign of Titus coincided with the destruction of Pompeii in AD 79. When he died in 81, his brother Domitian took over. Though Roman accounts describe Domitian as a tyrant, modern historians give him some credit for the peaceful, stable second century that followed his reign. He certainly made enemies, however, and in AD 96 he was murdered.

The second century AD saw the Roman Empire at its height, stretching from Babylon to the Atlantic coast, and from the edge of the Sahara to Hadrian's Wall. The five emperors who followed Domitian oversaw a period of wealth and calm. Nerva restored some freedoms to the people and the Senate, but it was Trajan who was held in the highest esteem, and all successive emperors were inaugurated with the prayer "*Felicior Augusto, melior Traiano*" ("Luckier than Augustus, better than Trajan"). Trajan expanded the empire to its largest extent and also added new buildings and monuments to the centre of Rome. He was generally tolerant of Christians, leaving them alone unless they were openly practising their religion. Other emperors were less forgiving of Christianity, and thousands were killed.

Hadrian followed Trajan and defended his conquests, notably by building a wall across northern England. Antoninus Pius continued in

a relatively peaceful vein, though his successor, Marcus Aurelius, had to deal with raids along the northern border of the empire.

The golden period came to a halt with the reign of Marcus Aurelius's son, Commodus, who was insane by the time he was murdered in AD 192, and the beginning of the empire's decline can perhaps be traced to this point. Much of the third century was marked by crisis. The huge empire was hard to govern, the sources of easy income had dried up, and numerous emperors came and went: 25 in less than 50 years. Diocletian, who took over in 284 and reigned until 305, alleviated some of the problems, but also took the decision to split the empire in half, creating two emperors and two centres of power. The system proved unworkable and collapsed into internecine struggle and civil war.

Diocletian is also notable for the most widespread, and probably most vicious, persecution of Christians, which did nothing to stop the spread of the faith. After his reign it began to be more accepted, culminating with the conversion of Emperor Constantine and the adoption of Christianity as the official Roman religion.

Constantine founded Constantinople, previously Byzantium, as the 'second Rome' and for a century or so there were times when one person controlled both halves of the empire, but the last attempt at unification died with Theodosius in 395. The Western Roman Empire ended in 476, when the last emperor, Romulus Augustus, was forced to

abdicate by Odovacer, who became the first Germanic king of Italy. In Constantinople the Eastern Roman, or Byzantine, Empire continued to exist in some form until the Ottomans finally overthrew it in 1453. For Rome, however, its time as the *caput mundi*, the capital of the world, was over.

Medieval Rome & the Holy Roman Empire

When the Visigoths, led by Alaric, sacked Rome in 410, it was seen as the definitive fall from grace of a once-great city. In reality, the city was already a shadow of its former self, the population reduced and its monuments in a state of decay. This process continued through the rest of the century, with further plundering by the Vandals.

The last monument to be erected in the Roman Forum, the column of Phocas (see page 67), was added at the beginning of the seventh century, but by then the recycling of Roman buildings was well under way, and the column itself was from an earlier period. When they weren't being trampled by waves of invading forces, the city's old buildings were used as a gigantic source of building materials for new churches – a practice that continued for around a thousand years. Apart from his column, Phocas is remembered for having donated the Pantheon to the Church, thereby saving it from ruin.

As the city's political power ebbed away, the role of the pope became increasingly significant. Rome's position at the centre of Christianity had been established under Constantine, when the Bishop of Rome had been referred to as pope, and from the beginning of the sixth century onwards the primacy of the role was widely accepted. This acceptance, however, was not enough to stop scholars in the ninth century feeling it necessary to forge documents, which came to be known as the False Decretals, purporting to show that from the earliest days of the Christian Church the pope had had dominion over it, and that Constantine had awarded secular power to Pope Sylvester I.

The struggle to assert secular as well as spiritual power has done much to define Rome ever since.

Above: Arc of Constantine. Opposite page: Palazzo Nuovo, one of the Capitoline Museums, designed by Michelangelo.

Initially the papacy as a power relied on the Eastern Roman Empire, but as that weakened it sought to form alliances at home, and increasingly took on secular powers. A new phase in this battle for power in Rome began when Charlemagne was crowned Holy Roman Emperor. In 799, Pope Leo III had been attacked and injured by two noblemen, challenging his power. A subsequent trial declared the legitimacy of his authority and laid the foundations for a bold new power-sharing arrangement. One of the most powerful men in European history, Charlemagne (also known as Charles I of France, Germany, and the Holy Roman Empire) was a Frankish king, the son of King Pippin the Short and Bertrada of Laon. He was already immensely powerful, but giving him the title of Holy Roman Emperor broke Rome away from the influence of the Eastern Empire, gave Charlemagne extra authority and created a new sense of a Europe that simultaneously looked back to Roman glories and embedded Christianity at its heart.

Both pope and emperor were integral to the arrangement, and they were dependent on each other. When this symbiosis worked well it was a powerful marriage: an effective melding of spiritual authority with economic and military might. At many times over the following centuries, however, tension as to which of the two roles took priority boiled over into bloody feuding.

From the mid-12th century, powerful families in Rome were either Guelph (pro-papacy) or Ghibelline (pro-emperor), and the rivalries between the factions were violent enough to turn the city's streets into battlegrounds. In 1309, Pope Clement V decided that he had had enough, and moved the whole papal court north to Avignon, in his native France. Rome was once again bereft of power, largely abandoned to shepherds and their flocks. But battles between the city's families continued. Cola di Rienzo, son of a washerwoman and an innkeeper, whose statue now stands at the foot of the steps up to the Capitoline Hill, launched a rebellion against the lawless nobility in 1347 and became, for a while, the most powerful man in the city.

In 1377 Pope Gregory XI brought the papacy back to Rome, moving it from the Palazzo Laterano to the better-fortified Vatican. A year later, however, he died, and as a new pope was elected in Italy, so a rival pope was ordained in France. It was perhaps the low point of papal rule, a time known as the Western Schism. It was ended in 1414 by the Council of Constance, which conferred legitimacy on the Roman line.

Renaissance

When Nicholas V became pope in 1447 he brought artists and intellectuals into his court, nurturing the beginning of the Italian Renaissance, a cultural and artistic re-birth that embellished the Italian peninsula and made Rome one of the most important places in the world. Both spiritually and temporally, the pope was once again the most powerful figure in the city, and through papal patronage the city's face was permanently changed. Artists such as Michelangelo, Titian and Raphael, and architects such as Bramante, were employed in the city to decorate such masterpieces as the Sistine Chapel, commissioned by Pope Sixtus IV – the first so-called 'pope-king' of the city – and the new St Peter's basilica.

During this artistic flourishing the city continued to be a violent place, and the successors of Sixtus IV had to deal with murder on the streets and, in 1494, French invasion. Popes such as Alexander VI were set on promoting the fortunes of their own families, and as money flowed in the city, corruption increased. The city's ancient ruins were newly appreciated during this period, but with the realization of their value came an increase in plundering. Artistic activity in Rome reached a peak under Popes Julius II and Leo X at the beginning of the 16th century, but it was not long before dissenting voices in northern Europe put an end to the party.

Sack & Counter-Reformation

Pope Clement VII, successor to Leo X, allied himself with France in a bid to throw off the imperial control of the Holy Roman Emperor, Charles V. At least partly in response to this move, in 1527 unruly imperial troops, having defeated the French in the north of Italy, marched on Rome and sacked it, killing most of the papal guard, destroying and looting the city and forcing the pope to take refuge in the Castel Sant'Angelo (see page 159). After months of siege, Clement eventually surrendered and had to pay for his life.

Rome subsequently embarked on another period of rebuilding, though this time the artistic driving force was not the humanism of the Renaissance but rather the Church's reaction to Luther and the Protestants to the north. Luther criticized the corruption of the Church and its obsession with money and decoration, and as the Churches of Germany and England defected, the very existence of the Church in its Roman form was threatened.

Sistine Chapel.

After the failures of Pope Paul IV, who set up the city's Jewish Ghetto (see page 98), his successors cut down on pomp and tried to emphasize the serious nature of the Church, though at the same time creating ever more overblown Baroque monuments. This style was designed both to impress the locals and to act as a counterpoint to the austerity of Protestantism. Their commissions did much to mould the Rome of today, with many of the city's ornate fountains and buildings dating from this period.

Unification

In 1798, during the French Revolutionary Wars, Rome was invaded by Napoleonic forces and became a part of Napoleon's empire. Pope Pius VI was exiled to France, where he died, and Rome was briefly controlled from Paris. The *Repubblica Romana* lasted only two years before papal control was restored in 1800.

Napoleon's Kingdom of Italy, however, established in the north in 1805, sowed the seeds of Italian nationalism. After his defeat, the Congress of Vienna in 1815 decided to return the peninsula's borders to more or less their pre-Napoleonic positions, mainly under the control of the major European powers. The papacy and European governments were largely against unification, which threatened their holdings, but popular sentiment and some powerful radical figures, notably Giuseppe Mazzini and Giuseppe Garibaldi, began to turn the tide toward establishing a single country. Garibaldi was sentenced to death for his part in an uprising in Piedmont and escaped to South America, where he lived for 14 years before returning to play a crucial role (see below).

In 1848, Pellegrino Rossi, the unpopular minister of justice of the Papal States, was assassinated in Rome. As the citizens demonstrated, demanding a democratic government, Pope Pius IX's reaction was to flee the city in disguise. In the power vacuum that followed, the Roman people set up a second Roman Republic. Garibaldi arrived in time to help defend it against the French troops of Napoleon III, who, under pressure from Catholics in France, felt obliged to defend the pope's right to govern. The city, led by Garibaldi, built defences on the Gianicolo hill and repelled the first French attack, though they could not withstand the reinforced second wave. Garibaldi and his troops were allowed to withdraw to San Marino, and Rome was once more under the control of the papacy, defended by French troops, who remained stationed there.

Garibaldi attacked Sicily and worked his way up the peninsula, aided by Camille Cavour, prime minister of Piedmont-Sardinia. For a while, reluctance to attack Rome meant that the city was not included in the nascent Italy, but once the Franco-Prussian War started, Napoleon III could no longer spare his French troops to defend the city. He withdrew them, and the Italian army marched into what was to become the new Italian capital on 20 September 1870, a date immortalized in the names of countless streets all over Italy.

The 20th century

It took some time for the papacy to accept the new order and its almost complete loss of temporal power. It was not until 1929 that Pope Pius XI signed the Lateran Pact, acknowledging the Italian state in exchange for sovereignty over the Vatican and various other churches and palaces around the city.

By that time there was a new figure of power in the city: 'His Excellency Benito Mussolini, Head of Government, Duce of Fascism, and Founder of the Empire'. A politically active socialist until the First World War, Mussolini had returned from fighting for the Allies determined that a 'third way' was necessary. His politics appealed to both aristocrats and the working class by expounding a classless society rather than class war. He marched on Rome with his National Fascist Party in 1922 and took power in a coup, albeit one that had a fairly broad base of support.

Increasingly totalitarian and self-obsessed, Mussolini promoted a new Italian nationalism that harked back to ancient Rome, though he also introduced a minimum wage and votes for women. In the city the fascist period added grand, futuristic architecture, under a regime that gloried in its ancient structures while at the same time bulldozing new roads through many of the monuments. As Mussolini became more dictatorial his regime became increasingly dependent on violence and suppression, and he sided with Hitler's Germany in the Second World War.

Rome was not too badly damaged by bombing in the war, having been declared a demilitarized 'open city' by defending forces after a brief bombing campaign by the Allies, who took it in 1944. In the aftermath of war, Mussolini having been executed, the Italian king Vittorio Emanuele III was forced to abdicate, and Rome became the capital of an Italian republic.

The 20th century saw enormous growth in the city: a population of less than a quarter of a million at unification rose to two and a half million by the millennium. Rome held the Olympics in 1960 and the World Cup final in 1990 and became especially fashionable in the 1960s in the wake of Federico Fellini's era-defining classic film *La Dolce Vita*.

The 1970s were known as the *anni di piombo* ('years of lead') and were a period of extreme instability, with political conflict boiling over into terrorism and violence. In the 1990s the city became the focus of the *mani pulite* ('clean hands') anti-corruption trials, which had some success in cleaning up Italian politics. While national Italian politics have been in an almost constant state of turmoil, governance of the city has been relatively stable, especially under recent mayors, Francesco Rutelli and Walter Veltroni, though Gianni Alemanno, a neo-fascist elected in 2008, is a much more controversial figure. In many cases, investment in the city's monuments has ground to a halt, and the construction of the new metro line has been dogged by interminable delays, but a handful of successful new projects have begun to add some contemporary spice to Rome's venerable streets.

Art & architecture

Architectural history

Built on, in and around the ancient world's biggest, greatest city, the Rome of the last 1500 years has had a hard act to follow. The contemporary metropolis still struggles to cope with the sheer quantity of extraordinary old architecture: the third metro line is continually hitting buried archaeological ruins, and Richard Meier's structure built to enclose Augustus's *Ara Pacis* has been controversial to a degree hard to imagine in any other world capital. In many ways Meier's building encapsulates the Roman dilemma of the 21st century: what to do with a significant past that is everywhere? Mussolini had a stab at creating a new Roman architectural style that looked forward as well as back, and a few notably modern buildings, such as Renzo Piano's Auditorium and the Jubilee Church at Tor Tre Teste have begun to infiltrate the Roman cityscape. But, for the most part, Rome's architectural scene is one that concentrates on its ancient glories.

Building blocks

At the heart of ancient Roman architecture was an understanding of arches, domes, vaults and – vitally – concrete. The extraordinary strength of these structures has enabled many to survive for thousands of years. With the decline and fall of the

Top: Ara Pacis. Above: Piazza del Campidoglio.

empire, many Roman architectural theories were lost, to be rediscovered centuries later.

More pragmatic than the Greeks, and less restricted by notions of beauty, much Roman building was highly practical, creating solutions to issues such as the provision of water, housing and transport. At the same time, competition between families and between rulers meant a constant race to create bigger and more impressive public structures.

Similar to modern Portland cement concrete, Roman concrete was made from quicklime, ash and an aggregate of pumice. It wasn't until the 18th century that anybody managed to recreate it successfully. The dome of the Pantheon, the most stunningly complete ancient monument in Rome, is made from different types of concrete, getting progressively lighter and thinner towards the apex. This helps hold the enormous structure and stops it collapsing under its own weight: a staggering 4535 tonnes.

The Pantheon is one of ancient Rome's most influential buildings, a good example of how Roman architecture was reused by subsequent civilizations, its motifs and structural elements reinterpreted and recycled to become the building blocks of Western architecture. The Pantheon, probably a temple to all the gods, was adapted as a Christian church, which ensured its survival, though it wasn't until the 15th century and the Renaissance that architects such as Brunelleschi began to properly appreciate and pay homage to its brilliance.

Medieval Rome

Early Christian architecture built on Roman foundations (both literally and metaphorically) to begin the creation of a distinctive architectural identity. Columns were brought in from elsewhere to create aisles, fragments of Roman marble were reused as flooring (see box page 75) and building materials from Roman structures were put to new uses. Good examples still exist in the city, including under the Basilica di San Clemente (see page 76).

Renaissance

As the second great centre of the Italian Renaissance, after Florence, Rome has a wonderful heritage of architecture from the period. Michelangelo's design for the piazza del Campidoglio (see page 72) was not finished during his lifetime, but it encompasses much that happened in the city during the period. Turning the focus of the highly significant Capitoline Hill away from the Roman Forum towards the modern city, he incorporated ancient statues into a modern interpretation of classical form, cleverly using an awkward, sloping, trapezoidal space and introducing a grand staircase, the *cordonata*, to emphasize the axis. The paving design includes an oval that is actually egg-shaped – a clever use of perspective to work with the space – and the twelve-pointed star of the original design (only finally carried out under Mussolini's orders) references the pagan zodiac at the same time as the orientation turns towards St Peter's and Christianity.

The two huge statues at the top of Michelangelo's stairs are ancient likenesses of Castor and Pollux, found, repaired and given new prominence at a time when contemporary Italy was beginning to realize the wonder of the ancient past. In some ways, however, the great rediscovery of ancient architecture had a poor effect on the city's ancient ruins, most of which were plundered for raw materials, with columns and stones carted away to build churches and palaces.

Baroque Rome

Much of modern Rome's look and feel comes from its Baroque embellishments: the extravagant fountains in its piazzas are permanently connected with the popular conception of the city, and many of its more heavily decorated buildings come from this period. With the Counter Reformation, a response to austere northern Protestantism, the Church in the 17th century demanded an architecture that was more emotional, more theatrical. The fashion spread and the sombre, classical designs of the Renaissance were swamped in cuteness, cupids and curlicues.

Above: Palazzo Civita di Lavoro,in EUR. Opposite page: Emperor Constantine.

The Fontana di Trevi is the city's most prominent Baroque monument, its operatic exorbitance gilded by its famous cinematic moment: Anita Ekberg wading out into the water. There are plenty more Baroque Roman fountains, and impressive buildings too, including the Palazzo Madama, home to the Italian senate.

Neoclassicism & the 20th Century

With the unification of Italy in 1870, the country once again looked to classical ancient architecture for inspiration. Neoclassicism was an attempt to use Roman style to create a new Italian look. The huge white marble Vittoriano, on the Capitoline Hill – usually called by one of a number of unflattering nicknames – now seems overblown, but it served to remind the newly united Italians of their shared past, as well as ushering in the most notable buildings of 20th century Rome, in Mussolini's fascist style.

Fascism & EUR

Where Roman neoclassical architecture elaborated on ancient forms, the fascist regime that ruled the country from 1922 to 1943 pared the influences back and created a much leaner, more futuristic, and in some ways, more pragmatic style. The EUR district, built for the cancelled 1942 World Fair, was Mussolini's attempt to recast Italian style in a forward-looking way. This suburb, now a business district dominated by cars and offices rather than a brave new world, is ultimately let down by the lack of a human aspect. It has, however, featured in many films, and visually it remains an interesting project. Other notable buildings of the era include the Palazzo della Poste all'Aventino and the Stadio dei Marmi at the Foro Italico.

Modern Rome

In a city centre with almost no new architecture, the Richard Meier building housing the *Ara Pacis*, opened in 2006, was always going to have a tough time, and it has been controversial. As a modern structure it has to contain one of ancient Rome's masterpieces in a way that lights and encases its exhibit without clashing with it, mimicking it or trying to upstage it. There is a certain mirroring of form and substance, a necessary similarity of dimensions, but, on the whole, Meier's neutral design allows the *Ara Pacis* space to breathe, to retain its dignity.

Meier's building uses travertine stone as well as 500 sq m of glass, through which natural light streams on to the monument. To the horror of architects and most visitors to the museum, Gianni Alemanno, Rome's mayor, has vowed to pull the building down, suggesting that a neo-Baroque structure would be more appropriate.

Meier's other contribution to Rome's architecture is more universally admired, partly at least because it was built in an unloved suburb. The Jubilee Church and community centre, formally known as Dio Padre Misericordioso, was built in Tor Tre Teste for the millennium and features three large, sail-like curved walls in a bravely striking design.

Renzo Piano's music venue, the Auditorium Parco della Musica, north of the city centre, has successfully breathed new life into Rome's music scene. Around Christmas the central space between Piano's three armadillo-like auditoria becomes an ice-rink, and the whole structure has a refreshingly approachable feel. It is a rare model of what a contemporary Rome could look like.

Art

The history of art in Rome is largely a history of religious patronage. While many of Italy's great artists were born elsewhere in the country, they were often enticed to the capital by the riches on offer here to decorate its great buildings and churches. Since the Renaissance, artists have also flocked here to study and paint the ruins of the ancient city, both as inspiration and setting. An extraordinary wealth of ancient Roman art lives on in the city's statuary, and in bas-reliefs on arches and pillars that are still standing.

In recent years, the city's plans for a great contemporary art space have been continually thwarted by endless delays to the MAXXI gallery, but growing appreciation means that it is possible to find good 21st-century art in Rome too.

Roman art
The art of ancient Rome owed much to the ancient Greeks – many Roman statues were copies of Greek originals – but also to the Etruscans of central Italy. In Roman times artists tended to have less prestige than their Greek predecessors, art being seen largely as a utilitarian decorative craft and a status symbol. There was, however, no shortage of very good art in ancient Rome, as demonstrated by the huge numbers of statues that survive today. The Capitoline Museums (see page 73), with their fascinating extension in the Centrale Montemartini (see page 82), are a good place to begin to.

Vatican Museums.

understand the superlative skills of Roman sculptors, perhaps the greatest of the ancient artists. Other examples are scattered around the city, on monuments such as Trajan's Column (see page 72). A prime example of the use of art in imperial times, the extraordinary bas-reliefs that wind around the huge triumphal column (for a close-up view, visit the Museo della Civiltà Romana, see page 254) were used for aggrandizement but were almost impossible to see in any detail.

Other good examples of Roman art are the mosaics, frescoes and pottery that can be seen in many of Rome's museums, and in situ in the Forum, Ostia and Tivoli. Landscape, often extolling the virtues of rural life, is one area where Roman artists moved on significantly from the ancient Greeks, developing some understanding of perspective. This was superceded only in the Renaissance, when artists developed a full appreciation of the mathematical rules of perspective. Ancient Romans considered wall painting not to be a 'high art', but very few of their more highly respected panel paintings have survived.

Early Christian art

Carvings and inscriptions of the early Christian period tend to be remarkably primitive in comparison with the fine precision of earlier Roman texts. The city has some fine examples of religious painting, however, including some of the earliest examples of now-familiar Christian iconography. On the Aventine Hill, the doors of Santa Sabina (see page 80) have one of the first depictions of the crucifixion; Santa Maria in Trastevere (see page 172) has one of the oldest images of the Virgin nursing her baby. In San Clemente, a fourth-century church exists below the level of the medieval structure, and includes some wonderful frescoes (see page 76). The catacombs, outside the city, where early Christians buried their dead, also have some early frescoes (see page 251).

Medieval

The medieval period in Rome is characterized by centuries of decorative Byzantine art. Some of the

Detail from Sistine Chapel.

Pietà.

finest examples are glitteringly complex mosaics, in churches such as Santa Maria in Trastevere and San Clemente. Eventually, Roman artists began to break out from the constrictions of the form, and in the 13th century Pietro Cavallini painted in a style that came to be known as Roman naturalism. Cavallini's fresco in Santa Cecilia in Trastevere (see page 176) is an important pre-Renaissance work: it's tucked away from the eyes of most visitors, but extraordinarily ahead of its time in its use of three-dimensional space and composition. Another work attributed to the artist is in San Giorgio in Velabro.

Renaissance
In 1418 the Pope returned to Rome from Avignon, and as the city became increasingly important again, money flowed freely. Though the heart of the Italian Renaissance was in Florence, many of its finest artists came south to Rome, creating some of the world's great masterpieces in the city. Michelangelo and Raphael were the two most prominent, and their masterpieces in the Vatican – the *Capella Sistina* and the *Stanze di Raffaello* – remain the most admired works of art in Rome.

The entwined Renaissance strings of humanism, science, mathematics and art produced paintings and sculpture with a sense of space and light that was revolutionary. At the same time artists looked back to classical Rome for inspiration and rediscovered forms that had been all but forgotten. Most important of all, Rome's Renaissance artists understood something

vital about what it is to be human. For all the awesome wonder of Michelangelo's Sistine Chapel, it is the artist's *Pietà*, in St Peter's, that better embodies something less tangible: empathy.

Baroque
The High Renaissance was a hard act to follow, and art in Rome after the mid-16th century generally declined into the contrivances of Mannerism, an ill-fated attempt to recapture some of Michelangelo's passion. Caravaggio was one glorious exception, and the intense human plasticity of his dark, brooding art enlivens many galleries in the city. The enigmatic artist had a short but never dull career, fleeing Rome in 1606 with a price on his head, having murdered a young man.

Contemporary
Though Rome's acronym-heavy new museums, the still-only-partially-open MAXXI and MACRO, both exhibit contemporary art, the city has some way to go before it is considered a hotbed of modern culture. MAXXI, a huge project in the Flaminio area designed by Zaha Hadid, has suffered innumerable delays and setbacks and has been christened 'the eternal building site'. It should, eventually, fully open as the Museum of the Arts of the 21st Century.

Rome today

You only need a chatty taxi driver to get to know the endless list of problems affecting Rome: constant road works, pollution and regular strikes, not to mention a catastrophic traffic system, which gets even worse whenever there is a football match or a head of state is in town. Rome may not be the best example of efficiency, but it is also true that Italians have a natural tendency to complain. Romans in particular have mastered the art of moaning, stuck as they are between the government on one side and the Vatican on the other. Their problems are, to some extent, undeniable, but it is also true that things are looking brighter than they were, say, 20 years ago.

Rome metro.

Roman Renaissance

Rome is changing – it is speeding up and, above all, it is becoming European. That became clear in April 2005, in the six days between the death of John Paul II and his funeral. A steady flow of over four million mourners thronged towards the Vatican, patiently waiting to pay their respects: a huge number, one and a half times the city's population (2.7 million in 2007). The world was watching – some probably expecting a disaster – but Rome did not just manage, it rolled up its sleeves and succeeded, coping with the crowds without incidents. This was no longer the city of (eternal) chaos; it earned its place in 21st-century Europe.

What everybody saw on those days was the result of a long process of transforming the face of the capital. Before the pope's death, the other major event had been the Holy Year in 2000. Again, the world was watching, and Rome wanted to show a *bella figura*. The mayor at the time was Francesco Rutelli, a centre-left politician who managed to pass the test, allocating funds effectively, creating new structures, cleaning up the city and reopening long-closed museums. This was how it started. The following year the baton of innovation passed to another enlightened centre-left mayor, Walter Veltroni, a hyperactive cinema- and jazz-lover. His commitment would be rewarded with his re-election in 2006 with an unprecedented 61.4%.

Veltroni put the accent on culture and raised the city's profile by staging a series of events. Cinema in particular had a massive boost, with a brand new international film festival (romacinemafest.com), while the city again became a film set (for *Mission Impossible 3*, *Ocean's Twelve* and the TV series *Rome*). Hollywood celebrities flocked to Rome in a way that was said to evoke *La Dolce Vita* – Fellini's masterpiece portraying the city as the playground of the rich and the famous.

Eye-catching new buildings were created by world-class architects – first and foremost Renzo Piano's Auditorium (see page 199), which took the Romans by storm, appealing to both connoisseurs and people who had never set foot in such a place. Not only does it sell more tickets than any other music venue in the world, it is self-funding and profitable – surprising, to say the least, in a country where the arts, sadly, are a financial black hole.

There is enough to keep the Roman intelligentsia happy. But cultural achievements mask civic failures: laissez-faire policies on the city's suburbs have led to urban degradation and the spread of shantytowns filled with illegal immigrants. Although crime is low, the murder of a housewife by a Gypsy in 2007 sparked a rising tide of xenophobia, particularly against Romanians and travellers. This contributed to the election of rightwinger and ex-fascist Gianni Alemanno as mayor in April 2008; he defeated veteran mayor Francesco Rutelli on a surge of support based on his promise to wield an iron fist against illegal immigrants.

Transport problems

More problems. Public transport is painfully inadequate. Uniquely among European cities of its size, Rome has just two metro lines with only one interchange. This may be partly due to over 2000 years of history below the surface, but the existing system does not impress with its efficiency. The *metropolitana* is hampered by vandalism, suffers a plethora of unauthorized buskers and beggars, and the service is not as frequent as it should be. Relying on buses is difficult, if not impossible – they are overcrowded and timetables are random. Suburban trains are not a great help either. Rome has only 195 km of suburban railway, compared to London's 337 km or Paris's impressive 587 km, and the region invests a mere 1.79% of its budget in rail improvement.

In spring 2006 the works for Linea C officially started. This will slice the city from northwest to southeast, right through the most visited areas.

The project sounds great: 30 fully automated trains running 24/7 along 34 km of brand new tracks. In practice, this dream of streamlined efficiency will not come true any time soon. The first part of Rome's third metro line should open by 2012, but work won't be completed until 2015 (needless to say, dates have already been shifted a few times).

So much for the highs and lows of the 'Rome of the Romans'. As for the city of tourists, there is definitely good news. There is more to keep you entertained: the list of events on offer during the long Roman summer is growing longer and longer. And there is more to see: the *Ara Pacis* is now enclosed within Richard Meier's brand-new museum that – love it or hate it – is the first modern architecture in that historical area (see page 122); the equestrian statue of Marcus Aurelius has been given new grandeur in the spacious glass hall in the *Musei Capitolini*. Archaeologists continue to dig along the via dei Fori Imperiali, and the recently opened *Museo dei Fori Imperiali* (see page 71) is probably the most important addition to Rome's new museums. The modern technology behind 3D Rewind (see page 71), inaugurated at the end of 2008, makes it possible to take a virtual stroll around ancient Rome. MACRO's new wing inside the Mattatoio in the Testaccio area provides more room for contemporary art – and so will the MAXXI building, which is scheduled to open by the end of 2009.

Nature & environment

The starling squad

Rome's autumnal evening skies are pockmarked by hundreds of thousands of starlings, wheeling and turning in extraordinary airborne displays of flock dynamics. In alternately stretching and tightening clouds over the Tiber, the starlings' shape-forming is awesomely beautiful, but also a problem for a city increasingly encrusted in bird shit.

In November 2008 a Ryanair plane carrying 168 passengers had to make an emergency crash landing at Rome's Ciampino airport after hitting a flock of starlings, which damaged both of its engines. An average starling weighs only around 75 g, but they fly in flocks of up to 10,000, of which there are often many in the sky at any one time over the Italian capital. It is estimated that there can be as many as five million starlings in Rome every year – the highest population of any Italian city.

The birds, having migrated from the colder climes of northern Europe, gather in Rome after spending the day in the surrounding countryside, attracted by the city's heat island. Cars, statues and riverbanks get coated in a thick layer of guano; a smell of stale aviaries pervades the city, pavements are made impassable and people walk under trees with umbrellas up, even when there's no rain. The city authorities' fairly futile response is a team of

Places to escape to the countryside around Rome

Castelli Romani These towns in the hills near Rome make good bases for walks (see page 270).

Parco dell'Appia Antica The Appian Way combines plenty of historical sites with some open countryside. If you really want to escape from the traffic, head for the part of the park where ancient aqueducts cross sheep-farming territory (see page 250).

Riserva Naturale di Monte Mario Not far from the city centre, 204 ha of greenery and pine woods with views through the trees to St Peter's.

masked, suited and ear-muffed birdscarers, dubbed 'the starling squad', who, at an annual cost to the city of around €120,000, carry machines that amplify the unpleasant sound of the birds' distress call. The screeches punctuate the Roman evenings but seem to do little other than move the birds on to the next tree.

Meanwhile, others are studying Rome's extraordinary aerial shows for what they say about flock behaviour, and have come to conclusions that may have implications for everything from economics to robotics. The dynamics of huge flocks of birds have long mystified and perplexed experts. When under attack from predators such as falcons, the flocks can spread out and then concertina again with exceptional precision, never colliding or losing a single bird from the group. The accepted wisdom was that each individual bird followed all the other birds within a certain distance. But STARFLAG, a three-year study led by an Italian physicist called Andrea Cavagna, mounted multiple cameras on Rome's rooftops, and built three-dimensional computer models of the birds' movements. Cavagna has concluded that distance is not in fact important, and that each bird tracks the movements of exactly seven neighbours, however near or far away they are. This behaviour, using a fixed number of reference points, enables the flock to expand and contract flexibly without losing its shape and without isolating individuals.

The study's conclusions suggest that starlings may be brighter than was previously assumed. STARFLAG's findings are also important for predicting the behaviour of groups of other animals, designing collaborative robot systems, and even for predicting how humans might interact. However, they may not be much help in keeping Rome's cars clean.

Rome's cats

Draped purringly over Roman monuments on countless postcards and calendars, here's where to find the real thing around the city: communities of Roman cats.

Area Sacra di Largo Argentina the Torre Argentina cat sanctuary.

Pyramid Cestius the cat colony of the Non-Catholic Cemetery.

Giardino degli Aranci with views to miaow for.

Festivals & events

January

Epiphany (6th)
La Befana comes down the chimney to deliver presents to Roman children during the night before Epiphany, and puts in an appearance in piazza Navona at the end of the Christmas market.

AltaRomaAltaModa
altaroma.it
The city's fashion festival runs towards the end of the month, with events in Santo Spirito in Sassia, between St Peter's and the river. Strengths include a concentration on fashion publishing, ethical clothes and fashion from around the world, although the centrepiece is Italian haute couture. Exhibitions around the city complement the fashion shows.

February

Carnevale
Carnival is a notably child-friendly event in Rome, with plenty of exuberant fancy dress and the copious throwing of confetti, which blows around the city's piazzas.

March

Festa di Santa Francesca Romana (9th)
St Frances of Rome has been nominated as the patron saint of motor vehicles, and her feast day is marked by taxis, vans and buses turning up to be blessed in front of the Church of Santa Francesca near the Forum.

April

FotoGrafia
fotografiafestival.it
The photography festival includes the Baume & Mercier photography prize and international photography exhibitions in the Palazzo delle Esposizioni, Museo di Roma in Trastevere and various other locations.

Foundation of Rome (21st)
The anniversary of the city's legendary birth in 753 BC is celebrated with parades, fireworks on the Tiber and candles on the Aventine.

Christmas market.

Primo Maggio (1st)
primomaggio.com
May Day is a holiday, and is celebrated with a free concert of indie rock and Italian music outside the Basilica of San Giovanni in Laterano. International acts occasionally put in an appearance.

Festival delle Letterature
festivaldelleletterature.it
There is usually some English-language interest in Rome's literary festival, which runs for about four weeks from May to June, with international writers and music. Each year the festival has an esoteric theme, and most events are staged in the vast Basilica di Massenzio.

June

Estate Romana
estateromana.comune.roma.it
Numerous arts events around Rome are loosely tied together under the guise of the summer festival. From June until the end of September, a huge range of music, dance, cinema and theatre performances take place, often in the open air in parks and historical settings. Some are free.

Fiesta
fiesta.it
A festival of Latin American music and dance runs from mid-June to mid-August at the Ippodromo delle Capannelle, on the via Appia Nuova, to the southeast of the centre.

About the city

Isola del Cinema
isoladelcinema.com

From late June there are open-air screenings of films on the Isola Tiberina, in the middle of the Tiber. New films, previews and themed retrospectives all feature, and the season runs through to September. A temporary restaurant is set up and there are accompanying exhibitions, wine tastings and multimedia events. As part of the festival, showings and events sometimes also take place in Trastevere.

Roma Pride
romapride.it

This gay and lesbian event has so far successfully withstood a political environment that has recently turned more hostile: 500,000 people danced and paraded their way through the city's streets in 2008.

The Music Festival of the Nations
tempietto.it

A programme of classical concerts in the ancient Roman Teatro di Marcello runs from June through to September.

Villa Celimontana Jazz
villacelimontanajazz.com

This jazz festival features al fresco evening concerts in the gardens of Villa Celimontana, and continues until September. Internationally known acts often appear, and the definition of jazz is a fairly loose one – Macy Gray is among those who have previously featured on the bill.

Festa dei Santi Pietro e Paolo (29th)

The feast day of Rome's patron saints, Peter and Paul, is a holiday. The celebrations focus on the two early Christians' namesake churches: San Paolo fuori le Mura and St Peter's. The day is one of the earliest Christian celebrations and was probably superimposed on an earlier ancient Roman celebration honouring Romulus and Remus.

Festa de' Noantri
festadenoantri.it

The Noantri ('we others') are the Trasteverini, the inhabitants of Rome's west bank, and they celebrate their otherness for a week beginning on the third Saturday of the month. Festivities begin with a procession carrying a statue of the Madonna from the Church of Sant'Agata to the Basilica of San Crisogno; there are stalls, games, concerts and street theatre all over Trastevere.

Festival Euro Mediterraneo
festivaleuromediterraneo.eu

The festival runs through much of July and August, with music, opera, dance and theatre in some of Rome's grand ancient ruins, such as the Mausoleo di Cecilia Metella and the nymphaeum of the Villa dei Quintili, both along the via Appia Antica.

Passaggi Segreti
labilancia.it

The Secret Passages series of promenade performances of dramas in ancient sites runs through July and August. The venues change every year, but past productions have included Shakespeare's Julius Caesar in the Forum of Caesar and the Forum of Augustus.

Festa di San Lorenzo (10th)

By tradition St Lawrence of Rome was roasted to death, so his feast day is celebrated with fireworks, particularly around San Lorenzo fuori le Mura on the via Tiburtini to the east of the city centre.

Ferragosto (15th)

The Feast of the Assumption is a public holiday, with dancing in the piazzas in the evening and a concert at the Teatro Marcello.

La Notte Bianca
lanottebianca.it

To celebrate the official end of summer, there's all-night entertainment in various forms at locations around the city on the first or second weekend of the month. Museums and galleries, including some places that are rarely accessible, open their doors, and there's also a retail angle, with many shops staying open too.

RomaEuropa
romaeuropa.net

A wide-ranging festival of music, theatre and dance runs until December at various venues, including the Auditorium Parco della Musica. As well as classical pieces, the festival is strong on intelligent contemporary music, with interpretations of Brian Eno compositions and electronica, alongside occasional stars such as Cesaria Evora.

Festival Internazionale del Film di Roma
romacinemafest.org

Rome's film festival is a relatively new event, but has already garnered a reputation on the international circuit; the city's cinema heritage attracts a selection of stars, and excellent new films are showcased.

Festival Internazionale di Musica e Arte Sacra
festivalmusicaeartesacra.net

From mid-October through November, a series of sacred choral and instrumental works are performed in the papal basilicas – St Peter's in the Vatican, San Giovanni in Laterano and other churches around the city.

Roma Gospel Festival

A 10-day festival at Auditorium Parco della Musica, with blues and gospel from the USA and around the world.

Christmas

Natale in Rome is generally a holy affair, with the Pope celebrating Midnight Mass on Christmas Eve in the piazza in front of St Peter's. Many other churches organize seasonal events, and there are plenty of impressive nativity scenes. Auditorium Parco della Musica is the place to go for more worldly pleasures, such as ice-skating and special performances, and there are also Christmas fairs around the city, including one in piazza Navona.

New Year's Eve

The city's piazzas are the places to go for end-of-the-year partying. Piazza del Popolo usually has the biggest fireworks, as well as music concerts. The following day, street performances usher in the New Year.

Sleeping

Let's face it: Rome doesn't have a great reputation for its accommodation, especially when compared to other capital cities. Apart from the expensive luxury hotels, mid-range alberghi haven't traditionally offered the standards you would expect from one of the most visited cities in the world. After all, when they're blessed with hordes of pilgrims and tourists all year round, there is no need to make a special effort and it's easy to rest on their laurels. As a result, rooms are often in need of a good revamp, featuring yellowed wallpaper and old-fashioned furniture. Even at their best, they lack charm and come across as rather anonymous. They are also terribly expensive. If you are on a tight budget, your best alternative to a standard room could be to stay in a convent, where you will find large, spotless rooms and friendly service for a fraction of what you'd pay in a hotel – as long as you don't mind sleeping under a crucifix or respecting a fairly early curfew.

Now the good news: although this kind of accommodation does still exist, hotel standards have improved considerably over the past few years. In particular, in the luxury market, so-called 'boutique hotels' have boomed. Having long been overshadowed by trendsetter Milan, Rome finally has a decent number of stylish, contemporary hotels. Funky places for a young, demanding clientele are springing up throughout the capital – hotels such as the Art in via Margutta (see page 212) or the music-themed Franklin (see page 164). Another very welcome new entry was the 2006 opening of Salvatore Ferragamo's *über*-cool Portrait Suites, right by the fashionistas' paradise of via Condotti – Rome finally managed to achieve its first designer hotel.

Where to stay

Although there are now a few elegant hotels around Termini, the area still offers affordable accommodation. The streets around the station are dotted with *pensioni* and two- and three-star hotels. The location is great for transport, with both metro lines and a bus terminal offering plenty of connections. It's brilliant if you are on a budget (and you don't have a problem sleeping in the boxiest of rooms), but after your first night there you might regret it and wish you had spent a little bit more to be somewhere else. The district is unattractive and – as is always the case with areas around large stations – relatively seedy, especially at night.

The *centro storico* is obviously more expensive. The streets around Campo dei Fiori have many mid-priced hotels, with the added bonus of a beautiful piazza, which is a lively market during the day and a hotspot at night. The areas around the nearby Pantheon and piazza Navona are even pricier.

Traditionally, the city's fanciest hotels are located around the Spanish Steps, piazza del Popolo and, of course, via Veneto. Although the heyday of *la dolce vita* is sadly over, this area has never ceased to be synonymous with elegance and luxury.

Across the river, funky Trastevere is a prime choice if you are a night owl, as many of the capital's trendiest bars are in this area. There is no metro, but fairly good tram and bus services make it easy to reach other parts of the city.

If you want to stay away from the hustle and bustle, more peaceful areas such as Celio and the Aventino could be better options. Prati (northeast of the Vatican) has a very good choice of hotels and is another excellent location – very busy during the day, it is quiet at night but has a few great music venues that will keep you entertained should you wish to stay up late. Due to its proximity to the Vatican, you can easily walk there – perfect if you are planning a morning visit to the Vatican Museums.

What type of accommodation

Italian hotels are classified on a star system (from one to five). One star usually indicates a family-run *pensione* – the cheapest accommodation, with basic rooms and limited facilities. In some cases you might have to share a bathroom. Generally, more stars mean a better hotel – but there are frequent exceptions. A higher rating is not necessarily a guarantee of friendliness or better service. On the other hand, you might stay in a three-star hotel that has all the facilities you would expect from a higher category.

Rome does not really have a high or low season, as it is busy most of the year. You might get a better rate if you visit in July or August – when most of the tourists prefer to go elsewhere because of the heat – or again in November or December, just before Christmas. There is plenty of accommodation available, but it's always a good idea to book in advance. You can very often benefit from discounted rates when you book directly through the hotel website. Alternatively, you can find good deals on search engines such as venere. com, expedia.com or lastminute.com.

Renting a flat could work out cheaper for a family or a group of friends. Websites such as at-home-italy.com, shortletsassistance.com and roma.cityapartments.it can be excellent resources, offering a variety of short-let apartments. If you want to do it in style, though, the most exclusive apartment on offer is without doubt the one in the house where John Keats lived and died, which is now run by the Landmark Trust (see page 214).

A B&B is another possibility. Check out the website of the Bed & Breakfast Association of Rome (b-b.rm.it) as well as sleepingrome.com. Both also offer apartment rentals.

Eating & drinking

Market in Campo de' Fiori.

If it's true that we are what we eat, the food of the Eternal City certainly says a lot about the nature of its inhabitants: strong, simple, perhaps a bit unrefined and with bags of character, just like the Romans.

There is a celebrated scene in *Un Americano a Roma* (Steno, 1954) that is illuminating in this respect. Roman actor Alberto Sordi decides to give up on his spaghetti-and-wine diet ("Food for peasants," he says) in favour of what he thinks Americans eat – a revolting concoction of mustard, jam, yoghurt and milk on toast. Quickly disgruntled with his new lifestyle, he turns back to the huge bowl of spaghetti on the table, uttering the immortal line, "*Maccarone, m'hai provocato e io te distruggo!*" ("Macaroni, you provoked me and I shall destroy you!") before forking it all into his mouth. The image is a classic of Italian cinema (the black and white poster of Sordi with his mouth wide open can be found at any souvenir stall in the capital) and well represents the conservative attitude Romans have towards food.

They certainly love their pasta – avoiding experiments and preferring the old, traditional recipes of their ancestors, using fresh, local ingredients. The dish that tempted American-wannabe Sordi could have been *spaghetti alla carbonara*, the most typical of Roman pasta dishes, made with eggs, pecorino cheese, *guanciale* (cured pork cheek) and a dash of pepper. Other big favourites are *bucatini alla matriciana* (with *guanciale*, tomato and pecorino), *gnocchi alla romana* (baked semolina dumplings) and *spaghetti cacio e pepe* (as simple as it gets: just black pepper and pecorino). Should you wish to try *rigatoni con la pajata*, it is advisable to eat first and then ask what the ingredients are! The best place to be initiated into the mysteries of this sauce is **Da Oio a Casa Mia** (see page 89), an authentic trattoria in the heart of the Testaccio district.

Meat courses are simple and tasty, such as *coda alla vaccinara* (oxtail) and *abbacchio alla romana* (milk-fed lamb). *Saltimbocca alla romana* (literally 'Roman-style jump-in-the-mouth') is slices of veal

Markets then & now

Shop like a Roman or simply browse around a local *mercato* (market), taking in the atmosphere. Roman markets date back to the early Republican period (from 509 BC), when the commercial *fora* became important centres of both business and social life. Among the most important were the Forum Boarium, strategically located by the Tiber, where Romans went to buy meat, the Forum Holitorum, which sold vegetables and herbs, the Forum Piscarum (fish) and the Forum Vinarum (wine). Here's a list of the most important markets in contemporary Rome:

Mercato di Campo dei Fiori (Mon-Sat mornings): The most famous and picturesque, in a spot dear to the hearts of locals, with a village atmosphere right in the city centre. It sells fruit and vegetables but also some of the best fish in town. When the market is over, you can browse in the area's food stores – equally mouthwatering.

Mercato di piazza Testaccio (Mon-Sat mornings): Located in one of the last tourist-free districts, this place is an absolute must if you want to sample authentic Roman life. It has fruit and veg, fish and meat, and a bit of everything else.

Mercato di piazza San Cosimato (Mon-Sat mornings): A traditional market in the heart of Trastevere, with an emphasis on locally grown food. Look out for the smaller stalls of the so-called *vignaroli*, who sell produce from their own farms only.

Mercato dell'Esquilino (previously known as Mercato di piazza Vittorio, Mon-Sat 0700-1700): Possibly Rome's biggest market, it offers a large range of groceries from all over the world, exotic fruit, herbs and spices from Africa and Asia – a lively, crowded and hectic slice of multicultural Rome.

Mercato di piazza dell'Unità (Mon-Sat 0700-2000, but most stalls open mornings only): In the upmarket Prati district, just off the shopping hub of via Cola di Rienzo. This is Rome's first covered market, housed in a beautiful Liberty-style building. It's mostly fruit and vegetables but also fish, meat and other foodstuffs.

Mercato della Moschea (viale della Moschea, Fri): In front of Rome's Mosque in the Parioli district. Spices and colours from India, Morocco and the Arab world.

Among the sweets, a special mention should go to *pangiallo*, a dried fruit and nut cake whose origins go back to imperial Rome, when it was given as a present at the winter solstice to invoke the return of good weather.

skewered together with wafer-thin slices of dry-cured ham and sage, then sautéed in butter and finished with wine. Another local classic is *carciofi alla giudia*, a dish of fried artichokes from the Judaeo-Roman tradition.

Among the sweets, a special mention should go to *pangiallo*, a dried fruit and nut cake whose origins go back to imperial Rome, when it was given as a present at the winter solstice to invoke the return of good weather.

Unless otherwise specified, the wine will most likely come from the Castelli Romani hills – possibly from the town of Frascati. Don't expect a

Top: Gusto café. Above: Pizzeria Li Rioni a Santiquattro in Celio.

cosmopolitan wine list, especially if you are eating in a trattoria. A carafe of *rosso* or *bianco della casa* (house wine) in quantities of *un quarto*, *mezzo* or *litro* will be served instead. Although wines from Lazio are little known outside the regional borders, the local wine industry has dramatically improved in recent years. This sudden rebirth has also seen a wine-bar boom in the capital, with plenty of *enoteche* replacing the old-fashioned, more traditional *osterie*. Many of them also offer innovative food and are therefore fashionable places, favoured by young crowds.

As far as eateries go, the categories can be quite confusing. Traditionally, osterie and trattorie have been inexpensive, family-run places offering typical food, often with rough-and-ready service. However, nowadays many of them have become quite exclusive, and a trattoria or osteria can be just as smart (and as pricey) as a restaurant. A ristorante is still top of the chain, and it is rarely as informal as a typical trattoria. If you are uncertain, look for a place where lots of locals are eating, and bear in mind that a bilingual menu usually means the place caters mainly for tourists.

Many restaurants offer a *menu turistico* – an often uninspiring two- or three-course set meal at a reasonable price. A much better option is the *menu degustazione*, proposed by more creative chefs, which allows you to taste more elaborate seasonal dishes and specialities. Sometimes wine is also included. Both these menus work out cheaper than ordering the same food *alla carta*. Remember that some places will charge a couple of euros for the *coperto* (cover charge): this should usually be specified on the menu.

For a cheap, fast-food alternative, head to a *tavola calda* (literally a 'hot table'), which offers a buffet menu, or a takeaway place selling *pizza al taglio* ('by the slice'), which is sold by weight and priced depending on the topping. The most traditional one is the simple *pizza bianca*, crispy, warm and plain or, even better, filled with mortadella.

Coffee culture

Rule number one: forget all the fancy names they use in the coffee places back home. No frappuccinos, frappelatte or the like. And be warned: if you order a latte in Italy you will end up with a glass of milk.

If you want an espresso – that tiny caffeine shot served in a small cup – just ask for *un caffè*. If you want it with a drop of milk, ask for *caffè macchiato* ('stained'). For regular coffee, order a *caffè lungo* or *caffè americano*, which are made with more water than espresso. Modern versions of the traditional Italian coffee bar have sprung up recently, and beside the usual things some might also offer *caffè marocchino* ('Moroccan'), made with cocoa and foamed milk, or *caffè al ginseng* – a real energy boost.

Rule number two: if you want to drink coffee like an Italian, a *cappuccino* (espresso with warm, frothy milk, often sprinkled with chocolate) is only a morning thing. Nobody would dream of ordering one after 1100 or – God forbid! – at the end of a meal. A *latte macchiato* is a weaker, milkier alternative – the equivalent of a latte at home.

If you're going to drink coffee standing up, pay first and show your receipt at the bar when ordering. If you sit down at a table you will get waiter service and pay at the end – service charges can be quite hefty, though, especially in tourist areas.

In Rome, the temple of coffee is **Bar Sant'Eustachio** (piazza Sant'Eustachio 82, T06-6880 2048, daily 0830-0100). Their undisputed speciality is their *Gran Caffè* (yes, with capital letters!), a frothy double espresso served ready sweetened. Another popular place is the nearby **Bar Tazza d'Oro** (via degli Orfani 84, T06-678 9792, Mon-Sat 0800-2000), which is especially famous for its much-admired *granita al caffè* – an espresso shot with crushed ice. For a high-calorie treat, order it *con panna sopra e sotto* (with whipped cream top and bottom).

Entertainment

Freni e Frizioni, Trastevere.

Until recently, people-watching was just about the best entertainment you could get in Rome. Apart from the city's traditionally sleepy nature, its public transport system doesn't make things easy for those who want to party: the metro shuts at 2330 (0130 at weekends) leaving you with a not-so-reliable bus service and rather expensive taxis. Things are looking brighter though, and there's much more on offer these days. Comprehensive listings – in Italian but with a small section in English – can be found in **Roma c'è** (Wed, €1.50 or free from some restaurants and bars).

Bars & clubs

The northern – particularly Milanese – ritual of the aperitivo has taken over the capital, and Romans love to chat over a drink at around 1900. Increasingly popular is the so-called *apericena*, which includes a light buffet meal in the price of the drink. At **Micca Club** (miccaclub.com, T06-8744 0079) €10 will get you a drink and yummy nibbles prepared by chef Giuseppe Annunzi. Other good addresses are **Freni e Frizioni** in Trastevere (piazza del Politeama 4, T06-4549 7499) or the osteria at **Gusto** (via della Frezza 23, T06-322 6273).

After their drink, Romans move on to a restaurant or back home for dinner. Proper nightlife does not start before 1130, and goes on until the early hours. Most bars are now obliged to shut at 0200, but nightclubs and live venues stay open till late. There's night action around piazza Navona and in Campo dei Fiori, both especially pleasant in summer. Very often, there is no need to plan your evening in advance. New places spring up all the time and leaflets and free tickets are always being handed out on the streets. Away from the *centro storico*, Trastevere and Testaccio are renowned for being the coolest spots.

Cinema

Despite the Italian tendency to dub all foreign films, original language movies are screened at **Alcazar** (via Cardinal Merry del Val 14, T06-588 0099), **Nuovo Sacher** (largo Ascianghi 1, T06-581 8116, usually Mon) owned and run by film director Nanni Moretti, and **Metropolitan** (7, via del Corso).

Gay & lesbian

In Testaccio you'll find Rome's first gay disco, **L'Alibi**. The gay scene in Rome isn't as open as in other European capitals, and many gay venues require you to purchase a membership card to get in (around €8 for three months' access to several clubs). Things are improving: a 300-m area called **Gay Street** was inaugurated in 2007 on via San Giovanni in Laterano, and the **Gay Village** open-air summer festival provides entertainment, music and performances (in 2008 it was held in the Parco del Ninfeo, in the EUR district; go to estateromana.comune.roma.it for information).

Music

Classical music lovers should check out what's on at the **Teatro dell'Opera di Roma** (via Firenze 72, T06-481601, operaroma.it), the **Accademia Filarmonica** (via Flaminia 118, T06-320 1752, filarmonicaromana.com) and the new **Auditorium Parco della Musica** (see page 199), home of the **Accademia Nazionale di Santa Cecilia** (T06-808 2058, santacecilia.it).

The jazz scene is particularly vibrant, with first-rate artists performing in the city almost every night. Apart from established names such

as **Alexanderplatz** and **La Palma**, check out the recently opened **Casa del Jazz** (viale di Porta Ardeatina 55, T06-704731, casajazz.it), a multifunctional musical venue in a villa that once belonged to underworld boss Enrico Nicoletti.

Festivals & events

In the summer many clubs shut and the action moves to nearby resorts such as Ostia and Fregene, which are dotted with beach discos. If you are staying in town, however, the **Estate Romana** is a three-month long festival of live music, events, theatre and outdoor film screenings (estateromana.comune.roma.it). Other themed festivals go on for most of the summer, such as the Latin-American **Fiesta** (Ippodromo delle Capannelle, via Appia Nuova, fiesta.it, Jun-Aug).

The opera moves outside in the summertime as well, against the superb backdrop of the Roman **Baths of Caracalla** (operaroma.it). Perhaps less famous than the Arena in Verona, it is nevertheless a magical experience. See also pages 46-49.

Tip...

It's easiest to book tickets for events or concerts online (greenticket.it). Alternatively, try **Orbis** (piazza dell'Esquilino 37, T06-474 4776) or the box office at **La Feltrinelli** (several branches, including largo di Torre Argentina 5, T06-6830 8596).

Late-night indulgence

A typically Roman tradition is to end a night on the tiles with a *cornetto* (the Italian equivalent to a *croissant* – plain, with cream, jam or chocolate). Knowing the address of a proper bakery, or *laboratorio artigianale*, that stays open all night means being a true *Romano di Roma*, and locals swear the best one is the underground Laboratorio Lambiase (see page 215). Try a *sorchetta* – a delicious pastry with cream and chocolate.

Shopping

For a European capital, Rome's shopping scene can seem surprisingly small-scale. Via del Corso has the standard European stores, and there are the high-end fashion labels, but otherwise small, family-run stores tend to dominate, offering a form of retail therapy that has nearly become extinct in many other capital cities. There are plenty of boutiques and old-fashioned bookshops and delicatessens offering personal service and a profusion of eclectic, individual products. Some of these shops may take some effort to seek out, but they reward the trouble.

A designer shop window on Via Condotti, Rome's prime location for luxury shopping.

The main area for the big-name shops is the Tridente, the area that spreads south from piazza del Popolo. It's filled with smart designer-label fashion, especially on and around via Condotti. Via Veneto is a little old-fashioned these days – for a younger, more mainstream and more Italian crowd, via Cola di Renzi and the nearby streets in Prati, just to the north of the Vatican, are more approachable.

In most of Rome, small local shops and markets are never far away – most districts have their local delicatessen and fruit and veg shops. And if fresh goats' cheese ricotta is a little impractical to carry home with you, there are plenty of shoes, gloves, items of kitchenware and statuettes of the Pope that will survive the journey.

While the big stores on via del Corso stay open all day and into the evening, many smaller shops still close for a couple of hours for lunch. Their basic hours tend to be 0930-1330 and 1530-1930, and they're closed on Sundays and sometimes

Monday mornings too. Nothing is fixed in stone, though, and opening hours often depend on how busy it is, whether it's raining or how late the shopkeeper got to bed the night before.

Antiques

The streets around piazza Navona, particularly via dei Coronari, are a good place to start looking, and via Giulia has numerous specialist dealers. Via Margutta and via del Babuino, near the Spanish Steps, make another rich hunting ground.

Arts & crafts

Design-led boutiques are scattered throughout the city, but Celio, Trastevere and the narrow streets to the north of Campo de' Fiori in the centre are hotspots. At one time nearly half of the city's registered artists lived on or around via Margutta: it remains an attractive street and still has some studios, though these days it's lost much of its bohemian atmosphere. Many of 21st-century Rome's more cutting-edge and contemporary studios are to be found in Testaccio or Ostiense.

Books

As the traditional area for Anglophones in Rome, Trastevere is unusually well endowed with English-language bookshops, both new and secondhand. Feltrinelli is a useful big bookshop with several branches in the city: notable central ones include the Galleria Alberto Sordi on piazza Colonna and Largo Argentina. For books on Rome and its antiquities, the bookshops in the city's museums are a good place to start. The one in Trajan's Markets has a particularly good selection.

Fashion

Via dei Condotti and the neighbouring streets are well worth a wander for the vicarious pleasure of window shopping, whether or not your wallet is thick enough to venture inside the big-name, big-price boutiques such as Armani, Gucci and Bulgari. If you're less interested in high-end glitz, via del Governo Vecchio has very good fashion outlets with fewer crowds and often a little more individuality. Locally made shoes and gloves can be good value. Another interesting area for fashion and jewellery is Monti, where there are plenty of independent boutiques and workshops, especially on and around via del Boschetto and via degli Zingari.

Food & wine

You can find good food and wine everywhere in Rome; apart from the markets (see page 53), there are plenty of good shops selling delicious cheeses, oils, olives and cured meats, and most of them will happily rustle you up a sandwich or wrap something for a flight home. Volpetti (in Testaccio) and Antica Caciara (in Trastevere) are two of the city's best delicatessens. Other traditional shops to look out for include *biscottifici* – literally biscuit shops, they often sell all sorts of homemade cakes and pastries.

Kitchenware

Modern-day Romans like stylish cooking equipment, and Gusto's kitchen shop (piazza Augusto Imperatore) – a small part of their food-centred empire – is cramped but hard to beat on both range and quality.

Markets

The fruit, veg and flower market in Campo de' Fiori is one of Rome's oldest, and although it's mainly tourists who dominate the Campo's famed *aperitivo* scene, in the morning it remains a place that locals frequent, drawn by the market's high-quality produce from the surrounding countryside.

The daily market in piazza San Cosimato, in Trastevere, is a notably cheaper alternative, as is the daily fruit and veg market in piazza Testaccio. Further south, along the river, the city's notorious Porta Portese market is a hubbub of cheap shoes, old magazines, fake label clothes and a fair quantity of tat.

Toys

The city's best toyshop is Città del Sole (via della Scrofa 65, T06-6880 3805, cittadelsole.it), a city centre den of exploration for kids of all ages.

Activities & tours

A good starting point when planning your activities in Rome is a visit to one of the tourist information offices. Apart from maps, they also have several free brochures with details of themed walks (which can also be downloaded from romaturismo.it).

Cycling

A bike is perfect for exploring the pedestrianized *centro storico*, and for getting off the beaten track. Proper cycle lanes are being created, but don't forget that Rome is famous for its hostility towards cyclists and pedestrians: keep your wits about you and stay away from busy roads.

Following in the footsteps of Paris, Rome has recently launched a bike-sharing system. **Roma'n'Bike** (toll-free T800-910658, roma-n-bike. com) has 19 pick-up and drop-off points in several areas of the centre, and a total of 271 bicycles, which can be picked up 0700-2300. The service is available to those over 18, using a smartcard that you can get at any tourist information office (€30 deposit; ID required). The first 30 minutes are free,

then you are charged for each 30 minutes up to a maximum of four hours. It's designed as a short-term rental service, so the longer you use your bike the more expensive it becomes.

If you want to rent a bike for a longer period, try **Top Bike Rental** (via dei Quattro Cantoni 40, T06-488 2893, topbikerental.com), centrally located between the Colosseum and Termini station. Prices start at €12 for a day (cheaper if you book online), and they also do guided tours.

Children

3D Rewind (via Capo d'Africa 5, T06-7707 6627, 3drewind.com, daily 0900-1900, €10) is a 30-minute interactive experience a stone's throw from the Colosseum. Opened in November 2008, it enables children to experience the atmosphere of ancient Rome, combining entertainment with historical detail (it's based on the *Plastico di Roma Antica* reconstruction by the Universities of Virginia and California). **Time Elevator** (via dei Santi Apostoli 20, T06-9774 6243, timeelevator.it, daily 1030-1930, €12) is another journey back in time that will speed you in 45 minutes through 3000 years of Roman history, from Romulus and Remus up to the present day.

Food & wine

The clubby **International Wine Academy of Rome** (vicolo del Bottino 8, T06-699 0878,

---

Tip...

A useful online resource is **romereview.com** (in English). Created by an American expat who has lived in Rome for over ten years, it has a constantly updated list of events, as well as being packed with unbiased reviews of hotels, restaurants, clubs and much more.

wineacademyroma.com) is the brainchild of Roberto Wirth, owner of the famous Hotel Hassler. Created as a sort of meeting place for wine lovers, it offers wine tasting courses and tours as well as 'meet the maker' and 'great chefs' dinners in the elegant setting of Il Palazzetto (see page 215).

For a unique experience, hop on to **Tramjazz** (T339-633 4700, tramjazz.com, Fri 2100 from piazza di Porta Maggiore, reservation required). It's a vintage tram transformed into a restaurant, so you can drink and dine in style, with some good music and Rome at night as a unique backdrop. You start off with an aperitivo before boarding, then the slow journey through the city begins, topped off by a jazz serenade in front of the Colosseum.

Tours & walks

If you don't feel like walking, a hop-on hop-off tourist bus might be a good option. Two similar tours of central Rome are **Rome Open Tour** (T06-9774 5404, romeopentour.com, daily 0900-1900, 0900-2200 in summer, €19 for 24 hrs or €24 for 48 hrs) and Trambus Open's **110open** (T06-684 0901 or toll-free 800-281281, trambusopen.com, daily 0830-2030, €20 for 24 hrs; non-stop night tours Thu-Sat from piazza Venezia at 2200 and 2230, €12; 10% discount when booked online). Trambus Open also operates the **Archeobus** (daily from piazza dei Cinquecento, outside Termini railway station, 0830-1630 every 30 mins, €13), a 90-min tour of the Forum and Appia Antica.

Appian Line (piazza dell'Esquilino 6/7, T06-4878 6604, appianline.it) has a variety of guided tours in and around Rome. Prices start from €30. You can join the tour at their terminal on piazza dell'Esquilino, or use their complimentary pick-up service, available from most hotels in the city.

Battelli di Roma runs a hop-on hop-off boat tour between Isola Tiberina and ponte Nenni (T06-9774 5403, battellidiroma.it, €12 for 24 hrs). You can board at Sant'Angelo dock, opposite Castel

Tip...

A phone call is all you need to buy museum, theatre and events tickets in the city. **060608** (060608.it, call centre daily 0900-2230) is a tourist helpline that also provides information on hotels, restaurant, attractions and cultural events. The website has a useful journey planner section.

Sant'Angelo, at Tiber Island dock (Trastevere side) or at lungotevere Marzio. If you have more time, they also run cruises to Ostia Antica (Tue-Sun, Nov-Mar 0930, Apr-Oct 1000, €13, reservations required).

Rome walks (romewalks.com, from €40) is a London-based company that offers several guided walks in English. For a different slant on the city, **Jewish Roma** (jewishroma.com, €300 for up to 6 people) looks at over 2000 years of Jewish life during an excellent three-hour tour of the Ghetto with witty local guide Micaela Pavoncello.

Contents

The ancient city

A bus passing the Colosseum

Introduction

What to see in...

...one day
Start in the **Roman Forum** for a relatively calm introduction to ancient Rome. Climb the **Palatine Hill** and then have lunch in a Celio **restaurant** before heading back to the **Colosseum**. If complete ancient Rome fatigue hasn't set in, the amazing **Capitoline Museums** stay open until 2000. Have a well-earned evening chill at a **jazz concert** in **Villa Celimontana**, or one of Celio's **wine bars**.

...a weekend or more
As well as the above, take the lift to the very top of the **Vittoriano** for great views over the city, then check out the **Imperial Forums**, including **Trajan's Column**, before heading to **Trajan's Markets** or **San Clemente** for some multi-layered history. The **Aventine Hill** is a haven of restrained calm before the liveliness of **Testaccio** and **Ostiense**, with the city's best **nightlife** and some great **restaurants** and **pizzerias**. And don't miss the **Centrale Montemartini**, an unusual museum in a power station, or the **Pyramid of Gaius Cestius**.

The Foro Romano, the heart of the ancient city, stretches from Campidoglio (the Capitoline Hill) to Rome's most famous icon, the Colosseum. This ancient stadium still pulls in the crowds, with good reason – it's an awesome sight, inside and out. To the south is the Palatine Hill and the Circus Maximus, with more extraordinary Roman remains. Many of the best pieces of statuary from this area are now in the Capitoline Museums. The Vittoriano, a 20th-century marble monstrosity dominating piazza Venezia, is a symbol of Italian nationhood. On the other side of the via dei Fori Imperiali, the Imperial Forums and Trajan's Market are relatively late Roman constructions.

To the east is Celio, with the multi-levelled history of the church of San Clemente. Two nearby churches, Quattro Santi Coronati and San Giovanni in Laterano, both have beautiful old cloisters, while Santa Croce in Gerusalemme has a magical vegetable garden.

South of Rome's centre is the leafy, well-to-do hill of Aventino, with peaceful churches and piazzas. Beyond, Testaccio is a much grittier area: a mix of working-class markets and young upwardly mobile bars, restaurants and nightclubs. Ostiense has fewer sights, though an ex-power station is now a permanent outpost of the Capitoline collection of Roman statuary. To the east are the huge ruins of Caracalla's Roman baths.

The hand of Constantine in the Capitoline Museums.

Foro Romano e Palatino

Entrances on via dei Fori Imperiale and via di San Gregorio, T06-3996 7700, pierreci.it.
Daily 0830 till 1 hr before sunset; joint ticket with Colosseum (valid 2 days) €9/€4.50 concession, plus €3 surcharge during exhibitions in Colosseum, or Archaeologia Card, free EU citizens under 18; €1.50 booking fee for phone and online reservations.
Metro: Colosseo. Map: below.

The centre of the Roman Empire, the Roman Forum is a huge, awe-inspiring, if often overwhelming, space. Stretching from the Capitoline Hill to the Colosseum, it is an area of ruined temples and triumphal arches, open squares, emperors' tombs, homes of Vestal Virgins and imperial drains. To the south, the Palatine Hill, etymological source for the word 'palace', was the site of the grand villas of ancient Rome.

After several years of free admission to the Forum, tickets were reintroduced in 2008; as yet there is little sign of the revenue being used to look after the site, much of which is shabby and poorly maintained, or closed to the public during 'restoration'. Don't expect much in the way of signposting or labelling either.

Tip...

Visiting the Forum and Palatine Hill first enables you to skip the much longer queues at the Colosseum ticket office.

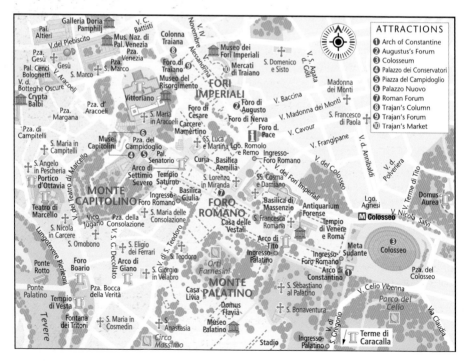

ATTRACTIONS
1 Arch of Constantine
2 Augustus's Forum
3 Colosseum
4 Palazzo dei Conservatori
5 Piazza del Campidoglio
6 Palazzo Nuovo
7 Roman Forum
8 Trajan's Column
9 Trajan's Forum
10 Trajan's Market

In early Roman times, the Forum was a marshy area, and became a key part of the city only after it was drained. Until the sixth century BC it was used for burials, but once the key drain of the *Cloaca Maxima* was built by the Etruscan Tarquins the Forum was paved for the first time. The first important Roman temples were constructed in the fifth century BC. Entering the Forum from the via dei Fori Imperiali deposits you in the heart of the action, just east of the Arch of Septimius Severus.

Arco di Settimio Severo This triple triumphal arch, nearly 21 m tall, was built in AD 203; its four panels depict the victories of Emperor Septimius Severus over the Parthians. After his death his sons Geta and Caracalla ruled jointly until Caracalla had his brother killed, and a line of text on the attic (the flat area at the top of the arch) was altered to erase any mention of Geta.

Umbilicus Urbis Just northwest of the Arch of Septimius Severus, the unprepossessing brick remnants of a round column are almost certainly the *Umbilicus Urbis*, the navel of the city, and thus of the Roman Empire. This monument was seen not only as the centre point of Rome, but as a connection to the underworld, as it probably stood above the *Mundus*, the point where Romulus had dug a circular pit at the founding of the city, into which new citizens of Rome threw handfuls of earth from their homelands as offerings. Ceremonial days when the *Mundus* was opened were considered unpropitious for business and legal transactions, as beings from the underworld could escape through the opening.

Tempio di Saturno The eight columns of a portico beyond are all that remain of the Temple of Saturn. From the third century, it replaced an earlier shrine to the god, and held the treasury. The festival of Saturnalia, held here each December, celebrated a mythical time of equality, and during it slaves were allowed to eat with their masters or even served by them.

Colonna di Foca This column was the last structure to be erected in the Forum, in AD 608, in honour of a visit by the Byzantine Emperor Phocas, though it was taken from an earlier building. The fig, olive and vine nearby were planted in the modern era to represent the venerated plants that, according to Pliny the Elder, once grew here in the central square – the hub of Rome and the forerunner of the Italian piazza.

Arch of Septimius Severus, Roman Forum.

Tip...

The **Archaeologia Card** (pierreci.it) costs €20/10 concession and is valid for the Forum, Palatine Hill and Colosseum, as well as various other sites, for one week; you can also use the **Romapass** (see page 11) at these sites and others.

Around the city

Tempio del Divo Giulio To the southeast of the Column of Phocas is the Temple of Deified Julius, erected by Augustus on the spot where Julius Caesar was cremated. Little remains except the altar, but it has great significance in Rome, and floral tributes are still regularly left there.

Basilica Giulia Simultaneous with his construction of a new forum to the east, Julius Caesar built this large basilica, later finished by his successor, Augustus. It kept its original name through various fires and subsequent incarnations. The central hall, 82 m long and probably three storeys high, housed a tribunal that heard important cases of the time.

Vicus Tuscus East of the Basilica Julia, on this Etruscan street off to the right, a door leads down to the *Cloaca Maxima* – the original sewer that drained the Forum. You can still hear the water coursing through it below.

Tempio dei Dioscuri Three white columns are all that remains of the Temple of Castor and Pollux, which once held the office of weights and measures. The senate also met here, as did bankers.

Tempio di Vesta e Casa delle Vestali Selected from noble families before the age of ten, and observing a vow of chastity for a minimum of thirty years, Vestal Virgins dedicated their lives to Vesta,

goddess of the hearth, home and family. They had special privileges but also had to live a pure life in the House of the Vestals, a cloister-like environment behind the round Temple of Vesta, where their principal task was to keep the goddess's sacred fire burning. The penalty for breaking their vow was to be buried alive – the man would be flogged to death.

Tempio di Antonino e Faustina At the northeast side of the Forum, the Church of San Lorenzo (the entrance is on the via dei Fori Imperiali) has been incorporated into the remains of this second-century temple to Faustina, the deified wife of Antoninus Pius.

Basilica di Massenzio e Costantino This gigantic structure was begun by Emperor Maxentius in the fourth century on the site of spice warehouses. Originally constructed on an east-west axis, it was completed by Constantine, who turned the plan 90 degrees so that the apse, which survives, was to the north. The huge head, hand and foot now in the Capitoline Museum were found here (see page 73).

Arco di Tito Built by Domitian in honour of his deified brother Titus, this arch, at the southeastern end of the via Sacra, marked victory in the Jewish War of AD 70-71. The internal bas-relief shows soldiers carrying plunder, including a menorah.

Palatino The Palatine Hill is linked to stories of the founding of Rome: it was on its lower slopes that Romulus and Remus were left in a basket, and here that Aeneas was greeted when he arrived from Troy. It was probably these myths, as much as the presence of other smart Roman villas, that led Augustus to site his home here, creating a connection between the office and trappings of the emperor and the very essence of Rome.

The immense **Imperial Palace** was first built by Tiberius and then enlarged by Caligula. Built over the top of other homes in the first century AD, it still dominates the hill. With fountains, courtyards and marble-lined halls, it is still possible to see

Above: The Roman Forum from the Capitoline Hill. Opposite page: Tempio di Antonino e Faustina.

what a grand, awe-inspiring place it must have been. The so-called **Stadium** was probably not used for sporting events, but was a huge private garden attached to the palace, complete with riding track. The curved area on its eastern side would have been where the emperor and his family would sit. The eastern part of the palace (confusingly labelled **Domus Augustana**, meaning 'Home of the Emperor', not to be confused with the House of Augustus) contained the emperor's private quarters; the **Domus Flavia**, to the west, was where official business was carried out. The square with an octagonal structure in the middle would once have been a peristyle – an internal courtyard with a central fountain.

Casa di Augusto Only recently opened to the public, the brightly coloured, well-preserved rooms of the House of Augustus come as something of a surprise after the crumbling stone of most of the rest of the site. To the north of the palace complex, it's badly signposted and only five people are allowed in at any one time. One room, upstairs,

can be viewed only through glass, but two more downstairs are completely open and have frescoes in vivid shades of ochre and terracotta, with trompe l'œil designs, decorative borders and barrel vaulting.

Museo Palatino On the top of the hill, the Palatine Museum contains various finds from the site, such as marble statues and detailed terracotta reliefs from the Temple of Apollo, made between 36 and 28 BC – the one of soldiers exhibiting the head of a Gorgon is a reference to the recently vanquished queen of Egypt. One of the highlights is a well-preserved fragment of fresco from the Augustan era of a woman playing a lyre.

Arco di Costantino The biggest of Rome's triumphal arches stands outside the main Forum area, next to the Colosseum. Dedicated to Emperor Constantine by the Senate after his victory over Maxentius, it is decorated with depictions of events from various eras – some taken from older monuments – presumably to place the Christian emperor in the context of earlier Roman greatness.

Around the city

Colosseo

Piazza del Colosseo, T06-3996 7700, pierreci.it.
Daily 0830 till 1 hr before sunset; joint ticket
with Forum and Palatino (valid 2 days) €9/€4.50
concession, plus €3 surcharge during exhibitions
in Colosseum, or Archaeologia Card, free EU
citizens under 18; €1.50 booking fee.
Metro: Colosseo. Map: Rome, F5, p84.

Completed in AD 80, Rome's amphitheatre was
built by the emperors Vespasian and Titus on
the site of the *Domus Aurea* (golden house) built
by their predecessor Nero. The construction of
such a massive public edifice in the place of the
much-hated emperor's extravagant palace must
have been a popular move. During Roman times
the stadium was referred to as the Flavian
Amphitheatre, Flavius being the family name
of Vespasian and Titus. The name 'Colosseum'

probably comes from a gigantic bronze statue,
originally of Nero but later adapted as the sun
god Helios, which stood, 35 m tall, outside it.

The precursor of the modern stadium, the
Colosseum probably held up to 70,000 people.
Spectators were protected from the elements by
a system of sails and curtains, operated by skilled
sailors. It is now Rome's most popular sight and an
icon of the whole country, its majesty dimmed
only slightly by the long queues to get in, the
hordes of souvenir sellers and costumed
centurions and gladiators that prowl the perimeter
hoping to be paid to have their photos taken.

Having been plundered for building materials for
centuries, and damaged by earthquakes, only around
half the mass of the original structure is still standing
– the southern half of the outer ring is missing
altogether, though the inner ring is much more intact.
Seats would originally have joined the two rings.

Inside the Colosseum.

What the locals say

It is difficult to choose one place not to miss. Rather than a monument, I'd recommend a viewing point: walking along via del Campidoglio, with the Senate House on your right, you will reach a terrace from where you can enjoy a breathtaking vista. The ancient Rome of the Colosseum and the Fora is at your feet. It is amazing, especially at sunset or early in the morning.

Stefano Corradino, TV journalist.

The best views are from the second floor, where a new museum has interesting temporary exhibitions. A part of the flooring has been reconstructed at the southern end, though the rest remains open, allowing visitors to see down into the complex of rooms that would have held animals, scenery and staff below arena level. When it was first built, a system of plumbing allowed the arena to be flooded for mock sea battles, but these declined in popularity in preference for animal and gladiatorial contests.

Despite the common myths, there is no evidence of Christians specifically being killed in the Colosseum, though many people certainly did meet grisly ends here, in savage gladiatorial combat or in fights with wild animals. The animals themselves fared even worse – sometimes thousands were killed on a single day. In all, as many as half a million people and a million animals may have died here.

Rome's biggest gladiator school was to the east of the site (some of its remains can be seen next to via Labicana). It was connected to the Colosseum by an underground tunnel; other tunnels connected to a hospital and to a morgue.

3D Rewind Rome

Via Capo d'Africa 5, T06-7707 6627, 3drewind.com.
Daily 0900-1900, €10.
Metro: Colosseo.

Using rigorously researched archaeological data to create a three-dimensional cinema experience of ancient Rome, this gimmicky attraction, opened in late 2008, is a missed opportunity. Wearing 3D goggles, viewers are taken through the streets and sights of the city at breakneck speed. The depictions of the buildings are fascinating. Unfortunately, crass attempts to get laughs and gasps from the audience obscure most of the interesting parts.

Mercati di Traiano e Fori Imperiali

Museo dei Fori Imperiali, via IV Novembre 94, T06-8205 9127, mercatiditraiano.it.
Tue-Sun 0900-1900; €6.50/4.50 concession, free EU citizens under 18 and over 65.
Metro: Colosseo. Map: Rome, E4, p84.

It was Julius Caesar who decided that a new forum was needed, outside the Forum of the republican era, and subsequent emperors, including Augustus and Trajan, followed his lead. Some of the Roman Empire's greatest buildings were erected in this area.

Sliced through by Mussolini's via dei Fori Imperiali, the Imperial Forums are these days the poor neighbour of the so-called Roman Forum – areas of overgrown broken columns, with little or no public access, that seem largely abandoned. However, a museum opened in 2007 in Trajan's Markets does an excellent job of interpreting the area and giving some idea of the one-time grandeur of this part of ancient Rome. In rooms off the two-storey *Grande Aula* (great hall) of Trajan's Markets, the museum dedicates a space to each element of the Imperial Forums, from Julius Caesar onwards. Above, hundreds of tons of groin-vaulted cement make up the impressive original ceiling.

The well-preserved remnants of the so-called markets themselves probably served as a combination of offices, schools and shops in Roman times, the building having the secondary purpose of shoring up the Quirinal Hill. Trajan's brick building is a grand, sweeping structure, full of arches and great views over the forums below and the rest of Rome beyond.

The **Torre delle Milizie**, the fortified tower behind the market, is one of the city's most significant medieval monuments. Probably

Around the city

constructed at the beginning of the 13th century, it has leaned to one side since an earthquake in 1348. It is still sometimes colloquially referred to as 'Nero's Tower', because of a belief that the emperor watched Rome burn from here in AD 64. In all probability there was no tower here in Nero's time, and in any case it is now thought that Nero was away from the city during the fire.

Colonna Traiana

In the ruins of his forum just off modern-day piazza Venezia, Trajan's Column, almost entirely intact, is one of the most extraordinary remnants of ancient Rome. Nearly 30 m tall and weighing over 850 tons, it held the ashes of the emperor; the 200-m spiralling bas-relief, illustrating scenes from his victories in the two Dacian Wars, is a sculptural masterpiece. In 1588 a statue of St Peter was placed at the top. A spiral staircase of 185 steps winds inside the column to the top, but is not open to the public.

Built in the second century, the design of the column was mirrored in the later Column of Marcus Aurelius (see page 73). You can see the carvings more easily in the form of reproductions in the Museum of Roman Civilization (see page 254).

Campidoglio

The second of Rome's founding hills, and the smallest in the city, the Capitoline Hill gives us the modern concept of a 'capitol'. A large part of the contemporary Capitoline is taken up with the 19th- and 20th-century marble monstrosity of the Vittoriano. Also here, however, is Michelangelo's **piazza del Campidoglio**, one of the city's most graceful squares and home to the excellent Capitoline Museums. Michelangelo's decision to reverse the traditional orientation of the hill, away from the ancient Forum and towards St Peter's and the modern city, was a symbolic as well as a practical one. The statues of **Castor and**

Below: Piazza del Campidoglio. Opposite page: Hand of Constantine in Capitoline museum.

Pollux, at the top of the wide stairway leading up from the traffic chaos of piazza Venezia below, are ancient, pieced together from fragments. The **equestrian statue** in the centre (a reproduction) depicts Emperor Marcus Aurelius – its prominence is largely because it was once thought to be Emperor Constantine. The original, from AD 176, is now in the Capitoline Museums; it is also depicted on the Italian 50 cent coin.

Musei Capitolini

Piazza del Campidoglio 1, museicapitolini.org.
Tue-Sun 0900-2000; €6.50/4.50 concession, combined ticket with Centrale Montemartini €8.50/6.50, free EU citizens under 18 and over 65. Bus: C3, 40, 63, 70, 81, 87, 95, 628, 716. Metro: Colosseo. Map: Rome, E4, p84.

Spellbinding, and much improved in recent years, the cream of Roman statuary is well displayed and well lit, and even the information boards are fairly good. There is Renaissance and Baroque art too, but it's the stunningly executed statues that really catch the imagination. The collection stretches between the two buildings that face each other across the piazza. You should allow three or four hours for a visit; tickets allow you to leave and come back later the same day – a break is not such a bad idea.

Palazzo dei Conservatori The ticket office is in this building, to the right as you come up the stairs, and it makes a good place to start. The courtyard contains some of ancient Rome's most iconic remains: the marble fragments of a huge statue of Constantine, made at the beginning of the fourth century. His hand, head and foot sit side by side. Only these naked parts would have been carved from marble, the remainder of the figure was probably of bronze.

At the top of the grand staircase, four extraordinarily sophisticated bas-reliefs, from the first and second centuries, are dedicated to Hadrian and Marcus Aurelius. The pose of Marcus Aurelius, on the left, is very similar to that of his equestrian statue, as he holds out a hand to a kneeling prisoner in an act of mercy.

The first floor has grand rooms frescoed with scenes of Roman history, mostly dating back to the 16th century. **Room XI, the Hall of Hannibal**, is one of the most impressive, decorated with giant, imaginative works, including the eponymous Carthaginian commander on an elephant, attributed to Iacopo Ripanda. Of the contents, the highlights are two bronzes: the first-century-BC *Spinario*, a boy removing a thorn from his foot, and the *Capitoline She-wolf*. The infant Romulus and Remus, the two legendary founders of Rome, were added to the wolf (cast in the fifth century BC) in the 15th century, and the ensemble is now one of the symbols of the city.

The naked marble bottom of the elegant *Esquiline Venus* welcomes visitors to a new, modern section of the museum, which houses some of its best statues. Though Venus' arms are missing, fingers show that she was once depicted brushing her hair. Also here is a finely wrought bust of

Speaking statuses

Speaking statues

The quintessentially Roman tradition of street writing goes back to the 16th century, when any form of criticism of the Church was severely punished, and frustrated Romans took to using a number of statues as billboards. The strictly anonymous messages – called *pasquinate* after the first person to write one – were sensibly posted at night. For centuries this was the only form of mass media in Rome and it is still popular today, as a visit to the statue in piazza Pasquino (off piazza Navona) will show.

Emperor Commodus (son of Marcus Aurelius) as Hercules, with a lion's skin over his head and the apples of the Hesperides in his hand. The highlight, however, is the original gilded bronze equestrian statue of Marcus Aurelius. Even familiarity with the copy outside does little to dull the wonder of the real thing.

Behind are the uncovered foundations of the Temple of Jupiter, dug 8 m into the ground. The *Horti Maecenatiani* were ancient private gardens with an eclectic collection of statues, many of which are displayed in rooms in this section, from an Egyptian dog to the Greek head of an Amazon.

On the second floor, the Renaissance and Baroque paintings can seem a little dull after the startling drama of the statues below, but there are some highlights worth seeking out. Titian's *Baptism of Christ*, from around 1512, is here, as are various Tintorettos and Guercinos. Two Caravaggios shine out – his *Fortune Teller* from around 1595 is an uncharacteristically light-hearted painting. Look carefully and you will see that the 'fortune teller' is actually stealing the man's ring. Next to it, his *St John the Baptist*, from 1602, is more typically shadowy, demonstrating the artist's almost photographic sense of light and dark.

Palazzo Nuovo A tunnel connects the two museum buildings, and also gives access to the *Tabularium*, an ancient porticoed bridge with great views over the Roman Forum.

The Palazzo Nuovo continues the Roman marble theme. The courtyard, with many

impressive, large works, centres on the second-century *Fountain of Marforio*, a work that in the 16th century became known as one of Rome's 'speaking statues': satirical verses, often mocking Roman leaders, were stuck to his manly limbs.

Upstairs, a hundred more statues line the hall, including a baby Hercules strangling snakes, Eros stringing a bow, and a drunken old woman with a jug of wine. The **Sala degli Imperatori** holds busts of the emperors; the **Sala dei Filosofi** contains philosophers, playwrights and intellectuals from ancient Greece. The **Great Hall** has precious black marble statues including one of Zeus and a slightly disturbingly large baby Hercules.

Finally, the **Hall of Gaul** saves some of the best until last. In the centre of the room is a stunningly human statue of *The Dying Gaul* – a soldier, wounded in the chest, having sunk on to his shield, exhausted but still resisting. By the window are *Cupid and Psyche*, a kissing couple charmingly oblivious to their surroundings.

Il Vittoriano.

Il Vittoriano

Piazza Venezia, T06-6920 2049.
Lifts to Terrazza delle Quadrighe Mon-Thu
0930-1930, Fri-Sat 0930-2330, Sun 0930-2030, €7.
Bus: 63, 75, 81, 87, 95, 170, 628.
Metro: Colosseo. Map: Rome, E4, p84.

Variously known as 'the typewriter' and 'the wedding cake', the gargantuan white marble monument to the first king of united Italy, Vittorio Emanuele II, sits at the edge of the Capitoline Hill. Encapsulating the *Altare della Patria* – the altar of patriotism – and various museums dedicated to the glory of Italy, its overblown size and absurd pomposity mean it is much gaped at but little loved. However, it's well worth climbing the steps up its terraces, not least for the great views it gives over the surrounding ancient forums and the rest of Rome. New lifts were opened in 2007 to the highest part of all, the *Terrazza delle Quadrighe*, giving the best views in the city.

Giuseppe Sacconi designed the structure in 1895 but did not live to see its completion in 1935. The tomb of the Unknown Soldier was added in 1921, beneath the equestrian statue of the king, and an eternal flame burns here in memory of Italy's war dead. Female figures representing Italian cities surround the statue, and there are more, in the grand sweep of columns behind, representing the Italian regions; information boards point out which is which.

Inside the building, the **Museo Centrale del Risorgimento** concentrates on military history, with statues, portraits, weaponry and costumes. The **Ala Brasini** wing, to the southeast, usually holds the most interesting exhibitions, for which there may be an entry charge. There is a café at the southeastern corner of the terrace.

Basilica di Santa Maria in Aracoeli

Piazza Campidoglio.
Daily 0900-1230, 1430-1730.
Bus C3, 40, 63, 70, 81, 87, 95, 628, 716.
Metro: Colosseo. Map: Centro Storico, G6, p96.

Squeezed between the Vittoriano and the Capitoline Museums, this basilica has its own set

Cosmatesque floors

The Cosmati family, working in and around Rome in the late 12th and 13th centuries, is usually credited with having invented the distinctive style of inlaid marble mosaic flooring found in some of Rome's most beautiful churches. The colourful geometric patterns have Byzantine influences, and Lorenzo Cosmati learnt his art from Greek craftsmen before making the style his own. The beautifully intricate and creative patterns incorporate squares, parallelograms, circles and purple (porphyry), green (serpentine) stone and paler marble. Over the centuries the harder porphyry and serpentine stones have worn less than the softer pale marble, leaving those parts raised. The Cosmati were recyclers – the materials for these floors were fragments of marble from ancient Roman structures. Good examples of the style can be seen in Santa Maria in Aracoeli (see page 75) and San Clemente (see page 76).

of stairs from the piazza below. The baroque interior hides a few details worth seeking out, especially the Pinturicchio-frescoed chapel, the first on the right as you enter. Illustrating the life of St Bernard and painted around 1483, the left-hand wall in particular is an impressive illustration of the Umbrian painter's Renaissance skills in perspective and the creation of three-dimensional space, as well as a very human characterization.

Possibly built over an earlier Roman temple, the church reused Roman columns to separate its three naves. In a chapel at the back, the *Santo Bambino* – a saccharine gold- and jewel-encrusted statue of the baby Jesus – is the centre of a popular ritual here on Christmas Eve (see page 21).

Piazza della Bocca della Verità

Metro: Circo Massimo. Map: Rome, E5, p84.

Nestled between the Campidoglio, the Circus Maximus and a constant barrage of traffic, the piazza della Bocca della Verità has a high density of sights. The **Bocca della Verità**, famously featured in the 1953 film *Roman Holiday*, is firmly on the coach tour circuit, and there is usually a queue of people waiting to have their photo taken with their hand inside the stone mouth. The legend, probably medieval, is that if you tell a lie the mouth will bite off your hand.

The church in which the stone is set, **Santa Maria in Cosmedin** (daily 0930-1700), gets far fewer visitors. Founded in the sixth century, it has an interior that has been stripped back to reveal some of its original features and a beautiful Cosmatesque marble mosaic floor. The columns in the church are all Roman; the bell tower is Romanesque, dating from the 13th century. An eighth-century mosaic of Mary, Christ and the Three Kings now hangs incongruously in the gift shop.

Around the piazza are various Roman monuments, none of which are open to the public. The *Arco di Giano* (Arch of Janus) is a triumphal arch from the fourth century, but much more battered than the city's other arches. Nearby, attached to the Church of San Giorgio in Velabro, is the ornamental third-century *Arco degli Argentari* (Arch of the Moneychangers). Towards the river, the round *Tempio di Ercole* (Temple of Hercules) is the city's oldest marble temple, dating from the second century BC, with all but one of its original columns still standing. The square **Tempio di Portuno** to the north is from around the same time; it is dedicated to Portunus, originally a deity of doors and entrances, who evolved into the god of ports and harbours.

Nearby, another Roman mouth can be seen: that of the ancient city's main drain, the **Cloaca Maxima**, where it discharged into the river just below the ponte Palatino.

Celio

Basilica di San Clemente

Via di San Giovanni in Laterano.
Mon-Sat 0900-1230, 1500-1800, Sun 1200-1800, upper level free, lower levels €5/3.50 concession. Metro: Colosseo. Map: Rome, G5, p84.

To the east of the Colosseum, the 12th-century Basilica of St Clement is impressive enough, but it is below the surface that the multi-levelled site really comes into its own. Here a fourth-century church

survives, with exceptional frescoes, and, further down, Roman remains comprise a temple, a large building and the streets and alleyways between them. The building is in the keeping of an order of Irish Dominicans, who were given refuge here by Pope Urban VIII in 1667 after they were expelled from England.

The early Christian church was covered over at the beginning of the 12th century, and the church that survives today was constructed over the top of it. The choir was rebuilt using materials from the earlier church below. There is a beautiful Cosmatesque mosaic floor and a sparkling 12th-century mosaic showing the Church as a vine, which sprouts from the blood of Christ and then curls artistically around the apse. The Renaissance frescoes in the chapel to the right of the entrance are by Masolino di Panicale, painted between 1423 and 1431, and illustrate the life and death of St Catherine. They alone would make a visit worthwhile.

Downstairs, in the earlier church, a wealth of frescoes dates back as far as the mid-ninth century, making it one of the world's best collections of early medieval Christian art. Descending into the atmospheric fourth-century structure, now with smart contemporary lighting, one of the first frescoes you come to is the 11th-century *Miracle of the Sea of Azrou*. The story it illustrates tells how once a year the sea drew back to reveal the watery tomb of St Clement. One year a boy was trapped by the returning tide and lost, but when the tide retreated again the following year he was found safe and well in the tomb. Fish swim around the tomb, with St Clement in the centre. The figures below are the donors who paid for the painting.

Below an 11th-century image of St Clement preaching to the people is the earliest known example of written Italian, explaining the story of Theodora (on the left) and her husband Sisinnius, who enters on the right to take her away but is struck deaf and dumb. Another 11th-century fresco illustrates the life of St Alexis: having gone to live as a hermit, he returned to his wife and family but, unrecognized by them, lived with them as a servant, his identity only becoming known after his death.

Other highlights include a ninth-century *Ascension*, with Jesus carried aloft by two angels, and a slab with a Roman inscription on one side and a much more primitively carved Christian inscription on the other.

Down more stairs are extensive, if rather cold and dank, Roman remains from the reign of Domitian in the first century AD – two buildings separated by a narrow alley. To the left is a temple dedicated to the god Mithras. This would once have been a public building, probably serving the amphitheatre in some way, which subsequently had an altar and benches added. The other building has unusually sturdy outside walls with few entrances, leading some scholars to the conclusion that it may have been a *moneta*, or mint. Several rooms are arranged around a central, unexcavated courtyard.

On the way out, look for a small eighth-century *Madonna*, in Byzantine style and flanked by two figures, probably St Euphemia and St Catherine, both wearing pearl crowns. This fresco, the oldest in the medieval church, was one of the first discoveries of Father Joseph Mullooly, who began the excavations in 1857. The hole in the wall above and to the left is where he first entered the old church.

Monastero dei Santi Quattro Coronati

Via dei Santi Quattro Coronati, santiquattrocoronati.org.
Daily 0615-2000, cloister Mon-Sat 1000-1145, 1600-1745, Sun 0930-1030, 1600-1745.
Metro: Colosseo. Map: Rome, G5, p84.

Devoted to four anonymous early Christians, martyred under Diocletian, this church and monastery date back to the fourth century, and there is an attractive 13th-century cloister. The Cappella di San Silvestro has 13th-century frescoes depicting Emperor Constantine crowning the pope.

Below: San Giovanni in Laterano.

Santo Stefano Rotondo

Via di Santo Stefano Rotondo, T06-421191.
Tue-Sat 0930-1230, 1400-1700, Sun 0930-1230.
Bus: 81, 673. Metro: Colosseo. Map: Rome, G6, p84.

A rare round church, Santo Stefano was first built in the fifth century to commemorate Christianity's first martyr. It's a beautiful space, with an inner circular colonnade and chapels off the outer ring. Around the outer aisle, graphic 16th-century frescoes illustrate various methods of torturing and killing Christians, from beheading and boiling them to squashing them under heavy rocks. Palestrina is said to have composed his music in the garden here in the 16th century.

Graphic 16th-century frescoes illustrate various methods of torturing and killing Christians.

Villa Celimontana

Via della Navicella, T06-589 7807,
villacelimontanajazz.com.
Bus: 81, 673. Metro: Colosseo. Map: Rome, G6, p84.

Southeast of the Colosseum, the gardens of Villa Celimontana are laid out in Renaissance style. Most of the year they are a pleasant place for a stroll or a picnic, but from June to September they come alive as a venue for evening jazz performances, with lights turning the park into a magically romantic place.

Basilica di San Giovanni in Laterano

Piazza di San Giovanni Laterano.
Cloisters Mon-Sat 0900-1800, Sun 0900-1745, €2.
Metro: San Giovanni. Map: Rome, H6, p84.

Until the 15th century this was the headquarters of the pope, and it remains a grandiose place, though

most of its decoration is now Baroque.

The cathedral of Rome, it is considered the most important of the four papal basilicas of the city. A 13th-century mosaic in the apse remains, and there is a beautiful Cosmatesque mosaic floor, but in the main it is the sheer scale that is most impressive.

Hidden on the back of the last column to the left of the main doors is a badly lit fragment of a fresco attributed to Giotto.

In the ornate 13th-century cloister, dotted with colourful mosaics, are various artefacts that were taken from the church before its Baroque overhaul. Highlights include the medieval tomb of Riccardo Annibaldi, a papal notary who died in 1289. His statue lies below a charming frieze of the funeral ceremony, in which a priest is shown sniffing the incense.

On the piazza outside the basilica is Rome's largest **ancient Egyptian obelisk**, commissioned by Pharaoh Thutmose III in the 15th century BC, and brought to Rome and erected in the Circus Maximus in 357.

Just to the east of the basilica is the **Scala Santa**, the holy staircase, said to have belonged to Pontius Pilate, to have been climbed by Jesus before his crucifixion and brought to Rome from Jerusalem by St Helena, mother of Emperor Constantine. So holy are these stairs considered that people are only allowed to climb them on their knees, and many do.

Basilica di Santa Croce in Gerusalemme

Piazza Santa Croce in Gerusalemme,
T06-701 4769, basilicasantacroce.com.
Church daily 0645-1930, garden Wed 0930-1300, 1530-1900 (may open more frequently in future, check website), shop Tue and Fri 1600-1800, Wed 1000-1230, 1600-1800, Sat 1000-1200, guided tours of garden and library on request at least 1 week in advance, free.
Bus: 649. Metro: San Giovanni.

Though it's a little out of the way, the church of Santa Croce in Gerusalemme is well worth a visit for its Cosmatesque floor, a stunning Renaissance

Above: Basilica di Santa Croce in Gerusalemme.
Opposite page: Santo Stefano Rotondo.

apse fresco, the chanting of its Cistercian monks and – most of all – its beautiful vegetable, herb and fruit garden, tended by the monks, inside the circular walls of what was once a Roman amphitheatre. The garden has recently been redesigned and has colourful new gates by Jannis Kounellis, using organic lumps of Murano glass woven into the ironwork. Roses and vines twine around pergolas, and a circular planting layout centres on a fountain at the middle of a cross formation. The garden is rich in symbolism as well as good practice in crop rotation. The fresh fruit and vegetables grown here are sold in a small shop, alongside other products made by the monks, such as jams and an *amaro* (herbal liqueur); it's hoped that a café, also selling garden produce, will open soon.

Around the city

The highlight of the church itself is the recently restored and now shiningly bright and clean fresco in the apse by Antoniazzo Romano. Previously attributed to Perugino or Pinturicchio, the painting has a stunningly realized landscape backdrop. It portrays stories of the Cross, a relic of which is supposedly held in the church, having been brought to Rome by Constantine's mother, St Helena.

Terme di Caracalla

Viale delle Terme di Caracalla 52,
T06-3996 7700, pierreci.it.
Tue-Sun 0900 till 1 hr before sunset, Mon 0900-1400, combined ticket with Villa dei Quintili and Tomba di Cecilia Metella, valid 7 days, €6/3 concession, or Archaeologia Card, free EU citizens under 18 and over 65.
Metro: Circo Massimo.

Built in AD 212 by Emperor Caracalla, the baths complex to the southeast of the Circus Maximus is impressive predominantly for its huge scale. The original structure, worked on by 9000 workers over five years, could accommodate 1600 people at any one time. The building was 228 m long and used some 20 million bricks and brick pieces. Many of these remain, as do some interesting fragments of mosaic. The rooms would have been heated by a hypocaust, conducting hot air under the floor from numerous furnaces burning wood and coal, which also heated the water for the baths.

Visitors enter through the *palaestra* at one end of the 56-m long *frigidarium*. The *palaestra* would have been used for exercise and sport, while the *frigidarium*, or cold room, formed the central hall of the complex. To the right is the *tepidarium* (warm room) and beyond, the scant outline of the circular *caldarium* (hot room). On the other side is the enormous swimming pool. The second *palaestra*, at the far end, has some of the best remnants of mosaics.

South of the Circus Maximus, and opposite Trastevere's lower reaches, the Aventine Hill rises above the Tiber into a rarefied atmosphere of villas, orange trees and quiet piazzas. There are almost no shops, cafés or restaurants, and the atmosphere is very different from most of the rest of central Rome, but it's well worth a wander for its views and its air of calm, as well as for some beautiful churches and a famous view.

Villa del Priorato dei Cavalieri di Malta

Piazza dei Cavalieri di Malta.
Bus: 23, 44, 95, 170, 280, 716.
Metro: Circo Massimo.

The Knights of Malta, now known as the Sovereign Military Order of Malta, having lost control of their eponymous one-time home, are now based here in Rome. Their grand villa on the Aventine Hill is most famous for the wonderful view through its keyhole, which lines up perfectly with an avenue of trees and the dome of St Peter's in the distance. Though the order produces its own stamps and retains a currency, it is no longer generally recognized as a sovereign state, despite its best efforts. Santa Maria del Priorato, the church behind the usually locked gates, was remodelled in the mid-18th century by Giovanni Battista Piranesi, famous for his engravings of Roman ruins and architectural fantasies; he also designed the piazza.

Giardino degli Aranci

Bus: 23, 44, 95, 170, 280, 716.
Metro: Circo Massimo.

At the top of the Clivo Rocca Savella, a cobbled and partially stepped path up from the river to via di Santa Sabina, this romantic little park has orange trees and cats and great views over the river to Trastevere and St Peter's beyond, as well as north to the Vittoriano.

The Basilica di Santa Sabina all'Aventino.

Basilica di Santa Sabina all'Aventino

Piazza Pietro d'Illiria 1, via di Santa Sabina.
Daily 0630-1245, 1600-1900, free.
Bus: 23, 44, 95, 170, 280, 716.
Metro: Circo Massimo. Map: Rome, D6, p84.

A large-naved, fifth-century church at the top of the Aventine Hill, this is the centre of the Dominican order. Restored to something like its original decoration, the rectangular basilica has the feel of a Roman structure: it's a plain but beautiful airy space with elaborate capitals atop its ancient columns, a starry ceiling and a frescoed apse, which probably matches the design of the original mosaic. The 6-m high cedarwood doors are the original fifth-century versions, and their 18 carved panels represent Bible stories, including one of the oldest existing depictions of the Crucifixion. Outside in the piazza, a fountain utilizes a rather sterner version of the face of the Bocca della Verità (see page 75).

Testaccio is an area thin on sights but with plenty of atmosphere, much of which stems from its working-class roots and its connections with the huge complex of the **ex-Mattatoio**: once Rome's abattoir, these days it's a higgledy-piggledy collection of workshops, galleries and dereliction, including a branch of the city's contemporary art gallery and an alternative food centre. Also here are an ancient pyramid and the graves of Keats and Shelley – together with a well-looked-after community of cats – in the wonderful Non-Catholic Cemetery. **Monte Testaccio** is a 30-m high Roman rubbish heap: it's almost entirely composed of broken amphorae, which once contained the ancient city's vast imports of olive oil, grain and other foodstuffs.

Macro Future

Piazza Orazio Giustiniani 4, T06-671 070400, macro.roma.museum.
Tue-Sun 0900-1900, may be closed in winter, €1 (may vary during exhibitions).
Metro: Pyramide. Bus: 719. Map: Rome, D7, p84.

Huge buildings in the ex-slaughterhouse are now a slick extension of Rome's contemporary art gallery, showing large-scale temporary exhibitions in an impressively huge and airy space.

Città dell'Altra Economia

Largo Dino Frisullo, Campo Boario, ex-Mattatoio, T06-5730 0419, cittadellaltraeconomia.org.
Tue-Sat 1000-2000, Sun 1000-1900.
Metro: Piramide.

A centre for the promotion of renewable energy sources, fair trade, organic food and events, the 'City of the Alternative Economy' has a food shop, bar and restaurant as well as a craft outlet selling some imaginative pieces made from recycled materials. The centre is also used for occasional special events.

Around the city

Cimitero Acattolico

Via Caio Cestio 6, T06-574 1900,
protestantcemetery.it.
Mon-Sat 0900-1700, Sun 0900-1300, last
entrance 30 mins before closing, free but €2
donation requested.
Metro: Piramide. Map: Rome, D7, p84.

The so-called Protestant Cemetery (sometimes
also referred to as the English or Foreigners'
Cemetery) is in fact for non-Catholics, making it a
sort of special members' club for dead ex-patriates
and a few atheist Italians. The prime attractions
here are the graves of the English Romantic poets
Keats and Shelley, though it's well worth buying
the €3 map to read about, and seek out, the
various other notable people buried here among
the cedar trees and cawing rooks. The place is
lovingly tended – a haven of peace among the
busy roads of Testaccio.

The cemetery is also the best spot from which
to get a view of the 36-m **Piramide di Caio Cestio**
just outside. Faced with marble, and Egyptian in
style, the pyramid was built in less than a year as
a tomb and memorial to Caius Cestius, who died
in 12 BC. He may also have been responsible for
the ponte Cestius, the first bridge between Isola
Tiberina and Trastevere. You can see the frescoed
interior of the pyramid, by prior appointment
(T06-3996 7700, pierreci.it), at 1100 on the second
and fourth Saturdays of each month. A **community
of cats** has lived by the monument for centuries,
and they are to be found prowling around the
graves of the cemetery. They now have their own
website: igattidellapiramide.it.

**The so-called Protestant Cemetery
(sometimes also referred to as the
English or Foreigners' Cemetery)
is in fact for non-Catholics, making
it a sort of special members' club
for dead ex-patriates and a few
atheist Italians.**

Centrale Montemartini

Via Ostiense 106, T06-8205 9127,
centralemontemartini.org.
Tue-Sun 0900-1900, €4.50/2.50 concession,
combined ticket with Capitoline Museums
€8.50/6.50, free EU citizens under 18 and over 65.
Metro: Garbatella.

Originally conceived as a temporary holding space
for some of the excess of the Capitoline Museums'
huge collection of Roman statuary and relics, this
gallery in an ex-power station has proved so
successful that it is now a permanent fixture.

On the ground floor, highlights include the
Barberini Togate, a first-century funerary statue of a
man wearing a toga and holding busts of his father
and grandfather – a work that demonstrates the
importance of social status. Here too is the funeral
bas-relief of a married couple from the first century
BC, he especially naturalistic, she noticeably more
mannered. Mosaics from the baths of via San
Lorenzo depict some very realistic sea creatures,
and a fifth-century BC *Aphrodite* stands seductively
in front of a 1912 extraction pump.

Upstairs is the **Sala Macchine** (Machine Hall),
the most impressive room of the thermoelectric
power plant, where huge industrial machinery sits
side by side with Roman statuary, and where the
huge scale of the power station is an appropriate
setting for the statues, the early 20th-century
industrial architecture matching the ancient
basilicas. The head, arm and feet of a huge acrolith
statue of a goddess – only the exposed body parts
would have been fashioned from marble, the rest
being made of bronze – indicate that she would
once have stood 8 m high.

In the **Sala Caldaie** (Boiler Room) is a Niobid
who once stood in Caesar's gardens, a panther
attacking a wild boar, which would also have been
a garden decoration, and a headless naked nymph
being hassled by an aroused satyr. Also in this
room are beautiful statues of a seated maiden
and a muse.

The statue of Hygieia inside the Centrale Montemartini power station.

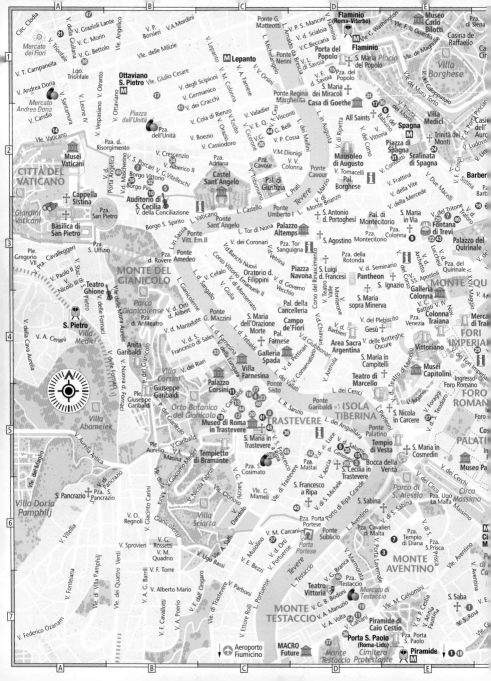

Rome listings

❶ Sleeping

1 Abitart E7
2 Aleph F2
3 Anselmo E6
4 Antica Locanda F4
5 Arco del Lauro D5
6 Art E2
7 Aventino E6
8 B&B Santiquattro G5
9 Boutique Hotel Trevi E3
10 Bramante B2
11 Buonanotte Garibaldi C5
12 Canada Hotel H2
13 Capo d'Africa G5
14 Casa di Accoglienza
   Polo VI A2
15 Casa di Santa Francesca
   Romana D5
16 Daphne Inn F3
17 De Russie E1
18 Donna Camilla Savelli C5
19 Exedra G3
20 Fawlty Towers Hostel H3
21 Franklin A1
22 Gladiatori G5
23 Grand Hotel Parco
   dei Principi G1
24 Hassler E2
25 Il Covo F4
26 Ivanhoe F4
27 Kolbe Hotel Rome E5
28 Locanda Monti B&B F4
29 Nerva F4
30 Palazzetto degli
   Artisti Suites F4
31 Portrait Suites E2
32 Radisson SAS es. Hotel H4
33 Residence Barberini F3
34 Residenza A F2
35 Residenza Arco de'
   Tolomei D5
36 Residenza Santa
   Maria C5
37 Ripa C6
38 Rose Garden F2
39 Sant'Anna B2
40 San Francesco D6
41 Santa Maria C5
42 The Beehive H2
43 Trevi B&B E3
44 Visconti Palace C2
45 Villa della Fonte C5
46 White E3

❷ Eating & drinking

1 Al Callarello E7
2 Angeli a Borgo B2
3 Asinocotto D5
4 bir & fud C5
5 Borgo Antico B2
6 Café Café G5
7 Colline Emiliane E3
8 Crab F5
9 Da Augusto C5
10 Da Enzo D5
11 Da Felice D7
12 Da Lucia C5
13 Da Olinda C5
14 Da Oio a Casa Mia D7
15 Dal Bolognese D1
16 Dar Poeta C5
17 Del Frate B1
18 Doppiozeroo E7
20 Glass Hostaria C5
21 Il Bocconcino G5
22 Il Chianti E3
23 Il Ciak C5
24 Il Palazzetto E2
25 Ivo C5
26 L'Arcangelo C2
27 La Gensola C5
28 Le Mani in Pasta D5
29 Le Tamerici E3
30 La Taverna dei Fori
   Imperiali F4
31 Margutta RistorArte D1
32 Maxela B2
33 Miraggio C4
34 Osteria Leonardesca B2
35 Osteria Margutta E1
36 Osteria degli Amici D7
37 Osteria del Pesce D7
38 Osteria dell'Angelo A1
39 Papa'Baccus F2
40 Papagiò G5
41 Piero & Francesco B2
42 Pizzeria ai Marmi D5
43 Pizzeria Li Rioni a
   Santiquattro G5
44 Quirino C5
45 Ripa 12 C5
46 Remo D7
47 Sicilia in Bocca A1
48 Trattoria degli Amici C5
49 Velando B2

The listings on this map are covered in the following chapters:
The ancient city; Vatican City & Prati; Trastevere & around;
Villa Borghese & Tridente; Trevi, Quirinale, Monti & Esquiline.

Sleeping

Forum & around

Hotel Capo d'Africa €€€€
Via Capo d'Africa 54, T06-772801, hotelcapodafrica.com.
Metro: Colosseo.
Map: Rome, G5, p85.
An expensive but elegant and approachable hotel in what was once a convent, adjacent to the Church of Santi Quattro Coronati, southeast of the Colosseum. It opened in 2002 and, though the 65 rooms are not especially spacious, they are light and modern, decorated in pale colours with free internet and flat screen TVs, plus extras such as slippers and bathrobes. Colourful modern artworks add splashes of colour, and the breakfast area and the best rooms have roof terraces overlooking the city.

Kolbe Hotel Rome €€€€
Via di San Teodoro 44, T06-6992 4250, kolbehotelrome.com.
Metro: Circo Massimo.
Map: Rome, E5, p85.
Between the Circus Maximus and the Forum, Kolbe is well placed for central Rome sights, with rooms that overlook the Forum on one side and an internal courtyard, planted with orange trees, on the other. The 72 well-equipped rooms incorporate original arches and some of the better ones have nice contemporary touches such as round beds and Jacuzzi baths. A bar on one of the lower roof terraces also has good views.

Hotel Gladiatori €€€
Via Labicana 125, T06-7759 1380, hotelgladiatori.com.
Metro: Colosseo.
Map: Rome, G5, p85.
Five-star refinement overlooking the 1930s excavations of the *Ludus Magnus* (the gladiator school), with the Colosseum behind. A roof terrace with great views catches the evening sun, and the style is refined and modern, with muted colours and fine fabrics. The downside is the busy via Labicana outside the front door.

B&B Santiquattro €€
Via dei Santi Quattro Coronati 64, T338-456 7436, bbsantiquattro.com.
Metro: Colosseo.
Map: Rome, G5, p85.
Under the same management as the excellent Il Bocconcino restaurant nearby, this B&B has seven rooms and apartments, simply decorated but with good comfortable beds and views along the street to the Colosseum.

Aventino

Hotel Anselmo €€€
Piazza Sant'Anselmo 2, T06-570057, aventinohotels.com.
Metro: Circo Massimo.
Bus: 23, 716.
Map: Rome, E6, p84.
An elegant hotel on a quiet piazza on the Aventine Hill, the Sant'Anselmo has a nice sprinkling of contemporary design elements among the antiques and sumptuous fabrics. The best of the 34 rooms has a private terrace with great views across the city. The rooms are never spacious, but they squeeze in plenty of style: floors are

Eating & drinking

polished, well-worn wood, there are claw-foot baths, and an uplit glass crystal chandelier cascades down the stairwell.

Hotel Aventino €€€
Via di San Domenico 10, T06-570057, aventinohotels.com.
Metro: Circo Massimo.
Bus: 23, 716.
Map: Rome, E6, p84.
Under the same management as the Hotel Sant'Anselmo just around the corner, the Aventino has 21 rooms, with parquet floors and the beds have elegant wooden headboards. There are antique touches such as inlaid wood furniture, and good modern bathrooms with hydromassage baths or showers.

Ostiense

Abitart Hotel €€
Via Pellegrino Matteucci 10-20, T06-454 3191, abitarthotel.it.
Metro: Piramide.
Map: Rome, E7, p84.
Packed with a bright and interesting collection of striking contemporary art, and with brightly coloured rooms, Abitart is a rare creatively designed hotel in Rome. It's not exactly central, though the transport links aren't bad, and it's well placed for Ostiense's grittier urban feel and the excellent Centrale Montemartini (see page 82). Next door, **Estrobar** (T06-5728 9141, estrobar.it) is a gallery, bar and restaurant.

Forum & around

Crab €€€
Via Capo d'Africa 2, T06-7720 3636.
Mon 2000-2400, Tue-Sat 1300-1500, 2000-2400.
Metro: Colosseo.
Map: Rome, F5, p84.
Smart and contemporary, Crab caters to the international side of Celio's new-found hip status. Oysters and seafood feature prominently on the menu, as do the eponymous crustaceans, once they've been hoisted from a tank near the door.

Papagiò €€
Via Capo d'Africa 26, T06-700 9800.
Mon-Sat 1230-1500, 1900-0030.
Metro: Colosseo.
Map: Rome, G5, p85.
Smart and very welcoming, Papagiò is a great little seafood restaurant with a traditional stone ceiling, tiled floor and wine bottles decorating the walls. Sea bass or tuna carpaccio make good starters and the seafood risotto is excellent, though for a real treat you should go for their trademark pasta with baby octopus, olives, cherry tomatoes and capers. There are also some vegetarian choices.

Il Bocconcino €
Via Ostilia 23, T06-7707 9175, ilbocconcino.com.
Wed-Mon 1130-1530, 1930-2330.
Metro: Colosseo.
Map: Rome, G5, p85.
A traditional Roman osteria that fills up with locals despite its proximity to the Colosseum. Red and white checked tablecloths, wooden panelling, a brick ceiling and old Roman cinema photos add to the old-fashioned feel. Daily specials might include an antipasto of fresh anchovies and chicory, or pasta with sausage and pumpkin, and there are sometimes good salads too, such as fennel, olive and orange.

Pizzeria Li Rioni a Santiquattro €
Via dei Santi Quattro Coronati 24, T06-7045 0605.
Wed-Mon.
Metro: Colosseo.
Map: Rome, G5, p85.
Though the fake outdoor-indoor decoration is a little twee, everything else about Li Rioni is spot-on, making it one of Rome's best pizzerias, though this fact is largely a secret kept by the locals of Celio. There is a good selection of traditional deep-fried *supplì* (rice balls) and the like, and the pizzas are archetypally thin and crunchy, without losing anything in the taste department. The atmosphere is almost always bubbling and service is impeccably friendly.

Cafés & bars

Bibenda Wine Concept
Via Capo d'Africa 21,
T06-7720 6673, wineconcept.it.
Mon-Thu 1200-2300, Fri-Sat
1200-0100.
Metro: Colosseo.
An *enoteca* with the strapline
"Making the image and culture
and wine more seductive", this is
both wine bar and shop, with a
huge selection of wines in a
bright, modern setting. You can
have a plate of cheese and
salami, and there are various
tasting options available, plus
lots of wine by the glass.

Café Café
Via dei Santi Quattro Coronati,
44, T06-700 8743,
cafecaferoma@libero.it.
Daily 1100-0130.
Metro: Colosseo.
There's an international feel to
this welcoming and cosy little
café, with none of the tourist-
centred attitudes that you might
expect to mar somewhere this
close to the Colosseum. Jazzy
tunes play, there's a Middle
Eastern-influenced menu of

assaggi or tasters, lots of teas and
some delicious freshly squeezed
juices too. Whether you want a
coffee, lunch (traditional Roman
dishes or a vegetarian option),
the Sunday buffet brunch or a
late-night drink, Café Café's
warm yellow walls and
collection of photography
books make it a great venue.

Il Pentagrappolo
Via Celimontana 21b,
T06-709 6301,
ilpentagrappolo.com.
Tue-Thu 1200-1530, 1800-0100,
Fri 1200-1530, 1800-0200, Sat
1800-0200, Sun 1800-0100.
Metro: Colosseo.
A bar with a young, hip clientele
and live music at the grand piano
on Thursday, Friday and Saturday
evenings. Aperitivi from
1800-2030 come with generous
plates of snacks, and more
substantial dishes are available
too, including a big selection of
cold meats and cheese. The wine
list includes an unusually high
number of organic vintages.

Wine Bar dei Contrari
Via Ostilia 22/22a, T347-706 4341.
Metro: Colosseo.
A theatre and cinema bar,
Contrari is a tiny venue with
nightly theatre, cabaret, or
arthouse films playing in a
corner and live music at a grand
piano in the refined cocktail and
wine bar. It's not a cheap place
for a drink, but the quality of
aperitivo snacks is high, and the

books, jazz, candles and elegant
decor give the place a cultured
edge over the competition.

Aventino

Al Callarello €€
Via Salvator Rosa 8,
T06-574 7575.
Mon-Sat 1200-1500, 1930-2300.
Metro: Circo Massimo. Bus: 715.
Map: Rome, E7, p84.
Popular with locals, the very good
value Callarello is well out of most
tourists' way, just off a quiet
piazza behind the church of San
Saba. Specializing in fish, they also
do good pizzas in the evening
and have an excellent self-service
buffet antipasto selection. The
eclectic decor mixes green and
pink walls, wagon wheels and
floral Art Deco touches.

Testaccio

Osteria del Pesce €€€
Via Galvani 24a, T06-5728 3840.
Mon-Sat 2000-0130.
Metro: Piramide.
Map: Rome, D7, p84.
Right in among the nightclubs
on the northern edge of Monte
Testaccio, this buzzing first-floor
seafood restaurant is one of
Rome's most fashionable spots,
serving impeccably fresh, high
quality fish dishes in a beautiful
setting, with high ceilings and
lots of faded, pastel-blue-
painted wood.

What the locals say

My ideal morning starts with a walk in a park – perhaps Villa Pamphilj, or maybe the Appia Antica, a beautiful fusion of nature and history. Then shop till you drop in the world's most fashionable *centro storico* and afterwards watch a traditional tea ceremony at the Japanese Cultural Institute in the Parioli district. For an aperitivo I go somewhere in Trastevere and for dinner I choose a traditional Roman restaurant such as Da Oio a Casa Mia in the Testaccio area, followed by some good blues at trendy Big Mama. If I want to party till the small hours, Testaccio has many good places to choose from – maybe I'd go for a hip alternative place like Radio Londra.

Simona.

Da Felice €€
Via Mastro Giorgio 29,
T06-574 6800.
Mon-Sat 1230-1445, 2000-2330,
Sun 1230-1500.
Metro: Piramide.
Map: Rome, D7, p84.
Smart, trendy, good value and almost always busy, it's usually necessary to book ahead for a table here. The menu rotates depending on the day of the week, but certain classics are permanent fixtures. The fettuccine with artichoke is fantastic, as is the *abacchio* (lamb) with roast potatoes. The modern interior, with open brickwork and hanging metal lamps, is chic but stops short of pretentiousness.

Osteria degli Amici €€
Via Nicola Zabaglia 25, T06-578
1466, osteriadegliamici.info.
Wed-Mon 1230-1500, 1930-2400.
Metro: Piramide.
Map: Rome, D7, p84.

A sophisticated, friendly little restaurant on a corner opposite Monte Testaccio, Osteria degli Amici serves both traditional Roman dishes and some more creative, mostly seafood-based fare. A daily blackboard menu may include octopus on a bed of *puntarelle* – a curly-leaved Roman variety of chicory – and fixed menu favourites include a tasty tagliatelle with sea bass. Pasta portions are generous, so you might want to skip the second course and save some room for a spicy chocolate soufflé.

Da Oio a Casa Mia €
Via Galvani 43/45, T06-578 2680.
Mon-Sat lunch and dinner.
Metro: Piramide.
Map: Rome, D7, p84.
Red and white checked tablecloths and old photos and newspaper clippings on the wall help keep this one of the most traditional of Rome eateries. The pasta carbonara is exceptional; there's soupy pasta *fagioli* and, for the brave, *coratella*: heart, liver, spleen and lung cooked with artichokes and onions.

Remo €
Piazza Santa Maria Liberatrice 44,
T06-574 6270.
Mon-Sat 1900-0100.
Metro: Piramide.
Bus: 95, 170, 280.
Map: Rome, D7, p84.
One of Rome's most popular pizzerias, Remo serves archetypally thin-crust Roman pizzas with the requisite degree of joyful chaos. The bruschette, piled high with fresh, sweet, juicy tomatoes, are also very good. A table near the front allows you to watch the *pizzaiolo* theatre in progress; a room downstairs at the back is marginally calmer.

Cafés & bars
Caffè Emporio
Piazza dell'Emporio 2,
T06-574 4241, caffemporio.com.
Aperitivo 1800-2200.
Metro: Piramide.
Bus: 23, 75, 280, 716.
Just across the river from the lower reaches of Trastevere, Emporio has an industrial chic that is a fitting welcome to Testaccio. Deep bass booms out across the red seating and aging locals drinking wine mix with hip young media types sipping cocktails, served from a long bar. The generous aperitivo snacks are carefully concocted and intricately designed.

Entertainment

Farinando
*Via Luca della Robbia 30,
T06-575 0674.*
Daily 0800-1400, 1700-2100.
Metro: Piramide.
An excellent bakery with a good
range of fresh bread, cakes,
savouries and pizza by the slice.

L'Oasi della Birra
*Piazza Testaccio 38/41,
T06-574 6122.*
Closed Sun.
Metro: Piramide.
A bar that springs up nightly out of
the Orazio Palombi wine shop,
offering bottled beer from
countries including Cuba, New
Zealand, Malta and Venezuela, as
well as some good stuff on tap. As
well as beer, they serve wine and
an abundant, if early, aperitivo
buffet between 1700-2000 –
probably all you'll need to eat all
evening. Hidden downstairs are
atmospheric rooms particularly
suited to beer drinking.

RGB 46
*Piazza Santa Maria Liberatrice
46, T06-4542 1608, rgb46.it.*
Tue-Sun 1000-1300, 1600-0100.
Metro: Piramide. Bus: 95, 170.
An art, architecture and design
bookshop, RGB (as well as Red,
Green and Blue, the name also
stands for 'Relax, Gallery e Book')
also hosts exhibitions and has a
lounge area serving lots of good
tea and wine; there's also
occasionally live music.
A very laid-back atmosphere.

Ostiense

Doppiozeroo €
*Via Ostiense 68, T06-5730 1961,
doppiozeroo.it.*
0700-0200, closed Sun lunch
and Mon evening.
Metro: Garbatella. Bus: 23.
Map: Rome, E7, p84.
A café, restaurant and bar,
Doppiozeroo is a sleek,
contemporary venue, with a
long bar serving coffee, *cornetti*
and delicious tarts in the
morning, very good value lunch
dishes served canteen-style, and
evening aperitivi. Underlining
their metropolitan chic, they
sometimes have special sushi
evenings.

Clubs
The circumference of Monte
Testaccio is packed with
nightclubs, many dug into the
Roman rubbish tip itself. Listings
magazine **Roma c'è** is a good
source of what's going on where;
otherwise just turn up and see
what looks good.

Akab-Cave
*Via di Monte Testaccio 69,
T06-5725 0585, akabcave.com.*
Tue-Sat 2300-0400, €10
depending on night.
Metro: Piramide.
Electronica, soul and disco in a
venue on two floors with a Zen
garden – one of the more serious
clubs around Monte Testaccio,
people come here to see and be
seen as well as to dance.

Caffè Latino
*Via di Monte Testaccio 96,
T06-5728 8556,
caffelatinoroma.com.*
Mon and Wed-Sat 2300-0430,
€10 including a drink.
Metro: Piramide.
A healthy mix of 70s and 80s
disco, R&B, transsexual nights,
Arabic music and dance, and live
gigs with a vaguely African/
Latino theme and one of Rome's
most mixed crowds – a wide
variety of colours, ages and
sexual orientations all having a
very good time.

Shopping

Art & antiques

Artigeco
Via dei Santi Quattro Coronati 34,
T06-677 209901,
artigeco@tiscali.it.
Mon 1630-2000, Tue-Sat
1100-1400, 1630-2000.
Metro: Colosseo.
A personal and eclectic mix of
art, fashion (Audrey
Hepburnesque numbers from
Simona Barbieri's Twin Set label),
homemade candles, lamps and
bags, this design boutique stocks
items made almost exclusively
by friends of the owners.

Cesaretti
Via Magnanapoli 9, T06-679 0058.
Metro: Colosseo.
One of central Rome's more
unlikely sights, this doll repair shop
has a dusty window display of the
results of previous operations.

Galleria Arte e Pensieri
Via Ostilia 3a, T06-700 2404.
Wed-Sat 1600-2000.
Metro: Colosseo.
Interesting exhibitions of
contemporary art in a little
gallery run by an art collective
noted for promoting up-and-
coming talent.

Food & drink

Negozio Benedettino di
Sant'Anselmo
Piazza Sant'Anselmo, T06-579 1365.
Tue-Sun 1000-1200, 1600-1900.
Metro: Circo Massimo.
Inside the grounds of the church,
this endearing shop sells
produce made by monks,
including beer, Trappist
chocolate, wine and honey, as
well as books and religious
artefacts.

Volpetti
Via Marmorata 47,
T06-574 2352, volpetti.com.
Mon-Sat 0800-1400, 1700-2015.
Metro: Piramide.
A culinary treasure trove, Volpetti
is just about everyone's favourite
Roman delicatessen. As a result it
is usually busy, but there are
plenty of staff on hand to offer
free tasters of everything from
deep-fried Roman savouries to
nougat. Just down the road, a
new canteen, **Volpetti Più** (via
Alessandro Volta 8, Mon-Sat
1030-1530, 1730-2130) offers the
chance to eat Volpetti delicacies
and hot dishes before you get
home.

Transport

The metro to Piramide is the
easiest way to reach Testaccio;
the 280 bus along the river is
another option, or you can walk
from Trastevere.

Music
Look out for regular free choral
concerts at the **Chiesa di
Sant'Anselmo all'Aventino**
(piazza dei Cavalieri di Malta 5,
T06-57911, santanselmo.net).

Casa del Jazz
Viale di Porta Ardeatina 55,
T06-704731, casajazz.it.
Tue-Sat 1900-2400 and Sun for
'jazz brunch', free-€10.
Bus: 118, 160, 714.
Also offering supper, this jazz
complex is not so simple to get
to (it's probably worth getting a
taxi), but worth the effort for
performances from some
top-notch musicians.

Contents

A florist on the aptly named Campo de' Fiori
(fields of flowers) selects stems for a bouquet.

Introduction

Nestling in a bend in the river Tiber that insulates it from the rest of the city, Centro Storico is more than Rome's historic centre. Built on the once swampy area of Campus Martius, or the Field of Mars, a military training ground, Centro Storico is arguably the essence of Rome. The warren of tiny medieval lanes packed with cafés, restaurants, boutiques and artisans' workshops transform a stroll into a series of discoveries.

The perfectly intact Pantheon, built in AD 120 as a temple, with its disc of sunlight beaming down to the floor, rightly attracts attention, as do the trio of fountains in lovely piazza Navona and Campo de' Fiori's busy market. Step down a side street though, and you'll find a little chapel with a Caravaggio that's just breath-stopping; one street over, a fresco by Raphael with a cheeky comment about women's intuition. Far from having to queue up, you might find next to no one around, making the gems you sight feel like your very own discoveries, and so much more memorable for that.

Centro Storico is also Rome at its most romantic, where you can eat outdoors under the shade of a grapevine or on a little piazza blissfully traffic-free, passed by just a horse-drawn carriage, a tiny electric bus or a market stallholder wheeling a handcart.

Go early to **Campo de' Fiori** then head to the worn but atmospheric temples in **Largo di Torre Argentina** and visit **Fontana delle Tartarughe**. Stroll through **Galleria Doria Pamphilj** before going to the **Pantheon** and then **piazza Navona** via **San Luigi dei Francesi**. Stop off at **Palazzo Altemps** then round off the day with drinks and dinner around **via dell'Orso**.

...a weekend or more

Next day, go into the **Pantheon** as soon as it opens. On the way to **piazza Navona**, visit **San Luigi dei Francesi**, then pop into **Santa Maria della Pace** and **Chiostro di Bramante**. Hunt for antiques along **via dei Coronari**. Recharge in **Palazzo Altemps** before aperitivi and dinner along **via dell'Orso**.

Neptune wrestling with a sea creature takes centre-stage in pizza Navona's Fontana di Nettuno.

Centro Storico listings

⚫ Sleeping

1 Adriano D3
2 Campo de' Fiori D5
3 Casa dei Fiori D5
4 Cesàri F3
5 D'Inghilterra F2
6 del Senato E4
7 Due Torri D3
8 Forte F1
9 Il Palazzetto F1
10 Locanda Cairoli D6
11 Maison Giulia Best
    Comfort C6
12 Navona D4
13 Pantheon E4
14 Ponte Sisto C6
15 Raphaël C3
16 Residenza Zanardelli C3
17 Santa Chiara E4
18 Smeraldo E4
19 Sole al Pantheon E4
20 St George B4
21 Teatro di Pompeo D5
22 The Landmark Trust F1

⚫ Eating & drinking

1 Al Bric C5
2 Angolo Divino C5
3 Armando al Pantheon E4
4 Bloom C4
5 Bottega Montecitorio E3
6 Caffè Fandango E3
7 Caffè Fiori di Campo C5
8 Caffè Universale D3
9 Casa Bleve D4
10 Coco E3
11 Cul de Sac C4
12 Da Francesco C4
13 Di Fronte A E1
14 Hosteria dell'Orso C3
15 Hosteria del Pesce C5
16 Il Bacaro D3
17 La Montecarlo C4
18 La Tartaruga D5
19 La Taverna del Ghetto E6
20 La Vecchia Bottega del
    Vino D6
21 Laganà D3
22 Le Volte D3
23 Maccheroni D3
24 Mimì e Cocò C4
25 Monserrato C5
26 Nino F2
27 Obika D3
28 Osteria ar Galletto C5
29 Osteria del Pegno C5
30 Osteria dell'Ingegno F3
31 Pagliaccio B4
32 Palatium F2
33 Pizzeria da Baffetto C4
34 Sangallo ai Coronari C3
35 Taverna le Coppelle D3
36 Trattoria Pizzeria
    Polese B4
37 Trattoria Tonino
    Bassetti C4
38 Tuna H2

Campo de' Fiori & the Ghetto

Tiny lanes weaving from the market on Campo de' Fiori to grander palazzi – Farnese with its Roman bathtub fountains, or Spada with its architectural folly – set a tone of contrasts that characterizes the area of Centro Storico between busy corso Vittorio Emanuele II and the river. A seat outside one of the Campo's dozen cafés is the perfect spot to soak up the sun and watch the market bustle, with workers scurrying to a *forno* to pick up lunch, old men playing chess, and an artist with an easel tucked discreetly behind the blooms of a flower stall.

The nightly police presence on Campo de' Fiori is a glum reminder of how rowdy it can get, but the neighbouring piazza Farnese has a grown-up air, with nearby via Giulia dotted with antiques shops. There are surprises round every corner: the weathered Teatro di Marcello is topped with luxury flats, while racing commuters ignore the tumbledown temples encircled by traffic at largo Argentina.

Amid the jollity are sombre historical reminders: a visit to the imposing riverside synagogue reveals the persecution and deportation suffered during the Second World War; a grave statue on the Campo recalls the dark days of the Inquisition. But nearby is a fountain that warms the heart: its sculptures of boys kindly helping tortoises into a pool make every passer-by smile.

Campo de' Fiori

Bus: 116. Map: Centro Storico, C5, p96.

The morning market starts the day early in Campo de' Fiori. When it's in full swing, it's hard to imagine a more cheerful local event. The pick of local produce is temptingly displayed alongside stalls specializing in cheeses and *salumi*. The regular customers each have their favourite stall, and several restaurants in the district also rely on a chosen stallholder to supply fresh produce daily. Up by the pair of fountains, the florists nip between their buckets of flowers, selecting stems to arrange into artistic bouquets.

Encircling all the activity are more than a dozen cafés, bars and restaurants. Even on a winter morning, tables on the sunny side of the square are full; all that's needed to fit right in is a smooth cappuccino and a big pair of designer sunglasses.

From midday till early evening, the Campo is best avoided: the departing stallholders leave a lot of rubbish behind, and the racket of street-cleaning vehicles is not the best accompaniment to a glass of *prosecco*. Aperitivo hour sees the punters heading back, some to spend the whole evening on the Campo. Some bars get packed out with foreign students – there are many US student residences in the neighbourhood – others have a DJ later on, or screen a big sports match.

It's been suggested that Campo de' Fiori's kicking atmosphere is down to the fact that there's no church on the square, but when the stalls are cleared the central statue is more noticeable: it's a memorial to a dark period in the Catholic Church's history. The gloomy, hooded figure on a high plinth is the philosopher Giordano Bruno. His radical opinions (for the late 1500s) resulted in a charge of heresy, and after eight years of interrogation by the Inquisition he was burned at the stake in 1600. His statue marks the spot and commemorates all the men who suffered the same fate; there is no memorial to the women who were similarly dealt with in the square round the corner, *piazza della Quercia*.

The presence of the *carabinieri* swells to half a dozen vehicles parked by the fountains on a busy weekend night; recent isolated incidents of drunken fights breaking out has resulted in most locals avoiding the area, although they haven't put the rest of Rome off.

Tasty looking cherry tomatoes, or *ciliengine*, on a Campo de' Fiori market stall.

Around the city

Galleria Spada

*Piazza Capo di Ferro 13, T06-683 2409,
galleriaborghese.it.*
Tue-Sun 0830-1930, €5/2.50 concession,
free EU citizens under 18 and over 65.
Bus: 23, 116, 280. Map: Centro Storico, C6, p96.

One block down from Palazzo Farnese, Cardinal
Bernardino Spada's palazzo is worth visiting even
if 17th-century Italian art isn't your thing. Most
visitors make a beeline for the elaborate joke the
erudite cardinal commissioned in 1651 for his
river-fronting garden. Set back from the orange
trees is Francesco Borromini's architectural folly: a
perspective-perfect colonnade that appears more
than 30 m long until a neighbourhood cat reveals
the trompe l'œil by strolling past the Lilliput-scale
statue at the far end (a mere 60 cm tall). The actual
length of the gallery is 9 m.

Upstairs, walls are crammed frame-to-frame,
partly to recreate a typical 17th-century gallery,
but also because only a small portion of the house
is open to the public. Two works by the trailblazing
female painter and feminist heroine Artemisia
Gentileschi are in Room IV: *Madonna Nursing the
Infant Jesus* (1610-1612), begun when she was only
17, and *Saint Cecily* (1613-1621). Her talent was
nurtured in her family's home-cum-atelier, where
she probably mixed pigments for her artist father
Orazio, whose *David and Goliath* appears in the
same room.

Labelling in English explains other treasures,
like a pair of large globes gifted to Spada by Dutch
cartographer Willem Blaeu. Both are intriguing,
with the 17th-century understanding of landforms
on the terrestrial globe (1622), and the position of
the stars updated by Spada in 1640 on the celestial
one (1616).

Don't miss a frieze in Room II painted on canvas
by Perin del Vaga: it was a model for a tapestry, never
realized, to be placed under Michelangelo's *Last
Judgement* in the Sistine Chapel. When Cardinal
Spada discovered it he commissioned Andrea
Gennaroli to make copies for the shorter walls and
had him add in the Spada shield for good measure.

Piazza Farnese

Bus: 116. Map: Centro Storico, C5, p95.

The piazza is smaller and calmer than
neighbouring Campo de' Fiori, partly because of
the constant presence of *carabinieri* parked outside
Palazzo Farnese (now the French embassy) but
mainly because, with just a couple of restaurants
and a café, the vibe is much more local.

A pair of massive, granite bathtubs from
the **Terme di Caracalla** (see page 82) have been
made into attractive fountains, their classic lines
topped by elaborate Gothic vases with extravagant
fleur-de-lis, the emblem of the Farnese family; put
together by Carlo and Girolamo Rainaldi in 1612,
the fountains are encircled by low railings, against

A bathtub fountain in piazza Farnese; massively heavy –
it's made of granite – yet it appears to float in its pool.

Tip...

Keep an eye on local listings (such as *Trova Roma*,
issued free with *La Repubblica* on Thursdays) in case
a concert or other event is scheduled on piazza
Farnese during your stay.

Piazza Farnese at night.

which locals lean as they read the paper, sip a coffee or munch on a slice of pizza bought from the *forno* on the edge of Campo de' Fiori.

There are occasionally free open-air concerts and cinema screenings here, and a handy bench running across the entire length of Palazzo Farnese is an ideal place to picnic in the cool shade of the huge building. The sounds of the piazza are soothing, whether it's the quiet hum of the electric bus passing, or the reassuring clatter of cups and saucers as a barista stacks them ready for the next customers. It's just a shame that the custom, in this otherwise pedestrianized piazza, is to park around the fountains.

Palazzo Farnese

Piazza Farnese, T06-6889 2818, france-italia.it. Bus: 116. Map: Centro Storico, C5, p96.

The palazzo was built principally by Antonio da Sangallo, and completed in 1589. Its frescoed gallery by Annibale Carracci is the stuff of urban legend as, although it's said to be beautiful, few have seen it. Occupied since the 1870s by the French embassy, the palazzo is frustratingly difficult to visit. Those who are both organized and patient can try emailing a polite request (visitefarnese@france-italia.it), preferably in French, up to four months in advance. Otherwise, wait for lights to go on at night to get a tantalizing view of the great ceilings. Sometimes, if a researcher is working late in the library of the Ecole Française on the upper level, you can also glimpse the elaborately carved wood panelled ceiling there.

During the day, walk around the palazzo's high, gloomy walls to get a glimpse into the small but pretty garden through the gate on via Giulia. The cheery *carabinieri* guarding the embassy don't seem to mind the curiosity of passers-by.

Fontana del Mascherone

Junction of vicolo del Mascherone with via Giulia.
Bus: 116. Map: Centro Storico, C6, p96.

The large, round face that forms the Fountain of the Mask behind the Palazzo Farnese has a benign if somewhat strange expression; its blown-out cheeks don't fit with the water spilling from its slack mouth. Sometimes mistaken for the **Bocca della Verità** (see page xxx) it was commissioned by the Farnese family, and local folklore says that during holidays wine, not water, would flow from its mouth. The sculptor has wisely remained anonymous.

Via Giulia

viagiulia500.net.
Bus: 116. Map: Centro Storico, B5, p96.

The long cobbled lane that runs parallel to the river Tiber is one of Centro Storico's most sought-after addresses. Its entire length is studded with enormous tubs planted with citrus trees, adding nicely to its air of exclusivity and providing a perfect setting for the antique dealers and little independent shops along it. Sadly, the Virginia creeper that once trailed romantically down from an overhead walkway arching over via Giulia from Palazzo Farnese has been removed. The arch, designed by Michelangelo, was the first phase of an unrealized plan to connect the palazzo with the Villa Farnese across the river.

Basilica di Sant'Andrea della Valle

Corso Vittorio Emanuele II 6, T06-686 1339.
Daily 0730-1230, 1600-1945.
Bus: 40, 46, 62, 64, 70, 81, 492, 628.
Map: Centro Storico, D5, p96.

Although a big church, Sant'Andrea seems friendly, partly because of its yellow-paned windows, which give it a warm glow even on a grey day. As the building was funded by three different families, complications meant that it took a long time to complete (1591-1665), and the decoration represents interesting changes in contemporary tastes.

It's a fact...

The first act of Puccini's opera *Tosca* is set in Sant'Andrea della Valle, though the family chapel featured in it was an invention.

The central cupola by Giovanni Lanfranco and the frescoes in the half cupola by Domenichino are very different stylistically. Domenichino's figures, placed between pilasters and windows high overhead, look as though they're aware of their very lofty position, and have charmingly tucked themselves firmly in place, or are holding on so they don't fall.

There are two papal funerary monuments, but neither Pius II nor Pius III was buried here originally: both were moved from St Peter's when their family, the Piccolomini, decided to donate land to build a church that would house only them.

The altar end of the church sits over the foundations of the Theatre of Pompey, an ancient Roman structure that is most infamous for being the spot where Julius Caesar was killed.

Barracco Museo

Corso Vittorio Emanuele II 166a,
T06-8205 9127, museobarracco.it.
Tue-Sun 0900-1900, €3/1.50 concession, free EU citizens under 18 and over 65, audio guide €3.50.
Bus: 40, 46, 62, 64. Map: Centro Storico, C5, p96.

If you feel like a change from ancient Rome, take the kids to count the lions among the antique sculpture from ancient Egypt, Greece and Cyprus (with, OK, some pieces from Rome) on display in this little Renaissance house two steps from Campo de' Fiori. Being greeted by a large alabaster lion that looks as if it's smiling (it's missing its jaw, but it does date from the fourth century BC) is a good start.

Remarkably intact and beautifully presented, the pieces were assembled by a passionate collector, Giovanni Barracco. Some of the mosaics, decorated amphorae and statues he left to the city in 1904 seem impossibly old, such as the wooden head of a lioness dating from 2000 BC. And some have the most expressive faces: a laurel-crowned head found in Cyprus dates from the fifth century BC seems to be suppressing a knowing smile. The pieces recovered from excavations in Rome between 1880 and 1900 offer an insight into just what was being dug up at that time, when gardens surrounding villas and swathes of farmland were swallowed up in the rush to build offices and houses for all those involved in administering the newly united Italy.

Area Sacra di Largo Argentina

Largo di Torre Argentina.
Guided tour with volunteers from Torre Argentina Cat Sanctuary (T06-4542 5240, romancats.com) Mon-Sat 1600, free but donations appreciated.
Bus: H, 40, 46, 64, 70, 81, 492, 628, 780.
Map: Centro Storico, E5, p96.

To see a collection of once-magnificent temples, away from the hordes at the Forum, you can't do better than a stroll around Largo Argentina. The medium-sized temples are presumed to be the offerings of triumphant generals returning victorious to Rome. In addition to these four, two of which were uncovered only in 1926, more may extend the line to the south. Just behind the temples is the site of the Theatre of Pompey, which is thought to include the Curia where Julius Caesar was assassinated: a circular paving stone is considered by locals to mark the precise spot the murder took place when, in 44 BC, Caesar was turned on by an estimated 60 conspirators who until then he'd thought of as his allies.

If the Area Sacra had its own world-class visitor centre and was not bounded on three sides by busy bus and tram routes, turning it into a traffic island, the precious remains of flights of steps and outlining walls would almost certainly make this a key sight. However, it suffers the double indignity of being largely ignored by locals and apparently abandoned by the state, with six remaining columns from a circular temple looking

A central temple, or the remains of one, in the atmospheric Area Sacra di Largo Argentina.

particularly weather-beaten. Aside from small descriptive panels set on each side of the square, the only information provided is on tours given by volunteers from the cat sanctuary which is tucked into a corner of the Area Sacra.

Crypta Balbi

Via delle Botteghe Oscure 31,
T06-3996 7700, pierreci.it.
Tue-Sun 0900-1945, combined ticket (valid 3 days) with Palazzo Massimo, Palazzo Altemps and Terme di Diocleziano, €7/3.50 concession, plus €3 during exhibitions, or Archaeologia card, free EU citizens under 18 and over 65; guided tour (in Italian) to archaeological site below ground, Sun 1500, free.
Bus: C3, H, 40, 46, 62, 64, 70, 87, 119, 492, 780.
Map: Centro Storico, E5, p96.

Airy and ordered, this museum, which opened to the public in 2000, is a pleasure to visit. From its beginnings as a *crypta* (courtyard) where refreshments were enjoyed by theatregoers spilling out of the theatre built in 13 BC by one Lucius Balbus, through to medieval times, Balbus' Courtyard has seen many changes of use, and they – and the fortunes of its inhabitants – are charted through well-documented displays of artefacts. The findings from the structures, which were used variously as tombs, workshops, places of worship or houses, are neatly put in context, with clear explanations in English.

Aside from the usual suspects – skeletons, coins and column fragments – the range of intricate shoe and stirrup buckles, secateurs, combs whittled from bone and perfume containers brings home just how much Romans enjoyed the good life.

Corresponding with changes in economic circumstances as the collapse of the western empire drew near (around AD 475), the findings chart a decline in the level of luxury. The museum's collections of tableware and kitchenware become ever simpler –crockery, once bronze-plated, became plain, then was not used at all; roasting dishes were replaced by large cooking pots, suggesting that soup was the staple meal instead of the meat enjoyed in more prosperous times.

Visiting the archaeological site below ground, where many of the objects showcased have been found over the last 20 years, completes the picture. There are two little aqueducts, and the lane where grain was dished out to hungry plebs, one of whom may have been responsible for rethinking a column capital. Found flipped up and hollowed out, it was used as a giant mortar for pounding grain into flour: a smart reaction to belt-tightening times.

Fontana delle Tartarughe

Piazza Mattei.
Bus: H, 40, 46, 62, 64, 70, 119, 492, 780.
Map: Centro Storico, E6, p96.

Four lithe boys half-dance and half-leap as each boosts a turtle into a basin of water overhead; the sculptures make the Turtle Fountain a firm favourite with everyone. Although less than five

One of the four bronze boys who hoist turtles to a pool overhead in Fontana delle Tartarughe.

minutes from Largo Argentina, the fountain is down a narrow back street and you'll often have the little piazza to yourself. The turtles are not the originals though. When one was sadly stolen, the remaining three were quickly removed and replaced by replicas.

The bronze boys and their pools date from a 1581 design by Giacomo della Porta, but were supposed to be erected in nearby piazza Giudea. When Muzio Mattei, a nobleman whose palazzo overlooks this piazza, saw the design, he begged for it to be put within sight of his house, offering to cobble the square and look after the fountain from then on.

Charming though the turtles make the scene, renewing a hope that boys could be kind to animals, they were not part of the original fountain but were added, probably by Bernini, around 1658, during restoration work. If you take a second look you can see the boys are not balancing on their shells in quite the way they would need to in order to support the creatures.

La Sinagoga e Museo Ebraico di Roma

Lungotevere de' Cenci 15, T06-6840 0661, museoebraico.roma.it.
Mid-Jun-mid-Sep Sun-Thu 1000-1900, Fri 1000-1600, mid-Sep-mid-Jun Sun-Thu 1000-1700, Fri 0900-1400, closed Sat and Jewish holidays, visits by guided tour only (available in English), every hour, €7.50/4 concession, free under 10.
Bus: H, 23, 63, 280, 780.
Map: Centro Storico, E6, p96.

The small Jewish Museum is dedicated to the history of Rome's Jewish community and its struggles in the face of adversity. The earliest Jews are thought to have arrived in Rome in 161 BC, making this the longest surviving Jewish community in Europe. In addition to precious silverware and an extensive collection of textiles, the museum chronicles the creation and destruction of the Ghetto. In 1555, Rome's Jewish population was given an ultimatum: move to the Ghetto (a very restricted riverside area, prone to flooding) or leave. For 300 years those Jews who

Top: Via del Portico in the Ghetto retains a strong community feel.
Above: The imposing façade of the Synagogue.

The weather-beaten Teatro di Marcello is even older than the Colosseum and is topped by luxury flats.

remained (some 4000 of them) were crammed within what was little more than an open prison.

Among the many severe restrictions imposed on everyday life was that only one synagogue was allowed. The community cleverly interpreted this as meaning one building, in which they built a separate synagogue on each of the five floors – the Cinque Scole – so that Jews from different traditions could retain their various rites. When liberation came with Italian unification in 1870, Rome's Jewish community celebrated by dismantling much of the old Ghetto and the Cinque Scole, from which many of the objects on display in the museum come.

The community had a new synagogue built, wanting it to feature a high dome as a symbol of their liberation. It was completed in 1904, and its square-based dome stands out on the Rome skyline. The synagogue was the site of a historic first: Pope John Paul II chose to visit it in 1986, and seemed to be talking as much to Christians as to the Jewish congregation when he apologized for the pain Catholics had caused Jews.

Portico d'Ottavia

Via del Portico d'Ottavia.
Walkway access daily 0900-1800, free.
Bus: H, 23, 63, 280, 780.
Map: Centro Storico, E6, p96.

Constructed in 146 BC, the ancient porch is so badly weathered and its four open sides are so jumbled it's hard to make sense of the structure. When it was built it was flanked by two temples. A much-eroded pediment sits atop a couple of columns, but it's made lopsided by a brick wall that replaces a further two columns to the right. Some of the columns to the rear, meanwhile, are incorporated into the Church of Sant' Angelo in Pescheria, named after the fish (*pesce*) market held here from ancient to medieval times.

To see the portico a bit closer up, head down the ramp that leads through to the Teatro di Marcello. There are lots of column fragments and marble and travertine blocks and even three tall, slim columns, the only remains of an ancient temple dedicated to Apollo, dating from around 400 BC. But while it's all pretty striking, and the absence of crowds makes for happy wandering, much imagination is needed, as there are no information panels or descriptions for any of the remains on view.

Teatro di Marcello

Via del Teatro Marcello 44.
Walkway access daily 0900-1800, free.
Bus: C3, H, 63, 81, 95, 170, 628, 715, 780.
Map: Centro Storico, E7, p96.

A medieval house perched atop two tiers of ancient limestone arches makes the Theatre of Marcellus an eye-popping sight. While it's slightly older (by 80-odd years) than the Colosseum, which its structure echoes, the Teatro di Marcello hasn't fared quite so well over the last two millennia. Only 12 of its original 41 arches remain, and the lower tier is so weathered that its Doric columns have all but disappeared. While some visitors to the Colosseum might grumble that it looks a bit dog-eared, comparing the two shows just how intact the Colosseum actually is. One reason for the Teatro's quarried appearance is that its cut and carved stone was considered a handy source for those needing building materials and embellishments for churches and houses back in the Middle Ages. Its third tier, which would have had Corinthian pilasters, has disappeared entirely, to be replaced by the Renaissance palazzo spread across the structure.

Begun on land cleared by Julius Caesar, the Teatro di Marcello was completed in 13 BC by Emperor Augustus, who named it in honour of his nephew; it could seat 20,000. Although it was abandoned around AD 300, when the games and entertainments it hosted petered out, its strategic position close to the river made it an ideal fortress. It was the Savelli family who, in the process of restoring the Teatro, had the novel idea of building a house for themselves in the upper levels. Now known as Palazzo Orsini, after a later owner, and divided into luxury flats, the residential part of the Teatro is not open to the public. Visitors can, however, stroll by its

time-ravaged arches via a walkway that drops down from the main road. Summer concerts held in the archaeological area beside the Teatro are a nice reminder of the structure's original function as a place of entertainment.

Five of the best

Columns & obelisks

❶ The soaring column on piazza Colonna, wrapped by its beautifully carved frieze (see page 119).

❷ The pink columns, even more than the grey ones, in the Pantheon's portico (see page 114).

❸ The crumbling columns of Hadrian's Temple on piazza di Pietra (see page 119).

❹ The stubby obelisk balanced on a sculpture of a baby elephant on piazza della Minerva (see page 117).

❺ Trajan's column, one of Rome's most amazing relics (see page 72).

Column of Marco Aurelio.

Piazza Navona & the Pantheon

It's hard not to be completely seduced by the maze of narrow streets criss-crossing Centro Storico between corso Vittorio Emanuele II and the shop-lined via del Corso. As architects and artists have been building and decorating palazzi and churches in this neighbourhood for centuries, there's a liberal sprinkling of breath-catching works of art. A delight to explore by day, at night the historic feel is shaken off as chic bars, restaurants and clubs transform the dinky lanes into hives of activity.

The perfectly proportioned Pantheon and the track-shaped piazza Navona – recalling its chariot-racing origins – are the best-loved legacies of the ancients. Take a stroll and you'll pass a sculpture of an adorable baby elephant on piazza Minerva, or the serene courtyard – and cool café – that is Bramante's Cloister. Even getting lost is good, because you might stumble on a rarely opened church and get to see a precious Raphael. Duck inside Palazzo Altemps to encounter a gallery completely wrapped in garden frescoes, or look for a trio of Caravaggio's paintings in San Luigi dei Francesi. When you're walked out, take a table outside Mimì e Cocò to watch the world saunter by, or recline on a sofa in the cool interior of Salotto 42.

Piazza Navona

Bus: C3, 70, 81, 87, 116, 492, 628.
Map: Centro Storico, F3, p96.

All roads might lead to Rome, but walking around Centro Storico it seems all *vicoli* converge on piazza Navona. During the day visitors come to marvel at the central fountain and its massive sculpture of four rivers personified, while at dusk the city's young crowd gathers round the same spot, as though attracted by the roar of the water. The tourists take pictures, buy an ice cream, try to avoid the fake bag sellers, peer over the shoulders of the portrait painters and then head off to the next sight. Once the teens arrive, though, their numbers just keep swelling: the fountain is not so much a spot to meet as *the* place to hang out. Too young to drink (or not interested in the area's above-average prices), they chat, check each other out and maybe amble to Campo de' Fiori and back before going for a pizza around 2300.

Piazza Navona's status as a vital hub stretches back to its origins around AD 86 as an arena enclosed by a track for races and games. It was called the *Stadio di Domiziano* (Domitian's Stadium) in honour of the emperor who had it built. It was even flooded on occasion so people could bob about in boats and re-enact sea battles – a spillover from the Colosseum (see page 70) – and the games were transferred to the stadium when the Colosseum had to be closed for repair work. The Pamphilj family rebuilt the piazza in the 17th century – when a Pamphilj elder was elected pope and needed a palace befitting the appointment – but retained the graceful, oval shape of the arena. In an echo of the fun and games 1400 years earlier, the Pamphilj had the piazza flooded on hot summer weekends in the mid-18th century, and invited friends to drive their carriages through the water for a bit of decadent entertainment.

Neptune in Fontana Nettuno on the north end of piazza Navona.

One of the enormous river gods in piazza Navona's Fontana dei Quattro Fiumi.

The fountains The piazza has three fountains, each – as was often the case – a construction of a simple, shallow basin that was then embellished, lavishly. The central fountain, the **Fontana dei Quattro Fiumi**, had so much added to it by its designer, Gian Lorenzo Bernini, that when it was completed in 1651 little more could have been crammed in. The world's four longest rivers, the Danube, Ganges, Nile and Plata (one from each of the continents known at the time), are personified as huge hulks of men, and for extra stature the assembly is topped by an obelisk. The marble representative of each river reclines on a leg of one of the interlocking arches of rough white granite, and the 16.5-m obelisk that tops the fountain (the total height is about 30 m) seems to be floating, thanks to Bernini's clever arch work, which leaves fresh air under its base. Although it was made in Egypt, the obelisk is a Roman copy, commissioned by Emperor Domitian, of an Egyptian original.

Three of the river gods are presented in odd poses. The Nile has a cloth drawn over his head: locals say that his face is hidden because the river's source wasn't known at the time. Facing the other side of the piazza, meanwhile, another is turning away as though in fear, and a third is on his back as though fallen, but with an arm defensively raised. Interestingly, the only thing in front of these two is the Church of Sant' Agnese in Agone. What can Bernini have been trying to tell us?

Amid the mermaids and seahorses wrestling with mean-looking sea creatures in the fountain at the north end of piazza Navona is Neptune, spear poised to despatch an octopus-like monster. Appropriately, it is called **Fontana di Nettuno**, and it was completed in 1574 by Giacomo della Porta. Less interesting is della Porta's 1576 **Fontana del Moro**, under the windows of Palazzo Pamphilj at the south end of the piazza, with mermen blowing on shells and an unhappy-looking central figure grappling with a fish.

Palazzo Altemps

Piazza di Sant' Apollinare 48, T06-687 2719, archeoroma.eniculturali.it.
Tue-Sun 0900-1945, combined ticket (valid 3 days) with Crypta Balbi, Palazzo Massimo and Terme di Diocleziano, €7/3.50 concession, plus €3 during exhibitions, or Archaeologia card, free EU citizens under 18 and over 65.
Bus: C3, 70, 81, 86, 116, 492, 628.
Map: Centro Storico, D3, p96.

Palazzo Altemps' serene atmosphere is a welcome antidote to the roar of traffic down corso Rinascimento and the jostle of visitors and vendors on piazza Navona just across the road. More like a private gallery than a museum, it retains a calm, uncluttered air that perfectly offsets the sculptures adorning the alcoves and archways in its courtyard and standing on pedestals in the spacious rooms.

The pieces seem so at home that it's surprising to learn that they were not collected by Marco Altemps, who bought the palazzo after becoming cardinal in 1561. Altemps did have his own extensive collection of ancient sculptures, but most of it was sold off by his heirs, and only 12 of the works remain on display. Many of the key pieces seen are from the Ludovisi Collection, bought by the state when their former home, the garden of Villa Ludovisi, was sold. As Palazzo Altemps was being restored and made ready to be opened to the public (in 1997), a detailed set of archives left by Marco Altemps enabled the new arrivals to be arranged more or less as he had laid out his own statuary four centuries before.

An enormous sarcophagus richly decorated in bas-relief shows a group of Barbarians being defeated by the Romans. Dating from the second century AD, it is carved from a single block of stone and is a classic piece of political messaging: the near-perfect appearance of the victorious Romans is set against the dazed expressions and huddled confusion of the Barbarians.

Frescoes have been uncovered throughout the palazzo (which required extensive restoration work after it was obtained, somewhat neglected, from the Vatican). Especially lovely is the fairytale trompe l'œil garden in the first-floor loggia overlooking the inner courtyard, where vines tumble over trellises overhead and painted flowers bloom.

Chiostro del Bramante

Via della Pace, T06-6880 9036, chiostrodelbramante.it.
Tue-Fri 1000-1930, Sat and Sun 1000-2100, free.
Bus: 70, 81, 87, 116, 492, 628.
Map: Centro Storico, C3, p96.

The arches and columns framing the courtyard that Donato Bramante built for the Monastery of Santa Maria della Pace are elegant in their simplicity. Where monks once paced, the cloister is now scattered with over-sized cushions – an extension of the chic café in the upper arcade that opens on to the courtyard. Bramante completed the classically inspired structure in 1504, before going on to

An imposing statue with an animated sword handle in Palazzo Altemps.

Around the city

St Peter's in 1506. Barely five minutes from piazza Navona, the cloister is a haven of tranquillity.

Temporary exhibits (admission by ticket) are held on the ground floor; state at the ticket office that you're going to look at the Chiostro del Bramante and you'll be waved through.

Chiesa di Santa Maria della Pace

Via della Pace.
Mon, Wed, Sat 0900-1200, free.
Bus: 70, 81, 87, 116, 492, 628.
Map: Centro Storico, C3, p96.

The baroque façade of this little church is elaborate, but given its irregular opening hours, most visitors don't hang about to admire its pretty, semicircular porch, but head inside to see the highlight of a visit: set above an arch in the first chapel on the right is Raphael's *Sibyls Receiving Instructions from Angels*, a fresco dating from 1514. The gentle beauty of the scene is as much in the

Tip...

The Chiostro del Bramante's neighbour, the Church of Santa Maria della Pace, is best known for its Raphael fresco (see below), but it has very limited opening hours. To glimpse the fresco, head to the cloister's modern art gallery (next to the café, 1115-1930) – through the handily positioned window there's a view down into the church.

billowing skirts as the lovely faces of the women. According to Greek mythology, sibyls were women who possessed prophetic powers; Raphael's fresco cheekily suggests that their powers were not intuitive but passed on from angels, so no wonder the sibyls are looking sceptically at the bossy angels hovering overhead, with their scrolls unrolled as though they have lists to go through.

Chiesa di Sant'Agnese in Agone

Piazza Navona, T06-6819 2134,
santagneseinagone.org.
Tue-Sat 0930-1230, 1530-1900,
Sun and holidays 1000-1300, 1600-1900.
Bus: C3, 70, 81, 87, 116, 492, 628.
Map: Centro Storico, D4, p96.

If the rivalry between the architects Francesco Borromini and Gian Lorenzo Bernini was even half as bitter as hearsay would have us believe, things must have got drama-serial sticky during the building of Saint Agnes in the Arena. When Pope Innocent X decided to build himself a mausoleum, he tore down the remains of the church next door to the family's palazzo on piazza Navona, only to promptly fall out with his nephew Camillo Pamphilj, who he'd appointed, along with architect Girolamo Rainaldi, to oversee the work

(see **Galleria Doria Pamphilj**, page 119). With Camillo and his team sent packing, Innocent appointed Borromini in 1653. Then Innocent died, prompting Camillo to return to the project, but, while he was squaring up to Borromini (whose work he was obviously going to find fault with), Borromini resigned. Camillo, delighted, brought back his old architect, but then Camillo himself died. His ever-capable widow Olimpia hired someone completely new to finish the job, unwittingly choosing Bernini to finish his rival's work (which he did, in 1672).

The church is named in memory of St Agnes, a girl whose vow of chastity so angered a would-be admirer that Emperor Diocletian, known for his persecution of Christians, got to hear about her. After a series of miracles saved Agnes from humiliation, enforced prostitution and even a pyre (the flames went out when she was thrown on to them), she was stabbed to death.

The frescoed cupola depicts poor Agnes's release in *The Presentation of St Agnes to the Glory of Heaven*. Cirro Ferri's mass of figures includes saints, angels, other martyrs and biblical characters, and took him so long he hadn't finished it when he died in 1689. Visitors often bring binoculars to get a proper look; its only lighting comes from eight windows, so visit when the sun's shining (and not after dusk) to see it.

Museo di Roma

Palazzo Braschi, piazza San Pantaleo 10, museodiroma.it.
Tue-Sun 0900-1900 (last entry 1800), €6.50/4.50 concession, free EU citizens under 18 and over 65.
Bus: 40, 46, 64, 116, 492, 628.
Map: Centro Storico, D4, p96.

The blue light playing over sizeable statues in the entry to the palazzo suggests a significant collection of statuary is in store, but up a very grand staircase, the museum's two floors are a quiet display of landscapes and portraits of Rome's moneyed families from medieval times up to the early 1900s. Many of the scenes, and not just those of socializing, picnics and parties, have as their backdrops the gardens, houses and squares that you can go and visit in the immediate vicinity of the museum. History is brought nicely alive, for example, when you see a painting of piazza Navona looking just the same as it does today, but all set for a late-medieval jousting tournament. On the other hand, the collection's watercolours and etchings of city panoramas offer a sharp contrast to the Rome of the 21st century: back in the early 1800s, before the construction boom that followed the unification of Italy, great swathes of what is now part of the city were still romantic, rolling fields. There are a few marble busts – practically the only handsome one is Antonio Canova's *Self-portrait* (1812), though picky commentators say that it's an over-idealized vision of the artist.

Via dei Coronari

Bus: 70, 87, 116, 492.
Map: Centro Storico, C3, p96.

Just north of piazza Navona this pedestrianized street is graced with many of Centro Storico's most knowledgeable antique dealers. It heads due west towards the Vatican, and gets its name from the rosary bead sellers who once traded there, selling sacred objects to pilgrims heading for St Peter's: a rosary was known as a crown or *corona*. Strolling down via dei Coronari can be interesting as much for the fun of browsing as actually shopping. You'll find antiquarian books (number 41), ceramics, lamps and paintings (159), antique clocks (215), furniture in luminous walnut veneers (6), telescopes and other scientific instruments (95), oriental furniture (150-153), paintings and prints (84 and 145), silverware (37), sculpture (79) and vases and urns (147).

Pantheon

Piazza della Rotonda. T06-6830 0230.
Mon-Sat 0830-1930, Sun 0900-1800, free.
Bus: 116. Map: Centro Storico, E4, p96.

This is one of the most eye-popping buildings of
ancient Rome. Although it somehow manages to
look quite small in images, standing under its porch
between pink columns that soar 14 m up to the roof
is a swift reality check. As you step through the huge
bronze doors – the originals, which makes them
almost 2000 years old – the 43-m diameter of the
drum-shaped interior appears to equate exactly to
the height of the hemispherical dome, creating the
scope for a perfect sphere to fit inside.

The Pantheon is at its most enchanting at noon
on the summer solstice, when the disc of sunlight
that beams down through the oculus, the 9-m
opening at the top of the dome, actually reaches the
floor. Standing in such a dazzling spotlight is almost
disorientating, as the fall of the beam seems so
focused. The light reaches different levels around
the Pantheon's walls according to the time of year.

The purity of the building's form is its great
appeal, even before taking in just how ancient it is,
how much planning went into its construction,
and how incredibly intact it remains. Picture the
Teatro di Marcello (see page 107) or the
Colosseum (see page 70); it is extraordinary
that, in comparison, the Pantheon has not been
damaged, built against, built over or left to tumble
down. Its survival is down to two pieces of luck.
First, when it was made into a church in AD 609 it
suffered no alteration, except for the addition of
the sculptures and frescoes seen today. These
adornments seem to clutter the Pantheon's
profound simplicity, but they don't stop you
getting a real sense of the space. Second, it was
able to stay standing without the material that
was plundered from it – the bronze that lined the
ceiling of the portico. It was the Barberini pope,
Urban VIII (1568-1644), who stripped this away,
to be melted down to make cannon at **Castel
Sant'Angelo** (see page 162). Locals were so angry
they coined the saying: *"Quello che non fecero i*

The architectonic Pantheon is Rome's most perfectly preserved ancient building.

Around the city

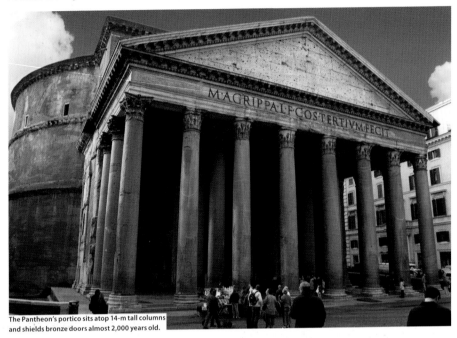

The Pantheon's portico sits atop 14-m tall columns and shields bronze doors almost 2,000 years old.

barbari, lo fecero i barberini." ("What the barbarians didn't do [to the Pantheon], the Barberinis did.")

Built around AD 120 by Hadrian, the Pantheon was dedicated to the worship of all the Roman gods; it was built on a spot where Marcus Agrippa had erected a smaller temple in 27 BC.

The dome is the showstopper. An amazing feat of engineering, it is made of concrete and was the largest existing dome for over 1000 years; it is still considered to be the largest non-reinforced concrete dome in the world. The cylindrical wall on which it sits is itself about 6 m thick. A quaint tale about the construction of the dome tells that the concrete was poured over a mound of packed earth that had been deliberately sprinkled with coins. Once it was set, the locals were lured to come and remove the earth with the promise that they could keep any coins they found. In fact it's understood that the concrete was poured in narrow layers over a hemispherical wooden

This temple, both open and mysteriously enclosed, was conceived as a solar quadrant. The hours would make their round on that coffered ceiling…the disk of daylight would rest suspended there like a shield of gold; rain would form its clear pool on the pavement below, prayers would rise like smoke toward that void where we place the gods.

Emperor Hadrian

structure that incorporated the moulds for the coffers, or recessed patterns, that encircle the dome, tapering in size towards the top. As well as being decorative, they help to reduce the weight of the dome; what's more, the materials used to make the concrete were adapted in view of the weight issue – more pumice was used in the mix for the upper reaches to make it lighter – and the shell is much thinner at the top than at the base.

Portions of the supporting structure are visible to the sides of the central altar: get as near as possible then look up to see the supporting arches. Better still, take a walk around the perimeter of the Pantheon to get an understanding of how thick the walls are.

Once the building was consecrated as a church, statues of the Roman gods were removed from the niches and replaced with religious art and sculpture; many of the works displayed were by the *maestri* (Great Masters) who were eventually buried here, including Raphael.

Pulcino della Minerva

Piazza della Minerva.
Bus: 116. Map: Centro Storico, E4, p96.

In the centre of a piazza just behind the Pantheon, Gian Lorenzo Bernini's design of a winning baby elephant is so adorable it's impossible to pass without smiling. Sculpted in marble, it shares the aesthetic assemblage so often seen in Bernini's fountains across the Centro Storico, where a work is composed of several different elements. This little elephant, affectionately known as 'Minerva's chick', supports a 5.5-m obelisk – the shortest of the 11 obelisks on view across Rome that were taken from ancient Egypt after the Roman conquest. Although the great weight doesn't seem to be too much of a strain on the little creature, it does look as if it needs a bit of a rub down, as it's streaked and marked from weathering.

Basilica di Santa Maria sopra Minerva

Piazza della Minerva 42, T06-679 3926, basilicaminerva.it.
Daily 0800-1900, free.
Bus: 116. Map: Centro Storico, E4, p96.

Just up from the Pantheon, Rome's only Gothic church is easily found thanks to Bernini's elephant monument on the piazza outside. Behind the church's plain façade, vaulted ceilings of blue studded with stars are supported by a colonnade

of Corinthian columns; further decoration runs ribbon-like under each arch. The church was begun in 1280, and its name is derived from its location, as it was built over (*sopra*) the foundations of an ancient temple dedicated to Minerva, the Roman goddess of wisdom.

In addition to a wealth of artworks, notably frescoes by Filippino Lippi in the Carafa Chapel, the Minerva houses many elaborate tombs, including those of a number of Tuscan nobles for whom it was a home-from-home until their own Florentine church (**San Giovanni dei Fiorentini** on via Giulia) was constructed in Rome. Memorials to no fewer than five popes compete for attention with that of St Catherine of Siena, who died in 1380. Her serene tomb belies the fact that her body is somewhat eerily missing its head, which is enshrined in Siena's San Domenico.

A 2-m marble statue by Michelangelo, *Christ the Redeemer*, holding a short cross, as though taking a quick rest while carrying it, is to the left of the main altar; it was finished in 1521 by Pietro Urbano. The flannel-like proportions of the bronze loincloth – added as an obvious afterthought in the Baroque era – seem to emphasize a disgruntlement at the prudery that required it.

Head out of the church through a little door to the left of the apse that takes you out to Beato Angelico, a lane running the depth of the church, to get a sense of just how big it is.

Chiesa di Sant'Ivo alla Sapienza

Corso del Rinascimento 40, T06-361 2562.
Sun 0900-1200, free.
Bus: C3, 70, 81, 87, 116, 492.
Map: Centro Storico, D4, p96.

The little church at the far end of the courtyard of palazzo della Sapienza gained its inspired shape when architect Francesco Borromini came up with a solution to fit the building (completed in 1660) into a small space left in the existing palazzo. He used a six-pointed star as his floor plan, with the internal walls alternatively concave and convex to ensure the end result was more rounded than overly linear. A little chapel is tucked into each tip of the star.

Around the city

The pretty spire of Sant'Ivo alla Sapienza is easy to pick out across the rooftops of Rome, thanks to its twisted shape.

Crowning this little jewel is a short twisted spire: a masterful flourish that distinguishes it from all others in this very heavily churched district.

The Palazzo della Sapienza, into which Borromini squeezed the church, was home to one of Rome's universities (founded in 1303) but since the opening of a big campus the other side of Termini (still called Sapienza after this little place), only a few lectures are now held on this site. A library, still used by students, looks as if it could date from the university's founding, but it is closed to the public. Also sadly not open to the public is the flight of steps that runs up inside the spire.

San Luigi dei Francesi

Via Santa Giovanna d'Arco 5, T06-688271, saintlouis-rome.net.
Daily 1000-1230, 1600-1900.
Bus: C3, 70, 81, 87, 116, 492, 628.
Map: Centro Storico, D4, p96.

The great attraction of the church also known as St Louis des Français (as it is the church of the French community in Rome) is a trio of paintings by Caravaggio dating from around 1600. All three hang in the Contarelli Chapel, furthest from the door on the left. On the left is *St Matthew's Vocation or The Calling of St Matthew*, depicting a barefoot Christ coming to call on an unwilling Matthew, in which the dramatic play of light across the shadows is mesmerising. Adding a mysterious element is the lack of clarity as to which figure represents Matthew: daylight shines on a youngster, flamboyantly clothed as Caravaggio himself would have been, who continues to count money at a table in an attempt to ignore the summons (if it's for him), but it also illuminates an older man looking pop-eyed with fright, who is pointing either at the boy at the table, or at himself in a 'Who, me?' gesture. In *The Inspiration of St Matthew*, above the altar, Matthew is being inspired by an angel as he writes his gospel; *The Martyrdom of St Matthew* shows the moment of his murder while celebrating mass.

Built between 1550 and 1568 by Giacomo della Porta, the church does have other great works, although Caravaggio's notoriety tends to see visitors heading straight for the chapel; don't miss frescoes by Domenichino (1616) in the Chapel of St Cecilia, second on the right, and the *Assumption* by the Venetian Francesco Bassano in the central nave.

Antica Vasca Romana

Via degli Staderari.
Bus: C3, 70, 81, 87, 116, 492, 628.

If it were anywhere else, the sculptural simplicity that defines the Antique Roman Basin would make it a principal sight. Placed between piazza Navona and the Pantheon, where it was found during excavations in 1987, however, it's sadly ignored among the wealth of things to be seen. A single jet of water bubbling up to the surface demonstrates its precision-perfect symmetry; the displaced water spills equally over the lip all around the granite basin, creating an infinity pool effect. To those seeking respite from fountains filled with fat-bottomed cherubs and muscular gods wrestling with sea monsters, the tranquil Vasca is the perfect antidote.

Tempio di Adriano

Piazza di Pietra.
Bus: 116. Map: Centro Storico, E4, p96.

Eleven towering Corinthian columns standing some five storeys high are the remains of an ancient temple dedicated to the deified Hadrian, the same emperor who completed the Pantheon and built his wall on the border between England and Scotland. Built in AD 145 by his successor Antoninus Pius, one of the original walls still stands behind seven of the massive columns, but the rest are now embedded into a new, and it has to be said, ugly, façade. To see a hypothetical and very impressive reconstruction of what the original complex may have looked like, take a look in the window of piazza di Pietra 36, which displays a scale model.

Now housing Rome's Chamber of Commerce, the temple's interior is occasionally open to the public during temporary exhibitions, allowing the enormous blocks comprising the rear side of the wall to be viewed.

Colonna di Marco Aurelio

Piazza Colonna.
Bus: C3, 62, 81, 85, 116, 119, 160, 175, 492, 628.
Map: Centro Storico, F3 p96.

The 30-m Column of Marcus Aurelius boasts not only incredibly detailed battle scenes spiralling up its exterior, but contains a stairway of some 200 steps hollowed out of its marble core that runs to the statue (once Emperor Marcus Aurelius, now St Paul) at the top. Climbing the Colonna was apparently wildly popular in the Middle Ages but is not permitted now. The minutely detailed frieze laps the column 20 times, creating (if only we could see properly – the column itself stands on a 10-m base) a continuous set of scenes. It is said to be less finely carved than the earlier **Trajan's Column** (see page 72), on which it was modelled, but with more drama. It is composed of 28 stacked marble drums, each almost 4 m in diameter. The column was designed and carved to commemorate the successful military campaigns of Marcus Aurelius, and was completed either just before or just after he died in AD 180.

Entirely surrounded by Renaissance (or later) architecture, the column is not paid much attention by shoppers heading for via del Corso or officials going for lunch: it is the perfect example of an out-of-context Centro Storico monument that you can gaze at unimpinged on by anyone else, let alone a crowd.

Mercato della piazza delle Coppelle

Piazza delle Coppelle.
Mon-Sat 0600-1430.
Bus: 116. Map: Centro Storico, D3, p96.

Frequented solely by locals, this three-stall market is not boasted about, so it retains a strong local feel. Pretty white umbrellas shelter the clutch of stalls from rain and sun. The fruit and vegetables stall, run by a brother-and-sister team, has been passed down through the family from their grandmother, typical of the family-run businesses in the area. Charmingly, they deliver their produce to restaurants in an old-fashioned handcart. Buckets of different varieties of freshly washed lettuce leaves jostle for space with different kinds of olives, making this a perfect spot to pick up goodies for a picnic. There's even a fish van (Tue-Wed, Fri-Sat) if you have access to a kitchen.

Galleria Doria Pamphilj

Via del Corso 305, T06-679 7323, doriapamphilj.it.
Daily 1000-1700 (last entry 1600), €9/6 concession (includes audio guide in English).
Bus: C3, 62, 63, 81, 85, 95, 119, 175, 492, 628.
Map: Centro Storico, F5, p96.

Stepping from noisy via del Corso into a courtyard planted with citrus trees is the perfect introduction to the Doria Pamphilj art gallery. Described as a miniature Versailles, the private gallery is still a family home – there's a wing and more to the rear where the youngest members of the Doria Pamphilj family still live. Exploring their very grand house – especially now the state rooms are back on view – is as much a reason to visit as spotting the masterpieces among the 500-odd paintings. In addition to Titian's *Salome* and two early Caravaggios, the gallery boasts Velázquez's celebrated *Portrait of Pope Innocent X* – the uncle of Camillo Pamphilj, the prince who started amassing this collection. There is also a pair of busts by Bernini in the sculpture collection; one has a big crack, which is said to have prompted the showman Bernini (when he noticed

it) to boast that he could chisel out a replacement in less than a week. You can compare the two – but history doesn't relate how quickly it was done.

Managed by the hands-on younger generation, Jonathan Doria Pamphilj and his sister Gesine, the collection is still owned by the family. Thanks to a computer programme used to tessellate the frames, the paintings are now displayed 'closely' as they were in the 18th century, with some even hanging in exactly the position their artists were commissioned to fill.

If the palazzo were in the middle of France or Germany, a million or more visitors might be expected annually. But with Galleria Borghese to compete with, Doria Pamphilj slips under many visitors' radar, attracting fewer than 60,000 a year.

Caravaggio's *Rest on the Flight into Egypt* in Galleria Doria Pamphilj; the notes Caravaggio painted form an actual melody.

That said, it is a luxury (for the sightseer at least) to be one of just a handful in such an extraordinary space.

Gallery Walk round the first floor gallery that encircles the entry courtyard to get a sense of the space, then dive into the rooms off it to look at the best treasures. In a tiny space at one end of the Mirror Gallery, which runs alongside via del Corso, is Diego Velázquez's *Portrait of Innocent X*, painted around 1650. The work is not immensely flattering to the ageing pontiff, who, so the story goes, exclaimed in horror on seeing the completed work, "*E troppo vero!*" ("It's too real!"). But it's the absence of idealism that makes us curious about Camillo's uncle, who fixes us with a gritty look.

One of the series of rooms at the opposite end of the gilded **Mirror Gallery** is the **Seicento room**, dedicated to 17th-century works, which contains two early Caravaggios. *The Rest on the Flight into Egypt* (around 1597) shows Caravaggio's bold move for the time: an angel busy playing the violin with its back turned to us. Joseph, an unexpectedly old man, holds up sheets of music for the angel – an endearing but astonishing detail (as though an all-perfect angel couldn't memorize a melody). You can actually read the music in the score, and during one of the concerts regularly held at Galleria Doria Pamphilj, the notes Caravaggio painted were played, to the absolute delight of the audience.

Alongside is a second early Caravaggio, *Penitent Magdalen*. Characterizing Caravaggio's unconventional approach is his choice of model: for both paintings, the Virgin Mary and the reformed prostitute, his sitter was the same woman.

In the next room, **Cinquecento**, the central beauty in Titian's *Salome* (around 1515) is almost unable to look at the severed head of St John the Baptist, despite having asked for it. Rumour has it that the ashen-faced St John was actually a self-portrait by the young Titian, and Salome a portrait of a woman who had broken his heart.

Back in the main gallery, the best of the series of half-moon shaped lunettes is Annibale Carracci's beautiful landscape *Flight into Egypt* (1603-1604). Carracci's designs for the others had to be

Five of the best

Pictures at Galleria Doria Pamphilj

❶ Velázquez's gritty portrait of *Innocent X*.

❷ The *Aldobrandini Lunettes*, a series of six paintings designed by Annibale Carracci.

❸ Caravaggio's *Rest on the Flight into Egypt*, and *Penitent Magdalen*.

❹ Titian's *Salome*.

❺ Kids can count the creatures in Jan Bruegel the Elder's *Earthly Paradise*.

completed by a pupil after he fell ill. Many of the statues in the gallery have cracks in them, either because only a fragment is original and the rest inspired guesswork, or because they were in the Aldobrandini room when its ceiling collapsed in the 1950s.

State apartments The star of the state apartments is the **Salone del Poussin**, which contains a phenomenal collection of landscapes, some 23 of which were commissioned from Poussin's rather less famous brother-in-law Gaspard Dughet.

Don't miss the leather-encased telescope locked in a cabinet in the **Yellow Room** – while uncle Innocent X was interrogating Galileo Galilei, Camillo was enjoying using his new toy. But before condemning Camillo, it's good to remember that he enraged the same papal uncle by renouncing the cardinalship he was offered in order to marry the fabulously wealthy Olimpia Aldobrandini – whose palace this was, so we also have her to thank for the collection on view today.

Chiesa Nuova/Santa Maria in Vallicella

Piazza della Chiesa Nuova, T06-687 5289.
Daily 0800-1200, 1630-1900.
Bus: 40, 46, 62, 64. Map: Centro Storico, C4, p96.

When angry youths in the 1400s stoned a fresco of the Madonna and Child painted on a communal wall, real blood trickled from the fresco, so the story goes. The medieval yobs were horrified, but when Filippo Neri heard the tale he was so moved he founded, in 1575, a church on the very spot, with the wall that bore the fresco, *La Madonna Vallicelliana* ('the Madonna of the little valley') forming the altar wall.

The church fathers remained very protective of their Madonna, and commissioned Peter Paul Rubens to provide a suitable canvas to hang in front to shield it. Rejecting Rubens' first attempt, they gave a more specific brief, asking for three paintings and, mysteriously, for a removable oval to feature in the central work. The resulting *La Madonna della Vallicella adorata dagli Angeli*, which Rubens finished in 1608 and is now gleaming from extensive restoration, is one of the main reasons visitors brave this large, rather gloomy church. Flanked by paintings of saints and martyrs, the central work shows Mary holding Jesus in a golden oval, as if in a family portrait, encircled by angels. Every Sunday, thanks to electronic wizardry, the oval containing Rubens' Mary is lowered to reveal the original fresco, in which Mary and Jesus are crowned in bright gold.

Ara Pacis

Lungotevere in Augusta (corner of via Tomacelli), arapacis.it.
Tue-Sun 0900-1900 (last entry 1800), €6/4.50 concession, free EU citizens under 18 and over 65.
Metro: Spagna. Bus: 224, 590, 628, 926.
Map: Centro Storico, D1, p96.

The state-of-the-art museum that houses the Ara Pacis, an ancient altar of peace, is so light-filled and lofty that visiting the poetic space has become one of the most memorable museum experiences in Rome. Designed by US architect Richard Meier and opened in 2006, the glass, steel and travertine building is a monumental hall, with the Ara Pacis bathed in light placed in its centre.

The Ara Pacis is an altar where sacrifices of animals and wine would have been offered to the gods, and it is encircled by an open-topped enclosure. Both elements are almost completely covered in intricately sculpted friezes. Built and carved around 9 BC to commemorate a period of peace following Rome's Gallic and Spanish campaigns, the Ara Pacis is a powerful work of Roman art. As it had been the altar of Augustus, and was unearthed nearby, it was fitting that it should be housed next to his mausoleum (see page 123).

Juxtaposing the ancient monument with Richard Meier's glass walls, which seem even lighter in structure up close, imbues the dramatic space with a sense of excitement. And not just for those inside, because thanks to the transparent façades, the design is democratic, with passers-by able to look in and see the Ara Pacis in its magnificent surroundings.

Meier's rhythmic, linear structure brought a very prominent and very welcome first to Rome: not only is the museum an exciting new space in the middle of the city, but it is the first modern architectural project to be built in the historic centre since the Second World War.

"The light in Rome is intoxicating," Richard Meier famously said, so he made sure natural light was a major feature. And as travertine is a very Roman material, it played an important part in shaping the raised piazza, complete with the fountain and wall of running water outside, which form an integral part of the museum.

The smaller exhibition spaces in the lower level chart the excavation of the fragments of the Ara Pacis and show how they were pieced together. Old and new are clearly shown in the monument itself, with the original fragments set against a new background of a different colour. The Ara Pacis then, is not just the main exhibit in the museum, but the sole draw.

Modern temporary exhibitions are staged here, and some have been super-successful, like the retrospective of Valentino's couture collections in 2007: set designers Patrick Kinmonth and Antonio Monfreda staged a representation of the Vestals who would have been in charge of the Ara Pacis 2000 years ago, with mannequins dressed in Valentino gowns 'processing' towards the altar.

The Ara Pacis is housed in a state-of-the-art museum designed by Richard Meier.

Clearly, as a very beautifully engineered space with a welcome degree of impact, the new museum's design has been controversial. It has been dogged by detractors who disapproved of a modern project, even in a square that was in need of an injection of energy, suffering as it does from unattractive Fascist architecture. When the museum opened, critics who heralded it as a masterpiece were confronted by those who found it necessary to compare it to a 'suburban swimming pool' or a 'petrol station'. Most people dismissed such remarks as the opinions of fuddy-duddies until, just after being elected in 2008, Rome's mayor Gianni Alemanno announced his intention to dismantle the museum and move it to the suburbs. This has, thankfully, turned out to be more about taking a swipe at his political predecessor, Walter Veltroni, who supported the project, than a serious plan.

Mausoleo di Augusto

Piazza Augusto Imperatore.
Metro: Spagna. Bus: 81, 224, 590, 628, 596.
Map: Centro Storico, E1, p96.

Work is under way to restore the Mausoleum of Augustus, built in 28 BC; the move is welcome, as the ancient tomb had become almost completely overgrown in recent decades. The project is part of an initiative to unite the public space between the mausoleum and two churches in the piazza with Richard Meier's Ara Pacis museum. The head of local university Roma Tre's architecture faculty, Francesco Cellini, is leading the project, which the city council estimates will cost around €20 million. The project was given an ambitious completion date of early 2009, but was not expected to meet it even before work was interrupted by winter rains. Conservative estimates now suggest 2011 is the earliest the complex will open.

Walk around Centro Storico

Head down via del Teatro Marcello, for a walk that starts at **Teatro di Marcello** and winds through the most atmospheric side streets to take in the best of Centro Storico. Allow yourself a day, making lunch en route a leisurely affair, with dinner at one of the choice restaurants at the end of the walk.

Begin by going down the walkway to Teatro di Marcello, and admire its crumbling bulk as you pass it on your left. Ahead is the city's **synagogue** with its striking square dome. Continue up the walkway to the street, stopping to wonder at the alterations that have left **Portico d'Ottavia** in its lopsided state. Follow via del Portico d'Ottavia, taking in the cinnamon-spiced scents from the bakeries and the sights of the Ghetto – the restaurants on the right are mostly kosher.

Take the first right, Via di Sant' Ambrogio, to Piazza Mattei, the site of the enchanting **Fontana delle Tartarughe** or Tortoise Fountain. Make your way up Via Paganica to the main road. **Crypta Balbi**, with its well-presented findings excavated onsite, is a block down via delle Botteghe Oscure – make a detour to look at the ancient sculptures in its windows.

We're headed to **Largo di Torre Argentina** next, a square known for its cats (there's a

The Synagogue, with its square dome, is a highlight of a visit to the Ghetto district.

sanctuary here) and its **Area Sacra**, the remains of four Roman temples that are best seen from the pedestrianized via di San Nicola de Cesarini. Across the busy corso Vittorio Emanuele II, continue straight down via dei Cestari, taking in Bernini's adorable baby elephant in marble, **Pulcino della Minerva**, on piazza Minerva.

Looking ahead toward piazza della Rotonda, you can already see the **Pantheon**, Hadrian's temple. Even if you've already visited, it's impossible to pass without walking through the giant doors to look up at the sun beaming through the aperture in its dome.

Take via dei Pastini to the **Tempio di Adriano**, the eroded columns of what was Hadrian's Temple, and look at the hypothesized model in the window of piazza di Pietra 36 to imagine what grandeur might have stood here two millennia ago. Recharge with a *cappuccino freddo* (if it's very hot) in the *über*-cool Salotto 42.

Turn left along via dei Bergamaschi to piazza Colonna, to marvel at the 30-m high **Colonna di Marco Aurelio**. Head across next-door piazza di Montecitorio and take via degli Uffici dei Vicario. At piazza Campo Marzio, take the tiny lane in the left corner, vicolo delle Coppelle, leading to piazza delle Coppelle and its market with a great local vibe. Outdoor tables at **Coco** make a good lunch stop. If it's too hot to sit outside, **Maccheroni** is the perfect alternative.

Walk along via delle Coppelle towards piazza Navona, but stop at via della Scrofa. Down on the left is **San Luigi dei Francesi** with its three Caravaggios – if lunch was very leisurely you can take a look, but it's not open before 1600, so chances are you'll want to come back.

Head up via della Scrofa until you reach via dei Portoghesi, and follow it as it becomes via dell' Orso; walking through these little lanes reveals the Rome of the locals: you can peek into courtyard gardens and see restorers busy in their workshops. Don't miss the old-fashioned barber's on the left, on the corner with via Pianellari.

Take a left into via dei Gigli d'Oro, which opens on to piazza Sant'Apollinare; on your

Tip…

When strolling down streets like via dell'Orso don't be too engrossed in conversation, because through open doors you can glimpse sculptors in their workshops, a restorer bent over a picture frame, a metal worker surrounded by tools, or a team repairing mosaics. For example, busy in the workshop at via dell'Orso 26 is a woodcarver and his mosaic-making and restorer daughters. This is Rome the way it's lived by locals, who've inherited their professions from hardworking parents and *nonno* or *nonna* before them.

Piazza Navona's oval shape was established in the days when chariots raced here (a couple thousand years ago).

right is **Palazzo Altemps**, a beautifully restored Renaissance palace – a lovely backdrop to the sculpture collection on display.

Cross straight over corso dei Rinascimento to reach theatrical **piazza Navona** with its **Fontana dei Quattro Fiumi** centre stage. If there's time for a detour, the church of **Santa Maria della Pace**, with Raphael's fresco of the Sibyls is a minute away to the west, as is the beautiful **Chiostro di Bramante**; if you have time, **Caffè Chiostro** in the upper loggia is the perfect place for a glass of wine.

Walk the length of piazza Navona and make your way south to **Campo de' Fiori**. The market will be over by now, so continue through to **Piazza Farnese** to admire the bathtub fountains and the ceilings of Palazzo Farnese, lit at night. The street that exits the square to the right, via di Monserrato, boasts several choice restaurants: Ristorante Monserrato has tables outside that are hard to beat.

Sleeping

Hotel Ponte Sisto €€€€
Via dei Pettinari 64, T06-686310, hotelpontesisto.it.
Bus: 116.
Map: Centro Storico, C6, p96.
The courtyard garden is enchanting: four palm trees stand metres high against the building's orange walls – a stunning contrast. Breakfast is served in the shade of the trees in summer. However, compact rooms featuring furnishings that look a bit dated and tired showers make the room rate seem high. That said, those overlooking the courtyard have floor-to-ceiling windows in both bedroom and bathroom. There's parking on site.

St George €€€€
Via Giulia 62, T06-686611, stgeorgehotel.it.
Bus: 40, 46, 62, 64, 116.
Map: Centro Storico, B4, p96.
Behind an ancient façade is the gem of a hotel that is St George. Calming hues of beige, chocolate and white are sharpened by black and white prints, and floor-to-ceiling windows overlook pretty via Giulia. Rooms have laptop-sized safes, TV and internet, and bathrooms are beautifully finished, with make-up mirrors and tubs. There's a blissout spa and a seriously beautiful-people-packed roof-terrace bar.

Hotel Campo de' Fiori €€€
Via del Biscione 6, T06-6880 6865, hotelcampodefiori.com.
Bus: H, 63, 116, 780.
Map: Centro Storico, D5, p96.
The elegant bedrooms and sleek bathrooms of this recently renovated hotel are the work of a set designer turned architect, whose theatrical sense shows in gold-framed TVs and customized headboards. The project has lost the hotel several rooms, to make space for the lift and en suite bathrooms throughout. Communal spaces include an elegant ground-floor sitting room and a roof terrace stretching over three levels. Two rooms on the top floor have their own balconies. Some rooms are small but so characterful the young clientele don't mind.

Locanda Cairoli €€€
Piazza Benedetto Cairoli 2 (1st floor), T06-6880 9278, cairolo@tin.it.
Bus: H, 63, 780.
Map: Centro Storico, D6, p96.
Architect Luciano Chisini opened this sensational space when, bit by bit, he'd expanded his home to buy the entire first floor of the palazzo. His input shows throughout, both in the layout and blonde wood fittings, and in the original paintings and photographs that adorn the walls and make the apartment a fascinating place to visit, let alone stay in. There's a very comfortable sitting room, and bedrooms are

Leisure in Rome

Via Metastasio 9, T06-6830 0335, leisureinrome.com.
A rental agency that specializes in high-end rentals, Leisure in Rome has apartments and villas on its books that are available from a minimum of three days to a maximum of one year.

spacious enough for a sofa, armchair or sizeable table. The concept of a home-from-home extends to the one long table that all guests share at breakfast.

Teatro di Pompeo €€€
Largo del Pallaro 8, T06-687 2812, hotelteatrodipompeo.it.
Bus: 116.
Map: Centro Storico, D5, p96.
Located between Campo de' Fiori and piazza Navona, the hotel is very aptly named since it sits on the foundations of the Theatre of Pompey. There's nothing theatrical about the rooms, however, which are all the more attractive for their honest presentation. The period furniture, marble-topped desks, classical mirrors and wood-beamed ceilings create a solid

atmosphere. The rooms are quite spacious, and the upper floors have lots of light. The breakfast room is below ground in the cave-like Roman structure itself.

Casa dei Fiori €€
Piazza del Biscione 83,
T06-6880 8922,
casadeifiori.hotelinroma.com.
Bus: 116.
Map: Centro Storico, D5, p96.
Up a pretty spiral staircase is this very attractive set of rooms on the first and third floors, opened just a year ago. The nicely renovated rooms are sizable; period furniture and wood-beamed ceilings are complemented by attractive dusky pink walls, and good bathrooms have large glass shower cubicles. It's in sight of Campo de' Fiori, but far enough away to not be bothered by the nightly racket, and breakfast is well above average, with fresh fruit and pastries.

Smeraldo €€
Vicolo dei Chiodaroli 9, T06-687 5929, smeraldoroma.it.
Bus: 40, 46, 64, 70, 81, 87, 119, 492.
Map: Centro Storico, D5, p96.
Divided between two addresses, one just around the corner from the main hotel, Smeraldo is just five minutes from Campo de' Fiori. There's a roof terrace, the rooms are pleasant and bathrooms quite bright, although some shower cubicles are on the small side. Although the basic standard is

fine, the rates reflect the hotel's location in a popular area, rather than any exceptional services.

Self-catering
Hotel Campo de' Fiori Apartments
Contact Hotel Campo de' Fiori, via del Biscione 6, T06-6880 6865, hotelcampodefiori.com.
Bus: H, 63, 116, 780.
Sleeping from two to five people, the 14 apartments managed by the Venetian owner of Hotel Campo de' Fiori are located near the hotel. Some have been renovated recently, others not. Ask for an apartment in a quiet location as it's better to have noisy Campo de' Fiori two minutes walk away than right under your window. From €160-180 per night for two.

Raphaël €€€€
Largo Febo 2, T06-682831, raphaelhotel.com.
Bus: C3, 70, 81, 87, 116, 492.
Map: Centro Storico, C3, p96.
The romantic sight of Raphaël's ivy-shrouded façade might suggest traditional interiors throughout, but happily nothing could be further from the truth. While US architect Richard Meier was working on the museum to house the Ara Pacis (see page 122) he was also busy at Raphaël, overseeing his designs for the third floor; his blueprint – with cool white bedding and sleek blonde oak – is now being rolled out across the second floor too. When the Meier-designed sixth-floor restaurant is completed (2010), breakfast, lunch and dinner on the rooftop with a view of a dozen domes will be a year-round affair.

Sole al Pantheon €€€€
Piazza della Rotonda 63, T06-678 0441, hotelsolealpantheon.com.
Bus: 116.
Map: Centro Storico, E4, p96.

A long history of welcoming guests to this Pantheon-fronting hotel goes back to the mid-15th century, when farmers bringing cattle to market would sleep in an upper room with the animals stabled below. Sole al Pantheon has come a long way since then, and is a rather grand affair, with rooms sumptuously decorated in great swathes of material; all baths are Jacuzzis. Breakfast is really good, both in its range – which changes daily – and quality; from spring on it's served in the courtyard.

Albergo Cesàri €€€
Via di Pietra 89a, T06-674 9701, albergocesari.it.
Bus: 116.
Map: Centro Storico, F3, p96.

The recently renovated fifth floor of this long-established hotel has resulted in a sleek breakfast room that spills out on to the spacious rooftop terrace in summer, where there's also an evening bar. The hotel is between the Trevi Fountains and the Pantheon, making it popular not just with people who want to go everywhere on foot, but also with local parliamentarians. Rooms, equipped with safes and Wi-Fi, are furnished in a classic style, and dotted with pretty period furniture and prints; upper-level rooms have gorgeous views across the rooftops.

Albergo del Senato €€€
Piazza della Rotonda 73, T06-678 4343, albergodelsenato.it.
Bus: 116.
Map: Centro Storico, E4, p96.

Although the reception is a bit pompous (perhaps to be expected from the name), the hotel's 50-odd rooms are very nice spaces, with not a hint of the red marble that overpowers the entry area. The decor is definitely classic, but not too heavy. All piazza-fronting rooms have a view across to the Pantheon, and there's a roof terrace.

Albergo Santa Chiara €€€
Via Santa Chiara 21, T06-687 2979, albergosantachiara.com.
Bus: 40, 46, 64, 70, 81, 119, 492, 628.
Map: Centro Storico, E4, p96.

Two minutes from the Pantheon, the hotel has a new wing with rooms that really appeal thanks to the pared-down colour scheme; as many of the rooms overlook piazza della Minerva, ask for a view on to the internal courtyard to ensure a good night's sleep. The main building retains its classical furnishings. Single rooms are small so ask for a double for single occupancy. Down on the ground floor, the bar spills out on to the pavement.

Hotel Adriano €€€
Via di Pallacorda 2, T06-6880 2451, hoteladriano.com.
Bus: 116.
Map: Centro Storico, D3, p96.

The comfortable, gorgeously furnished communal spaces make this feel like a big, inviting house. The long sofas in the winter garden lounge bar, the books and games encouraging guests to linger in the little library, and the offer of free bicycles to sail across the Centro Storico all contribute to the cocooned feeling. All the bedrooms, too, are luxuriously finished, with some bathrooms featuring Jacuzzis. Aperitivi nights are held in Adriano's bar, creating a lively exchange between locals and guests. Biannual shopping events, held at the end of April and November, are proving very popular.

Hotel Pantheon €€€
Via dei Pastini 131, T06-678 7746, hotelpantheon.it.
Bus: 116.
Map: Centro Storico, E4, p96.

Located on a side street mere minutes from the Pantheon, the hotel has been carefully restored: ceilings are wood-beamed and windows have traditional wooden frames. The classic style continues through to the marble bathrooms. Having just 13 rooms gives the hotel an intimate feel, with a lovely little sitting room next to reception providing a nice extra space.

Due Torri €€

Vicolo del Leonetto 23, T06-6880 6956, hotelduetorriroma.com.
Metro: Spagna. Bus: 70, 87, 116.
Map: Centro Storico, D3, p96.

With a private terrace as a complimentary extra for all fifth-floor rooms, and full-length windows opening on to a slim balcony for a little more space and light in all fourth-floor rooms (there is a lift), it's not hard to see why the pretty Due Torri sees a number of returning clients. If you don't want to chance your luck, put in a request when you book. Communal spaces are attractive, hung with antique mirrors, while the red-themed furniture reflects the hotel's history, explained with a wink from manager Cinzia: it's been both a hostel for cardinals and a bordello.

Hotel Navona €€

Via dei Sediari 8, T06-686 4203, hotelnavona.com.
Bus: C3, 70, 116, 492, 628.
Map: Centro Storico, D4, p96.

With a pair of columns and an ancient fountain to greet you in the courtyard, Hotel Navona immediately gets you in the Roman spirit. Upstairs, rooms in the family's palazzo-turned-hotel balance classic (antique tables, prints) with modern (transparent chairs). Several rooms have painted beamed ceilings; in some an ancient column capital or brick archway is visible. It all makes for a fascinating and authentic stay. A lift is planned for summer 2009 but the foundations will have to avoid the ancient Baths of Agrippa, on which the 15th-century palazzo was built.

Maison Giulia
Best Comfort €€

Via Giulia 189a, T06-6880 8325, bestcomfort.org.
Bus: 116.
Map: Centro Storico, C6, p96.

Furnished in a classic style that ties in with the beamed ceilings and wooden floors, rooms are comfortable and bathrooms are modern, with sunny lemon tiles and generously sized showers. The helpful staff will assist with sightseeing and dining plans and even cater for special requests, such as bacon and eggs for breakfast, if you ask in advance. There's a tiny gym with two machines and a cosy two-person sauna in the basement. This newly opened location has seven rooms, and there are another three in their Ghetto district B&B, where they also have a self-contained apartment available from €150-250 per night, depending on season and length of stay.

A note on B&Bs

Although there's someone manning a reception desk from 0800-2000, Rome's B&Bs are not part of a house, but a series of independent rooms. Visitors are given their own key, creating a nice home-from-home feel, and breakfast is served in a communal area.

Residenza Zanardelli €€

Via Giuseppe Zanardelli 7, T06-6880 9760, residenzazanardelli.com.
Bus: C3, 70, 81, 87, 116, 492, 628.
Map: Centro Storico, C3, p96.

This is run by the same family as Navona – they count among their illustrious relations one Giuseppe Zanardelli, prime minister in the early 1900s. Great attention to detail makes a stay here count. Furnishings have been carefully chosen, with mirrors in one room brought from Venice, and beautiful prints in the communal area. The rooms are very comfortable.

Self-catering
Hotel Navona apartments

Via dei Sediari 8, T06-686 4203, hotelnavona.com.
Bus: C3, 70, 116, 492, 628.

The family who run Hotel Navona and Residenza Zanardelli have a series of spacious one-bedroom apartments, with air-conditioning, priced from €155-250 per night depending on season and length of stay.

Eating & drinking

Here's a quandary: Italians, or Romans at least, don't seem to care too much about setting. While dishes are presented as, and taste of, perfection itself, the surroundings often leave much to be desired: not a single table outside, no matter how picturesque or quiet the street, (original) 1950s clutter as unintentional decor, harsh lighting with not a candle in sight. But if the setting really appeals, be warned: the place is run either by a genius inching the local clientele towards a more interesting ambience, or by a profiteer catering to tourists, with the associated climb in prices and slump in quality. Listen for Italian voices as you case the joint: if Italians are eating there, even if they're not local, it's an indication that the food is good.

Campo de' Fiori & the Ghetto

Al Bric €€€€

Via del Pellegrino 51-52, T06-687 9533, bric.it.
Tue-Sat 1930-2330, Sun 1230-1430, 1930-2330, closed 3 weeks in Aug.
Bus: 40, 64, 116.
Map: Centro Storico, C5, p96.

The focus here is as much on wine as on the menu. It's the bench containing 30-plus cheeses that has passers-by stopping to peer in. But once inside, the wine crate lids that decorate the walls indicate sommelier Maurizio's passion: he can offer a choice of over 600 wines, depending on the season. During winter the focus is on meat and hot cheese, with dishes such as *spaghetti con Roquefort e miele*, and in summer, fish. Piedmont is clearly an inspiration: *al bric* in Piedmontese refers to good wine-growing hills, and the bread, made in-house, is their own take on a Piedmontese staple.

Hosteria del Pesce €€€€

Via di Monserrato 32, T06-686 5617, hosteriadelpesce.net.
Mon-Sat 1900-2300.
Bus: 116.
Map: Centro Storico, C5, p96.
Step over the threshold of this fish speciality restaurant to be confronted with a bank of fish fresh from the sea off Terracina. You choose what you'd like and pay by weight. You also choose (with guidance) how you'd like it cooked, as the *secondi* on the menu aren't complete dishes, but ways of cooking. Scampi can be *crudo* (raw) or *in padella* (fried) while red snapper, turbot and sea bass all have their own recommended preparation. Sounds like too much work? Go for the *tartare di tonno crudo* (raw tuna steak) and you'll be set. Reservation recommended.

Pagliaccio €€€€

Via dei Banchi Vecchi 129a, T06-6880 9595, ristoranteilpagliaccio.it.
Mon-Tue 2000-2230, Wed-Sat 1300-1430, 2000-2230, closed 10-20 Jan, 5-20 Aug.
Bus: 40, 64.
Map: Centro Storico, B4, p96.
Two Michelin stars prove it's not just locals who are enjoying head chef Anthony Genovese and pastry chef Marion Lichtle's creative blend of Italian, Oriental and French dishes. Genovese's descriptions on the menu – "Pigeon 'my way' with tonka beans and chocolate" – are refreshingly unpretentious, as are the two dining rooms. For complementing flavours, a potato dumpling with mozzarella cream, oysters and wild trout eggs is a winner; for visual appeal, a dish of John Dory with fennel seeds, avocado and rhubarb couldn't be bettered. Carefully sourced produce and a focus on freshness is critical to what's being created. The tasting menu (five courses, one dessert) can be accompanied by a different glass of wine for each course. Reservations at least a week in advance are recommended.

Ristorante Monserrato €€€€

Via Monserrato 96, T06-687 3386.
Tue-Sun 1230-1500, 1900-2400.
Bus: 116.
Map: Centro Storico, C5, p96.
Inspired by his Sicilian wife, the

owner opened this restaurant to serve fish 20 years ago when such a place was needed. Fettuccine and taglioni are made inhouse; *paccheri con ragù di spigola* is a Neapolitan pasta with a sea bass sauce, and *bombolotti all'astrice* is another much requested dish – a crayfish pasta. The two indoor spaces give off a reassuringly traditional air that attracts an older crowd; with tables close together, there's a convivial feel among regulars and foreigners living locally. The 25 tables outside (for dinner only) are on the corner where a little electric bus turns; sometimes people have to pull in their chairs to let the little bus by.

Angolo Divino €€€

Via dei Balestrari 12-14, T06-686 4413, angolodivino@tiscali.it.
Daily 1000-1500, 1700-0200, closed Sun-Mon in Jul-Aug and 2 weeks in Aug.
Bus: 40, 64, 116.
Map: Centro Storico, C5, p96.
Really delicious dishes (Argentinian beef, goose with mash) are complemented by an astonishing range of wines. Sommelier/owner Massimo Crippa knows his stuff and is also passionate about the prosecco, champagne, *acquaviti* and whiskeys he offers. All set in a relaxed space with big windows and pale blue walls – a divine corner it surely is.

La Tartaruga €€€

Via del Monte della Farina 53, T06-686 9473.
Tue-Fri 1930-2245, Sat-Sun 1230-1500, 1930-2245.
Bus: 40, 63, 64.
Map: Centro Storico, D5, p96.
As this restaurant is small, and produce is bought each day from the market on Campo de' Fiori, it's seen as almost an extension of the family. Wines on the select list are from small vineyards, and unusual ingredients, like the *ortica selvatica di montagna* (mountain nettle) in a risotto, are typical of the fresh extras brought in from the family's home in the mountains outside Rome.

La Vecchia Bottega del Vino €€€

Via Santa Maria del Pianto 9a/11,
T06-6819 2210,
lavecchiabottegadelvino.it.
Tue-Fri 1200-1530, 1700-2230,
Sat 1200-1530.
Bus: 40, 63, 64, 780.
Map: Centro Storico, D6, p96.

A wine specialist in half the premises and a bar and restaurant the other side make a knockout combination. Buy wine by the glass or bottle, and then choose a plate of cheese or *salumi* and/or other dishes to accompany the wine.

Osteria ar Galletto €€€

Piazza Farnese 102,
T06-686 1714.
Mon-Sat 1215-1500, 1915-2300.
Bus: 116.
Map: Centro Storico, C5, p96.

It's the tables that spread out across piazza Farnese and the honest pricing of the simple, hearty dishes that draws the crowds to this friendly eatery. Trays of *dolci* lined up inside, where there are several large dining areas, look so temptingly fresh (they're made in-house) that you'll want to skip (or share) an antipasto to make sure you have room to try one.

La Taverna del Ghetto €€

Via del Portico d'Ottavia 7b-8,
T06-6880 9771,
latavernadelghetto.com.
Mon-Thu and Sun 1200-1500,
1800-2300, Fri 1200-1500,
Sat 1800-2300.
Bus: H, 23, 63, 280, 780.
Map: Centro Storico, E6, p96.

This restaurant in the heart of the Jewish district is the real deal, so good that diners extend beyond those who only eat kosher. Highlights include *carciofi alla giudia* (flash-fried artichokes, crisp and crunchy), *mezzemaniche con broccoli e salsicce di manzo kosher* (in-house pasta with kosher beef sausage), *stracotto di manzo* (braised beef stew) and *l'abbacchio ajo ed erbetta* (roast lamb with parsley and 'Jewish garlic sauce') – some of the Jewish community's best-known dishes.

Trattoria Pizzeria Polese €€

Piazza Sforza Cesarini 40 (off
corso Vittorio Emanuele II),
T06-686 9543.
Wed-Mon 1200-1600,
1900-2400.
Bus: 40, 46, 64.
Map: Centro Storico, B4, p96.

Filling the interior (and, in summer, extensive outdoor) space with cheerful diners are Paolo and his brother Lorenzo. Staples such as *saltimbocca alla romana* (sautéed veal and ham) or *polpettine di vitello con piselli* (veal olives with peas) get a firm thumbs-up from locals, who've enjoyed the family's cooking since the boys' father and uncle opened in the 1970s.

Caffè Fiori di Campo €

Campo de' Fiori 7.
Daily 0630-0200.
Bus: 116.
Map: Centro Storico, C5, p96.

Not very inventively named, but

very popular with twenty-something locals who come for a coffee in the morning, or a quick pizza at night. Salads are good too. For an aperitivo try an Italianized cocktail like *capirissima*. The staff are lovely.

Cafés & bars

Caffè ai Banchi Vecchi
Via dei Banchi Vecchi 6,
T06-6880 1170.
Mon-Sat 0630-2000.
Bus: 40, 46, 64, 116.
A friendly little corner café, with good pastries, sandwiches and *pizza bianca ripiena* (filled pizza base), it also has a good wine selection.

Caffè Farnese
Piazza Farnese 106,
T06-6880 2125.
Daily 0700-0200.
Bus: 116.
Aside from good coffee and having a name for being a decent *pasticceria* (they make their own *cornetti* and pastries), the ice creams here are tasty – they make their own in the summer. Don't drink at the bar – the view across the piazza outside is worth the extra euros.

Caffè Perù
Via Giulia 84.
Mon-Sat 0445-2000, closed 3 weeks in Aug.
Bus: 40, 64, 116.
Also known as Bar Alfredo, in honour of the friendly chap who runs it (who has been here since

he was nine), the dual names can make it hard to find. It is worth the trouble though, as this is the smallest, friendliest bar imaginable. There are a couple of tables outside for those who want to linger.

Crudo
Via degli Specchi 6, T06-683 8989, crudoroma.it.
Mon 1200-1600, Tue-Sun 1200-1600, 1900-0200, closed Aug. DJ Thu-Sun 2100-0200.
Bus: H, 63, 780.
A very cool lounge-style bar, and also part of EaTaly, a Slow Food movement, so the dishes laid out during aperitivo (1900-2100) are not just delicious but organic where possible and very carefully sourced. The food's *crudo* (raw) or as "little messed around with as possible". There's dining upstairs with the same great credentials.

Dada Umpa Caffè
Piazza Cairoli 2a, T335-607 7922. dadaumpa.net.
Daily 1100-0200, closed Aug.
Bus: H, 63, 780.
A café, restaurant and American bar, this all-white space has attracted a lot of attention in the weeks since it opened. It's not a club as such, but with lights in the Plexiglas bar changing colour and the music seriously clubby, it certainly feels like one.

Draft Book
Via del Pellegrino 196-197,
T06-6880 9709.
Mon-Sat 1200-0200, Sun 1600-0200.
Bus: 46, 64, 70, 116.
A mellow little bar just off Campo de' Fiori that uses second-hand books as decoration (all the reading matter is for sale) and has Wi-Fi. There's a big selection of draft and bottled beer.

Ducati Caffè
Via delle Botteghe Oscure 35,
T06-6889 1718,
ducaticafferoma.com.
Daily 0800-0200.
Bus: 46, 62, 64, 70, 87, 492, 780.
More lounge than café, this sleek space has a Ducati shop attached, but it's not sponsored by the brand. Slow Food influences see a startlingly good range of cheeses and meats, sliced to fill sandwiches while you wait. Aperitivo and dinner plans are afoot, so watch this space.

Il Nolano
Campo de' Fiori 12.
Mon-Tue 1800-0200,
Wed-Sun 1100-0200.
Bus: 116.
A really relaxed vibe makes Il Nolano popular with locals, who refer to it as alternative; it's certainly not frenetic like some bars round the Campo.

La Dolceroma

Via del Portico d'Ottavia 20b,
T06-689 2196, ladolceroma.com.
Tue-Sat 0800-2000, Sun
1000-1330, closed Jul-Aug.
Bus: H, 23, 63, 280, 780.

The Austrian-born Italian who established this bakery and *pasticceria* trained in Vienna and Seattle in order to bring authentic goodies like cheesecake (topped with tiny wild strawberries), *apfelstrudel* and much more to Rome. Eat in or take away.

Le Teste Matte

Via del Baullari 113-114,
T06-6880 1443.
Mon, Wed-Sun 0800-0200,
Tue 1700-0200.
Bus: 116.

Check out the chess playing early afternoons in this cheerfully cluttered bar. The late night vibe is scruffy and friendly; the speciality is absinthe.

The Drunken Ship

Campo de' Fiori 20-21, T06-6830
0535, drunkenship.com.
Daily 1600-0200,
happy hour(s) 1600-2000.
Bus: 116.

Loud and friendly is the vibe here; it screens sports on its two big TVs and there's a DJ from 2300 some weekends and holidays. Tucked in the fountains corner of the Campo, the Drunken Ship is easy to find thanks to its large, always-open window.

Piazza Navona & the Pantheon

Casa Bleve €€€€

Via del Teatro Valle 48/49,
T06-686 5970, casableve.it.
Daily 1030-1500, 1800-2230,
dinner from 1930.
Bus: 116.
Map: Centro Storico, D4, p96.

Known for its extensive wine cellar selected from small choice producers, Casa Bleve also does a good buffet lunch, with a range of delicious dishes on the bar for €30 for as much as you want. Delicate spring rolls are a current speciality – tiny wraps of pineapple or pepper. The dinner menu is à la carte.

Hostaria dell'Orso €€€€

Via dei Soldati 25b, T06-6830
1192, hdo.it.
Mon-Sat 2000-0100.
Bus: 70, 81, 87, 116, 492.
Map: Centro Storico, C3, p96.

A polished dream team has been appointed to shake up the bar, restaurant and club (on ascending levels) that is Orso. The 15th-century building, with its tunnel under the river connecting it to Castel Sant'Angelo, has long been a source of fables and mystery, but problems were caused for the church-owned space by an oblique reference to it in Dan Brown's *Da Vinci Code*. Whatever the truth, an order came from on high to have certain frescoes swiftly covered over in the Dante

room off the restaurant (Alighieri is said to have stayed there). Intrigued? So are we. And now, with 26-year-old Salvatore Bianco heading up the kitchen and an equally fresh-faced restaurant manager, we'll watch this place to see how it evolves.

A DJ transforms the space into a club from Thursday to Saturday (times vary) and it's sometimes closed for private parties so ring to check.

Laganà €€€€

Via dell'Orso 44, T06-6830 1161.
Mon-Sat 1300-1500, 1930-2330.
Bus: 70, 81, 87, 116, 492.
Map: Centro Storico, D3, p96.

Laganà is Rome at its best. Complementing the hearty, tasty dishes and good wine is

an atmosphere so warm that if you come regularly or on your own, you get drawn into the most entertaining chats. When the conversation lulled for a moment we asked if there was a menu, but Mimmo Laganà had nipped into the kitchen and a chirpy diner, clearly a good friend, chipped in, "Yes, but I never get to see it, and if I do order something, he brings me something else!" The fish and meat dishes are so good you need to come hungry so you can manage a couple of courses.

Sangallo ai Coronari €€€€
Via dei Coronari 180, T06-6813 4055, ristorantesangallo.com.
Daily 1200-2230.
Bus: 116.
Map: Centro Storico, C3, p96.
Buffalo meat is lean and low-cholesterol so it seems an obvious choice, but Sangallo seems to be the first in Rome to create dishes based on the meat. There's also a range of buffalo milk mozzarella and ricotta cheeses, brought in fresh each day by a staff member who lives near the huge buffalo herds of Frosinone. The tasting menu is a good option. There are lots of tables out on the piazza, but the beautifully restored interior is cool and welcoming.

Armando al Pantheon €€€
Salita dei Crescenzi 31, T06-6880 3034, armandoalpantheon.it.
Mon-Fri 1230-1500, 1915-2300, Sat 1230-1500.
Bus: 116.
Map: Centro Storico, E4, p96.
Although it looks like a humble trattoria, Armando's role feeding the government officials whose offices fill the area seems to have pushed prices up, along with the extensive list of wines now on offer. But dishes are honest fare, with occasional new creations such *spaghetti alla verde* – with a zesty sauce of wild rocket, Parmesan and lemon. And the presence of *trippa alla romana* and other offal dishes reassures that it does still serve locals.

Bloom €€€
Via del Teatro Pace 29, T06-6880 2029, bloomclub.it.
Oct-Apr, Mon-Tue, Thu-Sun 2000-2400.
Bus: 70, 81, 87, 116, 492.
Map: Centro Storico, C4, p96.
Recently refurbished, Bloom is now all soft grey with giant silk lamps that look like sea-urchin shells. As the space in the first floor restaurant is not large, dining is by reservation only on Saturdays and Tuesdays, when a DJ is scheduled to play in the club/bar below from around 2330. The set menu changes depending on the young chef's market picks.

Bottega Montecitorio €€€
Via della Guglia 62-63 (off piazza Montecitorio), T06-6920 0537, bottegamontecitorio.it.
Tue-Sun 1230-1500, 1930-2330, aperitivo 1730-2000.
Bus: 116.
Map: Centro Storico, E3, p96.
Down a side street two minutes from the Pantheon, a dinky entry bar area has space for a pair of couples; everyone else goes through to the comfortable white sofas and tables. The menu is based on *cucina romana* but with Mediterranean-wide inspiration. Salads are good: *arance e finocchietta* (orange and baby fennel) is light and super refreshing. Serving tiramisù in a teacup is a nice detail.

Caffè Universale €€€
Via delle Coppelle 16a, T06-6839 2065, caffeuniversale.it.
Mon-Sat 0900-0100.
Bus: 30, 70, 116, 492.
Map: Centro Storico, D3, p96.
A fabulous blend of a café, restaurant serving lunch and dinner, shop (for selected foody items) and day spa, this space really covers all bases. The wine list is so extensive that a sommelier is on hand to advise. The menu describes very refined dishes, listing, for example, four ingredients in the day's ravioli, which is enough to make your mouth water.

Coco €€€
Piazza delle Coppelle 54,
T06-6813 6545, cocorestaurant.it.
Tue-Sun 1230-1530, 2000-2400.
Bus: 70, 116, 492.
Map: Centro Storico, E3, p96.
On a piazza five minutes from the Pantheon, Coco comes into its own from April to October, when the umbrella-shaded tables in the car-free square are packed for lunch and dinner. Lunch is a *tavola calda*-style buffet on weekdays, brunch at weekends.

Il Bacaro €€€
Via degli Spagnoli 27,
T06-687 2554, ilbacaro.com.
Mon-Fri 1230-1445, 2000-2330,
Sat 2000-2330.
Bus: 116.
Map: Centro Storico, D3, p96.
The romantic canopy of grapevines and ivy that stretches over the lane in front of Il Bacaro makes the eight outside tables much sought after from April to October. The Italian-creative menu offers some nice surprises, such as *orecchiette con gorgonzola, pere, carote e timo* (pasta with Gorgonzola, pear, carrot and thyme) and *bocconcini di vitella alla arance con salvia e anice stellato* (veal with orange, sage and star anise). But €10 for a starter is excessive, and starring a dish in the menu as a warning that frozen ingredients might replace fresh ones, while honest, is a little lazy. Inside, the tiny space means the 14 tables are really elbow-to-elbow: ask for slightly more private table 5.

Le Volte €€€
Piazza Rondanini 47,
T06-687 7408.
Wed-Mon 1300-1500,
1930-2200.
Bus: 70, 81, 87, 116, 492.
Map: Centro Storico, D3, p96.
The big terrace outside gets very busy in good weather but inside is a beautiful space too: the high-ceilinged restaurant was a garage until two brothers-in-law restored it and uncovered lovely painted ceilings. The house speciality is *bistecca alla Fiorentina*, the thick-cut steak traditionally from cattle reared on the banks on Florence's river Arno: here it comes from Denmark, as they've found foreigners don't like strong-flavoured Italian meat.

Osteria dell'Ingegno €€€
Piazza di Pietra 45, T06-678 0662.
Mon-Sat 1230-1500, 1930-2400,
aperitivo 1500-1930.
Bus: 116.
Map: Centro Storico, F3, p96.
The deep colours in this restaurant set up just the right atmosphere in the candlelight; if you want an intimate vibe go for the mezzanine level, which is all but hidden. Tables in the pedestrianized piazza outside are perfect for relaxed outdoor eating. Portions could be less dainty – when food is this delicious, you don't want to be able to count your ravioli.

Osteria del Pegno €€€
Vicolo di Montevecchio 8,
T06-6880 7025,
osteriadelpegno.com.
Thu-Tue 1200-1500, 1900-2330,
closed 2 weeks Jan, 2 weeks Aug.
Bus: 70, 87, 116, 492.
Map: Centro Storico, C3, p96.
The duo who've spent 12 years shaping del Pegno know how to make your mouth water. Expect *cucina romana* with a kick, as many dishes have a magic ingredient – ravioli, for instance, might feature a *fiore di zucca* (with a saffron and orange peel sauce). The menu changes according to the local produce market and even the weather that day. They make their own bread and desserts daily.

Cul de Sac €€
Piazza Pasquino 73, T06-6880
1094, enoteca.culdesac@virgilio.it.
Daily 1200-1600, 1800-2430.
Bus: 40, 46, 64.
Map: Centro Storico, C4, p96.
An almost unbelievable number of wines, grappas, sparkling wines and champagnes fill the shelves of this Centro Storico institution. Plates of delicious French and Italian cheeses or *salumi* make the perfect antipasti, but Cul de Sac's pâté is also highly rated. The *primi* and *secondi* listings aren't extensive, but so good that clusters of locals will wait half an hour or more for a table: popping your head in the door is the only way of making a reservation.

La Montecarlo €€

Vicolo Savelli 13, T06-686 1877,
lamontecarlo.it.
Tue-Sun 1200-1530, 1900-0100.
No credit cards.
Bus: 40, 46, 62, 64.
Map: Centro Storico, C4, p96.
Hugely popular, with big queues
of locals happy to wait their turn
outside, as you can't book. Pizza
is the star of the show here; there
are pasta dishes but they're very
much secondary. Carlo, the
former banker who opened the
pizzeria, couldn't be lovelier.

Maccheroni €€

Piazza delle Coppelle 44,
T06-6830 7895,
ristorantemaccheroni.com.
Daily 1300-1500, 1930-2330.
Bus: 70, 87, 116, 492.
Map: Centro Storico, D3, p96.
Before Maccheroni opened
11-odd years ago, this was a
grocer's and butcher's shop.
The meat hooks are still there
to prove it, as are old black and
white photos showing how much
has changed. The accent is on
light dishes that are scrumptious.
On weekend nights the place is
packed with glam groups chatting
to the cheerful waiting staff.

Mimì e Cocò €€

Via del Governo Vecchio 72,
T06-6821 0845.
Daily 0930-0200.
Bus: 40, 46, 62, 64.
Map: Centro Storico, C4, p96.
It calls itself a *vinoteca*, but there's
breakfast, lunch, aperitivo and

dinner and, with plenty of tables
out on the pavement, the vibe is
a cheerful one. On a crisp
morning try a Mimì e Cocò
espresso, which comes with a
spoonful of melted chocolate
and cream. For a light lunch try
crostino di patate, *gorgonzola*,
raddiccio e noci.

Obika €€

Piazza di Firenze (corner of via
dei Prefetti), T06-683 2630,
obika.it.
Daily 1200-2330.
Bus: 116.
Map: Centro Storico, D3, p96.
Obika is a mozzarella bar, and
tastings of Campania's favourite
cheese (smoked, subtly flavoured,
more mature, and so on) are
popular at this chic corner spot.
There's a good range of salads
too. Stools and high tables
outside are especially popular,
even though the little piazza
doesn't have much of a view.

Taverna le Coppelle €€

Via delle Coppelle 38-39,
T06-6880 6557,
tavernalecoppelle.it.
Daily 1200-1500, 1800-2330.
Bus: 70, 87, 116, 492.
Map: Centro Storico, D3, p96.
Red and white checked table
coverings suggest the taverna
caters solely for the tourist
market, but the honest food
attracts plenty of out-of-towners
who want decent fare but don't
need flash surroundings. Dishes
are all the typical Rome basics,

but decently priced, which is
great only five minutes from the
Pantheon. The massive old pizza
oven means you can get a good
pizza too.

Caffè Fandango €

Piazza di Pietra 32-33, T06-4547
2913, caffefandango.net.
Daily 1100-0100, kitchen open
1200-2400.
Bus: 116.
Map: Centro Storico, E3, p96.
Opened by Domenico Procacci,
the producer of Fandango Films
(*Quiet Chaos*, *Gomorrah* and *Un*
Giorno Perfetto), this laid-back
space resounds to its own DJ
show, aired live online Monday
to Friday 1600-1800. In addition
to lunch and dinner, there's
aperitivo from 1830 to 2100,
when €10 buys you a cocktail
and all you can eat from the
tempting selection prepared
fresh throughout the evening.

Da Francesco €

Piazza del Fico 29, T06-686 4009.
Wed-Mon 1200-1500,
1900-0030.
Bus: 40, 64, 190, 571.
Map: Centro Storico, C4, p96.
Although Francesco isn't there
any more, this pizzeria, which
opened over 50 years ago,
continues to serve cheap and
cheerful food. The chirpy, cheeky
staff are welcoming, even when
you turn up around midnight.
Although they've conceded to
the demands of diners (only a
Roman understands that if you

go to a good pizzeria they won't serve anything else) and a small range of *primi* are on offer, there are still some quaint local traditions, like serving gnocchi on Thursdays only.

Pizzeria da Baffetto €
Via del Governo Vecchio 114, T06-686 1617.
Daily 1830-0030.
Bus: 40, 64, 190, 571.
Map: Centro Storico, C4, p96.
There are queues outside this pizzeria even at 2200, testimony to a magical word-of-mouth following of out-of-towners heading here to eat. You can't book, so turn up early (before 2000) or wait outside with the locals.

Trattoria Tonino Bassetti €
Via del Governo Vecchio 18-19, T333-587 0779.
Mon-Sat 1200-1500, 1900-2300.
Bus: 40, 64, 190, 571.
Map: Centro Storico, C4, p96.
The simple Roman dishes on offer at this humble little trattoria are priced with the kind of honesty that makes the place very popular: if they're too late to get a table, eager locals cluster outside, happy to wait for a second sitting. The two young sisters who run it grew up in the family cooking tradition, as their dad took the place over from their grandma, who opened the trattoria back in 1936.

Cafés & bars

Abbey Theatre
Via del Governo Vecchio 51-53, T06-686 1341, abbey-rome.com.
Daily 1200-0200, happy hour(s) 1500-2000.
Bus: 40, 46, 64, 492.
Cheerful, friendly Irish bar, with good snacks and food. The Guinness is from Ireland, which keeps connoisseurs happy. Sports screened live.

Bar Sant' Eustachio
Piazza Sant' Eustachio 82, T06-6880 2048, santeustachioilcaffe.it.
Daily 0830-0100.
Bus: 116.
Sant' Eustachio seems to have a magnetic pull; almost no Italian is able to pass by without stopping for a quick coffee. It's true they've turned the machines so you can't see what the barista is doing, and it is acknowledged that a 'magic ingredient' is added, but although it's unlikely to be the egg white, flour or bicarbonate of soda suggested by various locals, the super-frothy coffee is served sweet. They sell their coffee by the kilo, also handmade coffee-flavoured chocolates and other delicious coffee-related things.

Bar Tazza d'Oro
Via degli Orfani 84, T06-678 9792, tazzadorocoffeeshop.com.
Mon-Sat 0800-2000.
Bus: 116.
Visitors attracted by the smell of the daily roasting have turned a Pantheon institution into a bit of a touristy spot, but the coffee is still good enough to see the rather bare place packed with locals having a swift espresso. You can buy their freshly roasted coffee by the kilo.

Caffè della Pace
Via della Pace 3-7, T06-686 1216, caffedellapace.it.
Mon 1600-0200, Tue-Sun 0830-0200.
Bus: 70, 81, 87, 116, 492, 628.
Ivy-covered walls and pretty white umbrellas outside make this a popular stop, even if the surroundings push the price of a cappuccino up to €4.50.

Caffè Doria
Via della Gatta 1a, T06-679 3805.
Mon-Sat 0800-2000, Sun 0930-2000.
Bus: 40, 46, 64, 70, 81, 186, 492, 628, 850.
The stone horse trough in the middle of the tearoom is a leftover from the days when this was the stable-block of neighbouring Galleria Doria Pamphilj. Good selection of teas and cakes, but a little bit pricey.

Caffè Novecento
Via del Governo Vecchio 12, T06-686 5242.
Tue-Sat 0900-2100, Sun 1500-2100.
Bus: 40, 64, 190, 571.
The low sofas and pretty lights are perfect for this Paris-inspired tearoom. There's a delicious

range of cakes and pastries, but first you have to choose your tea (from a range of 50 varieties). It also serves coffee and lunch.

Giolitti
Via Uffici del Vicario 40,
T06-699 1243, giolitti.it.
Daily 0700-0130.
Bus: 116.
A gelateria, café and *pasticceria* supreme; there's a large room with tables for shoppers needing to take a seat and recharge, and it has Wi-Fi.

Kusha
Via degli Spagnoli 37,
T06-686 9965, kusha.it.
Tue-Sun 1800-0200.
Bus: 116.
Art, fashion and design merge at this appealingly unusual bar;

expect aperitivi amid exhibitions and interesting events.

Les Affiches
Via Santa Maria dell'Anima 52,
T06-686 8986.
Daily 1900-0200.
Bus: 116.
Opened by the five friends behind **Freni e Frizioni** (see page 184), this new bar promises to be one to watch: lunch openings are planned, as are exhibitions and book launches presented by the creative community the bar is aimed at.

Salotto 42
Piazza di Pietra 42,
T06-678 5804, salotto42.it.
Tue-Sat 1000-0200, Sun 1000-2400.
Bus: 116.

Purple-flowering bougainvillea rambles up the front of this tiny but cool café-club. Deep, comfortable sofas, a ton of fashion and design magazines to flick through between breakfast, lunch, aperitivo and dinner: what more could you ask for?

Vitti
Piazza San Lorenzo in Lucina (off via del Corso), T06-687 6304, vitti.it.
Bus: 81, 117, 119, 590, 628.
A large number of dinky round tables under umbrellas make this a very popular stop for shoppers seeking respite from neighbouring via del Corso. A seat on the pedestrianized piazza makes for good people watching.

Entertainment

Cinema
Nuovo Olimpia
Via in Lucina 16g (off via del Corso), T06-686 1068, circuitocinema.com.
Bus: 52, 61, 71, 80, 116, 119.
Part of an arthouse-oriented chain, it shows original-language films (marked VO, *versione originale*).

Clubs
Bloom
Via del Teatro Pace 29, T06-6880 2029, bloomclub.it.
Oct-Apr, Tue and Sat, 2330 till late.
Bus: 70, 81, 87, 116, 492.
Recently refurbished, Bloom's ground floor bar slides into club mode at around midnight. €180 reserves a table, with a bottle of vodka thrown in.

I Giganti
Campo de' Fiori 26, T06-687 4182, gigantibar@hotmail.it.
Tue-Sun 1700-0200.
Bus: 116.
Super popular, with a DJ from 2200 nightly, *i Giganti* (the Giants) can get pretty busy inside; even in winter the stools round the wine-barrel tables are packed.

Shopping

Mood

Corso Vittorio Emanuele 205,
T06-6880 8619.
Tue-Sun 1930-0400.
Bus: 40, 46, 62, 64.
A bar and restaurant that's
almost as silvery as it is huge; it
morphs into a lounge and club
(no entry charge) with different
DJs taking to the decks from
midnight on.

Festivals & events
Festa della Befana
Piazza Navona.
Dec-6 Jan.
Bus: C3, 70, 81, 87, 116, 492, 628.
Christmas markets and
funfair-style rides and games fill
piazza Navona right through to
Twelfth Night; the tackier the
games and toys, and the brighter
the lights, the better locals love
it, so it's not as traditional as you
might expect.

Music
Churches that host regular
evening music recitals include
Sant'Agnese in Agone (piazza
Navona, T06-2171 0027,
santagneseinagone.org), where
there's a concert most Fridays
at 1830, €12/10 concession.
Among the best of the
palazzi that host regular
classical concerts is **Galleria
Doria Pamphilj** (via del Corso
305, T06-7707 2842,
lastravaganzamusica.it).
Tickets are usually sold on
the door: €15/12 concession.

Estate Romana
(estateromana.comune.roma.it)
mounts a series of concerts
during the summer; part of the
programme is organized by
Concerti del Tempietto
(T06-8713 1590, tempietto.it)
with daily concerts in the area
beside the **Teatro di Marcello**
(Jul-Sep at 2030).

Jazz Café Zio Ciro
Via Giuseppe Zanardelli 10-12,
T06-6821 0119.
Daily 0800-0130, jazz Wed-Sat
2200-0130.
Bus: 70, 81, 87, 116, 492, 628.
Jazz from Lino Quagliero and
Gerardo di Lella. A bar and
Naples-themed menu caters
for groups wanting dinner.

Art & antiques
Browse in the specialist shops
along **via dei Coronari** (see
page 113) and **via Giulia** (see
page 102).

L'Image
Via della Scrofa 67, T06-686 4050.
Bus: 116.
Limited edition graphic prints
and original paintings by young,
emerging artists. Also a range of
good postcards.

L'Impronta
*Via del Teatro Valle 53, T06-686
7821, abuzzipuccini.it.*
Mon 1600-1930, Tue-Sat
0930-1300, 1600-1930.
Bus: 116.
A gallery that also sells prints of
scenes from across Rome.

Books
Altro Quando
Via del Governo Vecchio 80,
T06-687 9825, altroquando.com.
Sun-Fri 1030-0130, Sat
1030-0200.
Bus: 40, 64.
This newly opened bookshop
has a bar in the cellar, where the
books are a sumptuous selection
of titles (mainly in Italian) on wine
and just about every imaginable
aspect of food.

Fahrenheit 451

Campo de' Fiori 44,
T06-687 5930.
Mon 1600-2200,
Tue-Sat 1000-1330, 1800-2400,
Sun 1030-1330, 1800-2400.
Bus: 116.
Open till late with a good range of books on art, architecture, photography, cinema, philosophy, history and travel; some English titles.

Libreria Croce

Corso Vittorio Emanuele 156,
T06 6880 2269.
Mon-Fri 1000-2100,
Sat 1000-2400, Sun 1000-2000.
Bus 40, 46, 62, 64.
Two minutes from Campo de' Fiori, this long-established literary venue has an extensive stock. There's an English section, and chairs and a sofa are generously provided for browsers.

Libreria del viaggiatore

Via del Pellegrino 78,
T06-6880 1048.
Mon 1600-2000,
Tue-Sat 1000-1400, 1600-2000.
Bus: 116.
The concept behind this travel bookshop (with some English titles) is to get people to start travelling in anticipation of physically leaving.

Clothing

Via del Corso cuts right through the historic centre, running from piazza del Popolo to piazza Venezia. The shops are not exceptional, but you'll find all the usual high street brands here. From 1600 on Saturdays, Sundays and holidays, the top end becomes the place to *fare la passeggiata*, with enormous numbers of young teens clustered in cheerful groups, sitting on parked mopeds (not always their own) or dawdling along, getting in the way of impatient taxis – endearingly, the drivers almost never honk their horns at pedestrians in the Centro Storico.

Alternative

Piazza Mattei 5, T06-6830 9505,
alternative-roma.it.
Mon 1400-1900, Tue-Sat 1000-1900.
Bus: H, 40, 46, 62, 64, 70, 119, 492, 780.
Labels stocked by this small, kitsch boutique include Alessandro Dell'Acqua, Kenzo and Valentino.

Arsenale

Via del Governo Vecchio 64,
T06-686 1380, patriziapieroni.it.
Mon 1530-1930,
Tue-Sat 1000-1930.
Bus: 40, 46, 62, 64.
Women's fashion. The accessories are really fun: metal thread on felt bags, hats ranging from chunky to dressy, and chunky necklaces. All by Patrizia Pieroni.

Design Oriented

Via dei Falegnami 3,
T06-685 5399, design-oriented.it.
Bus: H, 40, 46, 62, 64, 70, 119, 492, 780.
Cute, girl-oriented fashion, frilly knickers, mad belts, 50s-inspired shoes.

Empresa

Piazza del Parlamento 32-33,
T06-686 7519.
Bus: 81, 119, 590, 628.
Men's collection from one designer, including shoes, belts and bags. Outlet Empresa (via Campo Marzio 9a-10), in a very raw industrial space, is nice to browse through, with prices up to 50% off.

Faire Dodo

Via Tomacelli 128,
T06-6880 9381, fairedodo.com.
Mon 1530-1930,
Tue-Sat 1030-1430, 1530-1930.
Metro: Spagna. Bus: 81, 119, 590.
Although it sounds French, the maternity wear – from elegant to sporty, with a youthful vibe – is Italian-designed.

Tip...

Roman street numbers can be frustrating, as the sequence usually goes all the way up one side, then down the other. Via del Corso is more idiosyncratic than most, because midway through the 400s, the numbers start again, this time going down from 60-odd.

Josephine de Huertas & Co
Via del Governo Vecchio 68,
T06-687 6586,
josephinedehuertas.com.
Mon 1530-1930, Tue-Sun
1000-1400, 1530-1930.
Bus: 40, 46, 62, 64.
Italian brands like Missoni but
French and Spanish labels too.

La Coppola Storta
Via del Piè di Marmo 4, T06-679
5801, lacoppolastorta.com.
Mon-Sat 1100-1900, Sun
1200-1900.
Bus: 40, 46, 64, 119.
Handmade caps from Sicily are a
Centro Storico institution.

SpazioEspanso
Via dei Bergamaschi 60,
T06-9784 2793,
spazioespanso60@interfree.it.
Bus: 116.
The beautiful space alone is
enough to draw people in:
elbow-high wooden blocks with
a pair of earrings or an
asymmetrical necklace on each
plinth, huge black and white
dishes and a 6-m long piece of
driftwood set installation-like in
the centre of the space. But it's
the clothing – emerging-talent
labels that industry insiders
barely even know about – that
have made this address such a
fashion magnet.

Food & drink
Ciuri Ciuri
Largo del Teatro Valle 1-2,
T06-9826 2284, ciuri-ciuri.it.
Bus: 116.
For Sicilian ice creams, cassata,
crispy fried rice balls, *cannolo*
with different fillings and lots of
different kinds of chocolate from
Modica, the Sicilian town famous
for its *dolce.*

Confetteria Moriondo & Gariglio
Via del Piè di Marmo, 21-22,
T06 699 0856.
Mon-Sat 0900-1930,
closed Aug.
Bus: 40, 46, 64, 119.
Before Valentine's Day, Easter and
Christmas, the most adorable
and inventive things are shaped
in chocolate in the adjoining
laboratorio, using only fresh
ingredients, then wrapped
beautifully. Clients can even put

in a specific order, such as
chocolate keys to celebrate a
new car.

Delizie di Sardegna
Via Giulia 195a, T06-686 7762,
cosaspreziosas.it.
Mon 1630-2030,
Tue-Sat 1030-1400, 1630-2030,
closed 2 weeks in Aug.
Bus: 23, 280.
Sardinian organic cheeses,
biscuits, liquors and more,
collected by the Sardinian owner
from across the island when he
returns home. Also books, music
and jewellery.

Enoteca al Parlamento
Via dei Prefetti 15, T06-687 3446,
enotecaalparlamento.it.
Bus: 116.
Slightly uptight staff, but an
extensive range of wine and
spirits on shelves that curve all
round the store's long walls.

L'Antico Forno
Via della Scrofa 33 (corner via della Stelletta), T06-4548 1408.
Bus: 116.
Bread and sweet pastries for picnics, fresh from the ovens you can see if you look in the windows as you walk up via della Stelletta.

Antico Forno Roscioli
Via dei Giubbonari 21-22, T06-687 5287, anticofornoroscioli.com.
Mon-Sat 0600-2000.
Bus: 116.
Bread, biscuits and cakes, plus pizza hot out of the oven, and cheese and cold meats in the adjoining deli counter area.

Forno Castel Sant' Angelo
Via del Banco di Santo Spirito 44, T06 6880 8305.
Daily 0800-2100.
Bus: 40, 46, 62, 64.
Perfect for picnics or for snacking right there in the store, as the

pizza comes hot out of the oven. The bread is also baked on-site, and the decent range of *salumi* comes from the family's farm and butcher's in Norcia, Umbria. Also cheese, cookies (the *botticcini del nonno* almond biscuits are especially good) and wine, and the friendly young Sicilian server couldn't be nicer.

Homewares
D Cube
Via della Pace 38, T06-686 1218, dcubedesign.it.
Daily 1100-2400 (Jan-Mar 1100-2100).
Bus: C3, 70, 81, 87, 116, 492, 628.
Hip design products, like Tord Bontje paper lamps, and lots of clever things for the kitchen and home, plus accessories.

Gusto
Piazza Augusto Imperatore 28, T06-323 6363, gusto.it.
Daily 1000-2400.
Metro: Spagna. Bus: 81, 224, 590, 638.
Gusto's book and wine shop also has sleekly designed kitchen products, from pestles to pans by Alessi; the first floor is devoted to wine and related products.

Magazzini Associati
Corso Rinascimento 7, T06-6813 5179.
Mon 1530-1900,
Tue-Sat 1000-1900.
Bus: C3, 70, 81, 87, 116, 492, 628.
A furniture shop that's so cool people stroll in simply to look; it also has gorgeous accessories from linen bathrobes to scented sachets by Ode Rosae.

Magie di Casa
Via Giulia 140c, T06-6813 6717.
Mon-Fri 1000-1300, 1630-1900, Sat 1000-1300, closed Aug.
Bus: 116.
This tiny shop is just bursting with must-have accessories, decorations and bed- and bathroom products. Bertozzi hand-printed linens are a big seller, but come at Christmas and you'll want to buy one of each and every irresistible decoration in stock.

Activities & tours

Cultural
Società Dante Alighieri
Piazza Firenze 27, T06-687 3722,
dantealighieri-roma.it.
Bus: 116.
Italian language and cultural courses for foreigners – courses for those staying longer in town, and day trips.

Cycling
Collalti
Via del Pellegrino 82,
T06-6880 1084.
Mar-Oct Tue-Sat 0900-1300, 1530-1900, Sun 0930-1300,1530-1800, Nov-Feb Mon-Sat 0900-1300, 1530-1900, closed Aug.
Bus: 70, 87, 116, 492.
You just need a passport to hire bikes here, from €3.50 per hour to €42 per week.

Cyclò
Via di Monte Brianzo 46-47,
T06-481 5669, scooterhire.it.
Mon-Sat 0930-1730.
Bus: 70, 87, 116, 492.
Bike rental.

Walking tours
Blu Aubergine
T347-260 7465,
bluaubergine.com.
A New York chef, Dana Klitzberg, runs culinary walking tours in Centro Storico.

Jewish Quarter tours
Museo Ebraico di Roma,
Lungotevere de' Cenci 15,
T06-6840 0661,
museoebraico.roma.it.
Bus: H, 23, 63, 280, 780
Le Cinque Scole Group operates daily walking tours through the Jewish Quarter. Book at the museum, €8/5 concession.

Wellbeing
Acqua Madre Hammam
Via di Sant' Ambrogio 17,
T06-686 4272, acquamadre.it.
Women only Wed, Fri, Sun 1100-2100, men and women (swimwear compulsory) Tue 1400-2100, Thu and Sat 1100-2100.
Bus: H, 40, 46, 62, 64, 70, 119, 492, 780.
Although it advertises itself as a hammam, Acqua Madre is more a modern-day interpretation of a Roman bath, basing itself on the three principal elements: clients go from the warm bath of the *tepidarium* (36°C), to a marble bench in the *caldarium* (45°C), and then, relaxed by gentle light and the sound of splashing water, into the *frigidarium* (28°C). To move through the spaces at least two hours are recommended. Massage treatments take place in the *tepidarium*.

Yoga
Libreria Sei Sensi, Via del Pellegrino 167, T06-689 2280, sensiattivi.it.
Shop: Mon 1600-2000, Tue-Sat 1000-2000.
Bus: 46, 62, 64, 116.
Regular classes (also in English) are held in the tranquilly-lit basement of a bookshop specializing in yoga.

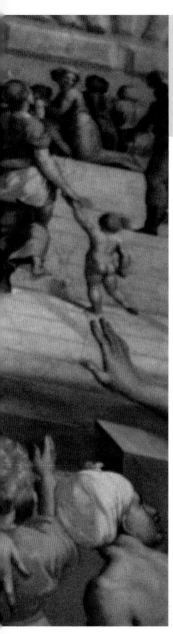

Contents

A detail of the *Fire of the Borgo* fresco by Raphael
(Raphael Rooms, Vatican Museums).

Vatican City & Prati

Introduction

The world's smallest state, yet one of the most important, Città del Vaticano is the City of God, spreading its arms wide open to embrace humanity, just like Bernini's spectacular colonnade on St Peter's Square. Aside from its spiritual importance, the Vatican has plenty to offer, to believers and non-believers alike. Raphael and Michelangelo are the two big names in the Vatican Museums, which feature over 4,000 years of art and antiquity. After all that, should you still have some energy, you can climb Michelangelo's dome – which the Romans fondly refer to as *Er Cuppolone* – for one of the most breathtaking views of the Eternal City.

Città del Vaticano has been an independent state since 1929. Apart from being the head of the Apostolic Roman Catholic Church, the pope is also a head of state, with full legislative, executive and judiciary powers. Although it has a population of about 800 and an area of only 44 ha, the Vatican is a self-sufficient community, with its own stamps and currency (the Vatican euro), radio station and newspaper (*L'Osservatore Romano*). Latin is still the official language – it's used even by ATM machines here – and is experiencing a revival under the current pope, who encouraged the old Latin mass. Sadly, for most of us, much of this Lilliputian country is strictly off limits.

Famously, the Swiss Guards have been protecting popes since 1506. They are still recruited from the three Catholic Swiss cantons, and can be seen in their colourful uniforms created by Michelangelo, history's first fashion designer.

Gallery of the Geographical Maps.

What to see in...

...one day

The **Vatican Museums** will require most of your day. Get there early to avoid the crowds. Afterwards head to **St Peter's square**, visit the **Basilica** and marvel at **Michelangelo**'s *Pietà*. Later, stroll over to **Castel Sant'Angelo** and enjoy one of Rome's finest views from its terrace.

...a weekend or more

Dedicate a whole day to the Vatican area, visit the **Vatican Museums** and **St Peter's Basilica**. If you have some energy left, climb all the way up to **St Peter's dome** for fantastic views of the city.

Next day, start with some retail therapy along **via Cola di Rienzo** in the Prati district, then head to a restaurant in the quiet **Borgo** area. Pop into the **Museo delle Anime del Purgatorio**, Rome's quirkiest museum, then stroll along the river and head to the terrace of **Castel Sant'Angelo**. Round the day off with some great music at **Alexanderplatz**, Rome's finest jazz venue.

Piazza San Pietro

Guided tours of St Peter's (in English) start from Vatican Information Office, Tue and Thu 0945, Mon-Fri 1415, Thu 1500, free.
Metro: Ottaviano. Map: Rome, A3, p84.

A spectacular prelude to the Basilica of St Peter, Gian Lorenzo Bernini's vast elliptical piazza (240 m wide) is rightly considered the outstanding example of Baroque architecture. It dates from 1656-1667.

The symbolism of the piazza fascinates many. Its 284 columns, arranged in four rows and topped by 140 statues of saints, famously represent the arms of the Church embracing all of humanity. Stand on either of the two circular stones (between the fountains and the obelisk), which mark the foci of the ellipse, and you will see all the columns line up perfectly, giving the illusion that

Vatican essentials

General information T06-6989 2425, vatican.va. The Vatican Information Office (T06-6988 1662) is located on piazza San Pietro, towards the entrance of the Basilica, on the left hand side (next to the Vatican Post Office).

Papal audience For tickets to the Wednesday morning audience, held at 1100 in the piazza or in the Nervi Auditorium, apply in advance to the **Prefettura della Casa Pontificia** (Prefecture of the Papal Household, T06-6988 3114), located just inside the bronze door by the right-hand colonnade of St Peter's square. Tickets are free and can be collected 1500-1930 the day before the audience or 0800-1030 on the day.

Dress code No shorts, miniskirts or sleeveless dresses are allowed, and the code is strictly enforced on entry.

Security Airport-style security checks are now the rule before admittance to the Basilica and the Vatican Museums. Sharp items will be confiscated.

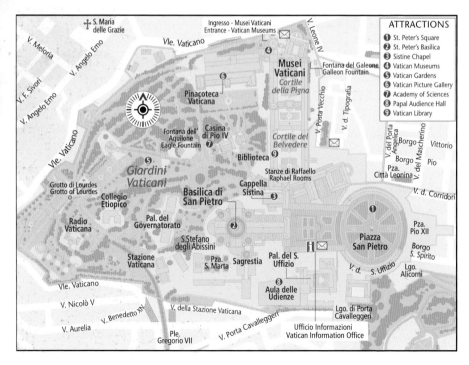

ATTRACTIONS
1 St. Peter's Square
2 St. Peter's Basilica
3 Sistine Chapel
4 Vatican Museums
5 Vatican Gardens
6 Vatican Picture Gallery
7 Academy of Sciences
8 Papal Audience Hall
9 Vatican Library

you are looking at a single row. The twin fountains, one by Carlo Maderno and the other built to match it by Bernini, symbolize the purification needed to access the house of God. The size of the square almost exactly matches that of the Colosseum – after all, St Peter's was supposed to be the last of the *fora* – the Christian one. Its elliptical shape also evokes the orbits of the planets, according to the Copernican theories of the time, while the obelisk in the centre functions as the gnomon of an immense sundial: it represents the sun itself, alluding to the central figure of the pope as an ideal 'sun king'.

The **Vatican Obelisk** is one of Rome's most impressive relics, and dates from the 13th century BC. Caligula brought it from Egypt to Rome in AD 37 to decorate Nero's Circus, which once stood on the site of the Basilica. There, it witnessed Peter's martyrdom. It stood to one side of the old St Peter's in the Middle Ages, and was moved to its current location by order of Pope Sixtus V in 1586.

It's been calculated that the square has room for 300,000 people, with no crowding. Most papal events take place here, from the Wednesday audience and the Angelus on Sundays to major religious celebrations. This is also where people wait for the white smoke to come out of the chimney of the Sistine Chapel to signal the election of a new pope, who then emerges on the balcony of the basilica to give his blessing *urbi et orbi* ('to Rome and to the world').

View from top of St Peter's Basilica.

Basilica di San Pietro

Piazza San Pietro, T06-6988 5518.
Daily Apr-Sep 0700-1900, Oct-Mar 0700-1800
(closed during official ceremonies held in the
square), free; dome daily Apr-Sep 0800-1800,
Oct-Mar 0800-1700, €7 by lift, €5 by stairs.
Metro: Ottaviano. Map: Rome, A3, p84.

The original St Peter's, begun over the apostle's tomb
by Constantine around AD 320, was an opulent
basilica resplendent with marble, mosaics and gold,
bearing a vague resemblance to San Paolo fuori le
Mura in Ostiense. Its six-storey bell tower was topped
by a golden cockerel, which, according to popular
belief, would one day announce the end of the world.
By the end of the 15th century, however, this glorious
church, immortalized by Dante and painted by Giotto,
which witnessed the crowning of Charlemagne and
22 other emperors, was in decay. It was time for the
artists of the Renaissance to think about a new one.

Most of the original structure was destroyed by
Donato Bramante, the first architect commissioned
to design the new basilica (his contemporaries
nicknamed him *Maestro Ruinante*, 'the Destroying
Master'). He had a 'modern' building in mind,
based on a Greek cross plan and inspired by the
Pantheon. His work was carried on first by Raphael
and later by Michelangelo, who came up with the
idea of a massive dome. Work began on the dome
in 1588 (24 years after Michelangelo's death) and it
was completed in just 22 months by a team of 800
men. It is the largest brick dome ever built and still
the tallest point of any building in Rome (137 m to
the top of its cross).

Pope Urban VIII celebrated the first mass in the
new basilica on 18 November 1626 – after 120 years
of construction. Many great artists had applied
their skills to its fabric (Fontana, Della Porta, Bernini
and Maderno, to name a few). Had Bramante and
Michelangelo had their way, in spite of the Baroque
spirit of the time, St Peter's could well have been
the celebration of Renaissance architecture that
everybody hoped it would be, but the most
substantial change came in 1607, when Paul V
decided that a Latin cross should replace the
original Greek plan. The result was Carlo Maderno's
massive extension of the nave, which blocks the
view of Michelangelo's dome from the square.

Interior Entering this amazing building, the first
highlight is in the first chapel on the right:
Michelangelo's *Pietà*. The only sculpture bearing his
signature, it was carved in 1499, when he was only
23. Before and after him, artists have consistently
portrayed a grief-stricken Virgin, but Michelangelo
delivered a much more spiritual view of human
suffering, conveying in a youthful-looking Mary an
almost supernatural feeling of serenity and
acceptance of her sorrow.

Tip...

Masses are celebrated in the basilica at the following
times: Monday-Saturday 0900, 1000, 1100, 1200, 1700,
Sunday and holidays 0900, 1030, 1130, 1215, 1300,
1600 and 1730.

Michelangelo's *Pietà*.

The pope giving a public address, piazza San Pietro.

A masterpiece of Baroque art is Gian Lorenzo Bernini's **baldacchino** (1633), which occupies the huge space under the dome and rises to a height of 29 m. The sumptuous canopy, supported by four spiral columns and richly decorated with gold, is the world's largest known bronze artwork. Also admired is Antonio Canova's neoclassical **monument to Clement XIII** (1784-1792) in the right transept, in which the figure of the pope is kneeling in prayer in an otherworldly state.

Pilgrims head for the last pilaster on the right before the main altar, to touch and kiss the now worn foot of Arnolfo di Cambio's statue *St Peter* (c 1296), in a tradition that goes back to medieval times.

Grotte Vaticane In the crypt beneath the basilica are the Vatican Grottoes (daily Apr-Sep 0700-1800, Oct-Mar 0700-1700, free). Dating from the Renaissance, they contain the tombs of dozens of popes, including John Paul II. The entrance is from

Tip...

For a truly impressive view of St Peter's dome, head to via Niccolò Piccolomini (off via Leone XIII). When you reach this road coming from Villa Doria Pamphilj the dome looks huge, then it progressively shrinks as you move towards it, thanks to a strange optical illusion.

the right side of the basilica porch. Beneath the grottoes, St Peter himself is said to be buried in the **Necropolis** (pre-booked guided visits only, contact Ufficio Scavi, via Paolo VI, T06-6988 5318, scavi@fsp. va, Mon-Sat 0900-1700).

Tesoro di San Pietro The Treasury (T06-6988 1840, daily Apr-Sep 0800-1850, Oct-Mar 0800-1750, €6) is entered from the left nave of the basilica. It houses all those treasures that neither the Saracens nor Napoleon managed to plunder, as well as several archaeological remains from the original Constantine basilica (such as the famous golden cockerel from the bell tower).

Musei Vaticani

Viale Vaticano 100, T06-6988 3860, vatican.va.
Mon-Sat 0830-1800 (last admission 1600), €14/8
concession, last Sun of each month 0830-1400
(last admission 1230), free; audio guides €7
(passport/ID required).
Metro: Cipro-Musei Vaticani. Map: Rome, A2, p84.

Mostly famous for the frescoes of the Raphael
Rooms and the Sistine Chapel, the Vatican
Museums contain an immense amount of artwork
divided into numerous collections – a total of some
7 km of exhibits. The papacy's first art collector was
Pope Julius II (1503-1513), but the Vatican Palaces
became a proper museum only in the 18th century,
thanks to Clement XIV and Pius VI: the Museo
Pio-Clementino was named after both of them.
Shortly afterwards the Museo Chiaramonti was

instituted, arranged by Antonio Canova.
All the other museums came later, with the most
recent being the *Museo Missionario Etnologico*
(Ethnological Missionary Museum), created in 1926.

Museo Gregoriano Egizio   Founded in 1839 by
Pope Gregory XVI, its 10 rooms house a series of
important archaeological finds from ancient Egypt.
Some of the rooms offer fine views over the *Cortile
della Pigna*, the courtyard named after the ancient
Roman fountain in the shape of a bronze pine cone.

Of particular interest among the exhibits are
(in **room V**) a monumental statue of Queen Tuya
(c 1250 BC) mother of Rameses II, several statues of
the goddess Sekhmet (c 1360 BC), and the head of
Pharaoh Mentuhotep (c 2000 BC). **Room II** contains
personal ornaments, mummies, painted sarcophagi
and other elements of funerary furnishings such as

Above: A giant sculpture – probably of Emperor Augustus – inside the Cortile della Pigna. Opposite page: The sculptural group of the Laocoon.

Tip...

The museums are closed on Vatican holidays (1 and 6 Jan, 11 Feb, 19 Mar, Easter Sun-Mon, 1 May, Ascension Day, Corpus Domini, 29 Jun, 14-15 Aug, 1 Nov, 8 and 25-26 Dec). Check the calendar on the website when planning to visit. Tickets can be reserved online to avoid queuing (€4 booking fee). Guided tours of the Museums (Mar-Oct Mon-Sat 1030, 1200, 1400, Nov-Feb 1030, €30/25 concession) and Vatican Gardens (Mar-Jul Tue, Thu and Sat 1100, Aug-Sep Tue, Thu and Sat 0930, Oct-Feb Sat 1100, €30/25 concession) are also available; prices include museum admission.

scarabs, which were put in place of the heart of the deceased and bore an inscription to protect them at the moment of their final judgement, and *ushabti* figurines, which were inserted into tombs (theoretically 365, one for each day of the year) to act as substitutes for the deceased in case they were called on to do any manual work in the afterlife.

Also in Room II, and notable for its high artistic merit, is the so-called *Dama di Antinoe* or *Lady of the Vatican* (third century AD), a beautiful linen shroud on which the portrait of a young woman is painted. Found in Antinoe, it was used to cover the dead inside the coffin.

Museo Chiaramonti Founded by Pius VII (Barnaba Chiaramonti) in 1808, it houses a plethora of Roman statuary and inscriptions. The Galleria Lapidaria section contains the *Augustus of Prima Porta*, portraying the emperor with a cherub (the symbol of Venus, protector goddess of the Julian family) at his feet. Also here is a statue of the *Nile* (first century AD), which, together with the *Tiber* (now in the Louvre), originally decorated the temple of Isis and Serapis near the Pantheon. The *Doryphoros* ('spear carrier') is a Roman copy of the bronze original by the Greek scultor Polykleitos.

Museo Pio-Clementino This museum houses some of the finest statues of the ancient world, including the dramatic sculptural group of the *Laocoön* from the first century AD, which has recently celebrated the 500th anniversary of its

rediscovery in Nero's **Domus Aurea** (see page 237). Inspired by an episode of the Trojan War (in which the priest Laocoön and his sons are strangled by two serpents sent by Athena after he warns the Trojans against accepting the Greeks' 'gift' of the wooden horse), it had a huge influence on the art of the Renaissance, particularly on Michelangelo, as did the *Apollo Belvedere*. Considered the epitome of classical perfection, this Roman copy of a Greek bronze from the fourth century BC, probably by Leochares, was rediscovered at the end of the 15th century near the church of San Pietro in Vincoli. Antonio Canova's neoclassical *Perseo* (1800), which can also be seen here, was inspired by Leochares' work. Last but not least among this celebration of fine art is the *Apoxyomenos*, the only Roman copy of a work by Lysippos, portraying an athlete scraping the sweat from his body.

When you reach the **Sala Rotonda** (circular room) look out for the massive bronze statue of *Hercules* (second century AD). It was found in Campo de' Fiori in 1864 under a slab of travertine, whose inscription suggests the statue had been struck by lightning and then buried on the spot, according to Roman custom.

Museo Gregoriano Profano Established by Gregory XVI in the Lateran palace in 1884, the collection was later moved to the Vatican and reopened in 1970. The featured works come mainly from excavations and discoveries in the pontifical territories. It is divided into five main sections: Greek

A detail of Raphael's *Transfiguration*.

sculptures (with a head of Athena dating back to around 460 BC and fragments of sculptures from the Parthenon), Roman sculptures based on Greek themes, Roman sculptures from the imperial era and finds from excavations in Ostia. The adjacent **Museo Pio Cristiano** houses perfectly preserved sarcophagi from the cemeteries of early Christian churches.

Pinacoteca Founded by Pope Pius VI (1775-1799), this exceptional collection of paintings – mostly on sacred themes – dates from the 11th to the 18th centuries. Although many works went to Napoleonic France after the Treaty of Tolentino (1797) and only 77 paintings were recovered through the efforts of Antonio Canova, the picture gallery grew over the years, taking in artworks from other papal collections.

Room II houses Giotto's *Stefaneschi Triptych* (c1320): originally commissioned for the main altar of the Constantine basilica, it represents

Tip...

In the Vatican Museums there are not many things you can afford to miss, so make sure you wear sensible shoes, carry a bottle of water and don't forget binoculars to admire the details of the Sistine Chapel. Large bags and backpacks are not allowed in and must be left in the cloakroom at the entrance, and the Vatican dress code applies.

Christ enthroned and surrounded by angels, flanked by scenes of the crucifixion of St Peter and the martyrdom of St Paul. **Room III** has works by Beato Angelico, Filippo Lippi and Benozzo Gozzoli.

Room VIII is entirely dedicated to Raphael. Among the highlights are the 10 tapestries created by the Flemish weaver Pieter van Aelst after Raphael's cartoons, which used to hang in the Sistine Chapel on special occasions, and the *Transfiguration* (1516-20). This painting, generally considered to be his last, is the superb result of the artist's competition with Sebastiano del Piombo, who was commissioned to paint an altarpiece for Narbonne Cathedral after Raphael, snowed under by other projects, delayed. Annoyed by the thought of being replaced by his rival, he created a daring painting depicting the transfiguration of Christ. The highly charged scene of the possessed boy in the lower part of the picture is generally seen as a reference to his rivalry with del Piombo, showing that Raphael had taken up the challenge.

Room IX has a striking, unfinished *St Jerome* (c1482) by Leonardo. In **room XII** look out for Caravaggio's theatrical *Deposition* (1600-1604), one of the first works to show his revolutionary approach to religious subjects.

Museo Gregoriano Etrusco Founded by Gregory XVI in 1837, the finds housed here are mostly the result of excavations carried out in the territories of Etruscan cities such as Vulci, Tarquinia and Cerveteri. Apart from an excellent collection of vases and funerary urns (check out the exquisite seventh-century BC Calabresi urn in **room II**), look out for the nearly life-sized bronze statue, the *Mars of Todi*, in **room III** and the Collezione Guglielmi in **room IX**, made up of about 800 objects including Villanovan bronzes and Etruscan and Greek ceramics.

Other collections Should you have any energy left before joining the hordes of tourists that crowd the Raphael Rooms and the Sistine Chapel, the **Museo Filatelico e Numismatico** houses a collection of Vatican stamps and coins. Far more interesting is the **Museo Missionario Etnologico**, containing collections put together by missionaries, which offers glimpses of different cultures, particularly those of East Asia. The **Padiglione delle Carrozze** houses carriages and cars. The highlight is the richly decorated *Berlina di gran gala*, a carriage commissioned by Leo XII (1823-1829) and used only four times a year, on very special occasions.

The **Galleria degli Arazzi** houses the so-called *Scuola Nuova* tapestries, woven in the workshop of Pieter van Aelst from cartoons by Raphael's pupils,

Top: Piazza San Pietro. Above: The Cortile della Pigna, named after the ancient Roman fountain in the shape of a bronze pine cone.

Stanze di Raffaello

Built under Niccolò V, these rooms were later transformed into an apartment by Pope Julius II, who commissioned several artists such as Perugino, Baldassarre Peruzzi and Lorenzo Lotto to decorate them. They were all dismissed as soon as the young Raphael started to work there.

Sala di Costantino This is the largest in the apartment, and is used for all papal ceremonies. Leo X commissioned Raphael to decorate it, but the sudden death of the artist in 1520, and then of the pope in 1521, meant the frescoes had to be done almost entirely by Raphael's pupil Giulio Romano. As the name implies, its walls depict four episodes from the life of Constantine, the first Christian emperor, symbolizing the downfall of paganism and the triumph of Christianity.

Stanza di Eliodoro Painted in 1512-1514, the frescoes show the miraculous protection bestowed by God on the Church at different moments in history. *Expulsion of Heliodorus from the Temple* refers to the pope's struggle against the enemies of the Church. *Encounter of Leo the Great with Attila* is an allegory of the triumphs of the Counter-Reformation papacy. *Miracle of Bolsena* illustrates the transformation of communion wine into the blood of Christ in 1263, which led to the institution of the Corpus Domini celebrations. *Liberation of St Peter* depicts, in three episodes, an angel freeing Peter from prison; it also alludes to the escape of Leo X after the Battle of Ravenna, and is notable for its rendering of a spectacularly lit night-time scene.

Stanza della Segnatura Raphael's most celebrated frescoes, also the first he painted in the Vatican (1508-1511), line this room, so-called because the pope used to sign documents here. The ambitious iconographic programme is meant to represent the three greatest aspirations of the human spirit: truth, goodness and beauty.

School of Athens famously depicts the most notable philosophers of ancient times within an imposing Renaissance structure inspired by Bramante's designs for the rebuilding of St Peter's. In the centre, Plato, pointing upwards, holds his dialogue *Timaeus* in his hand, a work in which he refers to a triple-natured god; beside him, Aristotle holds *Ethics*. Pythagoras, busily writing on the left, is being shown a diagram of a 'perfect' musical chord, while over on the right Euclid demonstrates geometry. Heraclitus, writing on a sheet of paper in the

Above: *School of Athens*. Opposite page: Castel Sant'Angelo bridge.

foreground, is a portrait of Michelangelo (who at the time was working in the nearby Sistine Chapel), and the figure with the black cap in the group of astronomers on the far right is a self-portrait of Raphael.

On the opposite wall, the *Disputation over the Blessed Sacrament* is a glorification of the Eucharist, while *Parnassus* is a superb allegory of the arts, depicting gods and muses along with the greatest writers of all time, such as Virgil, Dante, Catullus and Sappho. In the ceiling medallions and panels, Raphael painted a series of allegories of the sciences and arts (*Theology, Justice, Philosophy, Poetry, Astronomy*) together with important episodes related to the frescoes below (*Adam and Eve, The Judgement of Solomon, Apollo and Marsyas*).

Stanza dell'Incendio del Borgo The room takes its name from its most important fresco, *The Fire in the Borgo* (1514-1517), depicting a fire that broke out in 847 in the nearby Borgo district, which was miraculously extinguished with a solemn blessing by Leo IV. In the background of the fresco is the façade of St Peter's as it appeared in Raphael's day.

and exhibited for the first time in the Sistine Chapel in 1531. The adjacent **Galleria delle Carte Geografiche** is frescoed with accurately painted maps of Italian regions, commissioned from the cosmographer Ignazio Danti by Gregory XIII (1580-1583).

Aside from some frescoes by Pinturicchio painted in 1492-1495, the **Appartamento Borgia** (where the popes resided until the early 16th century) features over 800 works of modern religious art donated to the Holy See by more than 250 artists. Wandering through its 55 rooms you will come across works by Rodin (a small bronze cast of *The Thinker*), Dalì, Chagall, Van Gogh, Morandi, Kandinsky, Modigliani and Boccioni, to name but a few.

It's a fact…

The castle owes its name to the legend that the Archangel Michael appeared on its summit in AD 590, sheathing his sword to signal the end of the plague.

Castel Sant'Angelo

Lungotevere Castello 50, T06-681 9111, castelsantangelo.com.
Tue-Sun, 0900-1900 (last admission 1830), €5/2.50 concession, free EU citizens under 18 and over 65.
Bus: 23, 40, 280. Map Rome, C2, p84.

Yet another example of the fine Roman art of 'recycling': built between AD 123 and 139 as a peaceful resting-place for Emperor Hadrian and his successors, the mausoleum became a military post and, after undergoing continuous changes, was ultimately acquired by the pope on his return to Rome from Avignon in 1377.

Had this impregnable fortress not been there, the papacy probably wouldn't still exist, at least not as we know it. In the face of constant revolts, the popes started to use the castle as an alternative residence, connecting it to the Vatican Palace by a fortified corridor, the **Passetto di Borgo**, which allowed them to reach it quickly in case of danger.

Cappella Sistina

Named after Pope Sixtus IV della Rovere, who had the existing Cappella Magna restored between 1477 and 1480, the Sistine Chapel is the most stunning example of papal patronage from the entire Renaissance period.

Its architecture is simple; it consists of a large rectangular hall, 40.5 m long and 13.5 m wide, with a barrel-vaulted ceiling 20.7 m high. The pictorial decorations were completed in three distinct phases. The first cycle of frescoes was painted on the lower walls by Tuscan and Umbrian artists, between 1481 and 1483. Most notable are the scenes from *Exodus* by Botticelli, Perugino's *Donation of the Keys* and Signorelli's *Legacy and Death of Moses*.

The second decorative phase dates from 1508 to 1512, when Julius II asked Michelangelo to repaint the vast **ceiling**, which at the time depicted a rather uninspiring starry sky. The artist went up against his will, after a long hesitation. He then exasperated the pope by making him wait and refusing to hire assistants to speed up the work. He spent four years on the project, working under impossible conditions on 18-m-high scaffolding. The result is his genial version of the Book of Genesis, in a set of images that were brand new, both spiritually and intellectually.

Michelangelo believed that complex ideas could be conveyed in the human body alone, without background noise. This explains the blankness of the settings, which make the biblical characters really stand out. The *Creation of Adam*, possibly the most famous representation of God in the history of art, is the one that keeps visitors most transfixed, together with the elegant figures of the *ignudi*, the 12 softly rendered nudes who support festoons and medallions.

Twenty years went by before Michelangelo returned, once again reluctantly, to paint the *Last Judgment* (1536-1541) on the wall behind the altar (look out for the artist's self portrait in the flayed skin that St Bartholomew is holding). This powerful depiction of the *Dies Irae* is rightly considered the breaking point for the optimism associated with the Renaissance – after all, the Sack of Rome of 1527 must have had some consequences. It is centred on the figure of Christ, captured in the moment preceding the final verdict. Next to him the Virgin, the saints and the patriarchs anxiously await the sentence. In the centre of the lower section, the angels of the Apocalypse are awakening the dead to the sound of their trumpets. On the left the risen ascend towards heaven, while on the right angels and devils topple the damned down to hell, where Charon and Minos (the judge of the underworld) are waiting for them.

The approximately 400 characters that cram into the scene are almost all naked, and in some cases portray people of Michelangelo's time. Minos, with a snake biting his testicles, has the features of Biagio da Cesena, a papal master of ceremonies who criticized the nudity in the frescoes. Needless to say, the nudes were way too shocking for the time. At one point the whole wall was in danger of being pulled down, but luckily a less dramatic solution was reached. While Michelangelo was still alive, Pius IV had the more contentious images painted over by Daniele da Volterra, who is remembered by the derogatory nickname *Il Braghettone* ('the breeches maker').

Between 1979 and 1999 the frescoes were subjected to an extensive and controversial restoration, paid for by a Japanese television network, which removed centuries of candle smoke and grime, bringing back their original brightness. Until then, critics had focused on Michelangelo's sombre tones, while the restoration brought to light the real shades of intense blue and sea-green, splashes of yellow and dramatic shadows, more striking than ever. Michelangelo's genius was reignited, leaving his audience breathless even after 500 years.

Opposite page: Michelangelo's *Last Judgement*.

> **"**
> Without having seen
> the Sistine Chapel
> one can form no
> appreciable idea of
> what one man is
> capable of achieving.
> **"**
>
> *Johann Wolfgang von*
> *Goethe, 1787*

Above: Sant'Angelo angel. Opposite page: Hall of Justice, Prati.

Leo X, with a 16th-century high-relief *Madonna with Child* attributed to Raffaello da Montelupo, who also sculpted the statue of *Archangel Michael* (1544) in the Courtyard of the Angel – this originally graced the central tower until 1747, but was later replaced by the bronze sculpture by Pieter Antoon van Verschaffelt.

The castle terrace, immortalized by the tragic ending of Puccini's *Tosca*, offers some of Rome's finest views, with St Peter's in the foreground. The elegant pedestrian bridge in front of the castle, **Ponte Sant'Angelo**, was originally built during the reign of Hadrian, but it owes its current aspect to Bernini, who brought it to life by sculpting the figures of angels that line it on both sides.

Necropoli Romana della via Triumphalis

T06-6988 4947, visitedidattiche.musei@scv.va. Fri-Sat 0900, 1030, 1200, 1500, pre-booked guided tours only (some in English), in groups of up to 25 (apply by email with preferred dates), €8; join group at guided tours entrance to Vatican Museums.
Metro: Cipro-Musei Vaticani. Map: Rome, A2, p84.

Its rooms were decorated as lavishly as those in the Vatican. Even spaces for entertainment were created – an example is the **Cortile del Pozzo** (Courtyard of the Well), also known as the Theatre Courtyard because of the performances that took place there, especially under the Medici pope Leo X.

Castel Sant'Angelo was last used militarily during the sack of 1527, when Clement VII took refuge there while Rome went up in flames. It was later converted into a prison, whose inmates included Giordano Bruno, Benvenuto Cellini and Beatrice Cenci.

Inside, a 125-m long helicoidal ramp (originally intended for funeral processions in the mausoleum) leads up to the papal apartments, which are decorated with an eclectic collection of sculptures, paintings, marble finds, weapons and furniture. Highlights are the **Sala Paolina**, richly frescoed with events from the history of Rome by Perin del Vaga and his pupils in 1546-1548, and the **Cappella di Santi Cosma e Damiano**, added by

Recently discovered while digging the foundations of a multi-storey car park under the Vatican, and opened to the public in 2006, this is one of the most complete burial grounds of imperial Rome, with about 40 large tombs, some with frescoes and mosaic floors, and over 200 well-preserved individual graves of lower- and middle-class Romans, ranging from simple trenches to marble sarcophagi and dating from the first century BC to the early fourth century AD. The tour lasts about 90 minutes.

The castle terrace, immortalized by the tragic ending of Puccini's *Tosca*, offers some of Rome's finest views, with St Peter's in the foreground.

The area to the north of the Vatican derives its name from the *prati* ('meadows') that characterized it until Rome became the national capital in 1871, after which most of the city's green spaces succumbed to property speculation. With streets laid out on a regular grid, the new quarter was developed by the end of the century, employing an eclectic mix of architectural styles. Its palazzi house the staff of several institutions – such as the **Palazzo di Giustizia** (1888-1911) on piazza Cavour, which is also known by the disparaging nickname *Il Palazzaccio* because of its über-Baroque architecture.

An affluent bourgeois area, Prati offers the shopping delights of via Cola di Rienzo, which is always busy but never overcrowded, and therefore a perfect alternative to the more central shopping hubs. It is also the location of one of Rome's eeriest museums.

Museo delle Anime del Purgatorio

Lungotevere Prati 12, T06-6880 6517.
Mon-Sat 0700-1100, 1630-1900, free.
Bus: 70, 81, 280. Map: Rome, C2, p84.

This is one of Catholic Rome's least known and weirdest experiences. Next to the small neo-Gothic Chiesa del Sacro Cuore del Suffragio, it is dedicated to souls in Purgatory.

The collection was created by French priest Victor Jouet, whose mission was to look for proofs of the existence of an afterlife in attempts at contact between the deceased and their relatives. The result is a macabre display of hand- and fingerprints apparently left by the dead, scorched into articles such as clothes and prayer books. These are said to signal that the dead are asking for masses so that their souls can be released from Purgatory. Take it with more than the usual pinch of salt, as many of the items have been deemed unsatisfactory even by church officials.

Sleeping

Visconti Palace Hotel €€€
*Via Federico Cesi 37, Prati,
T06-3684, viscontipalace.com.*
Bus: 70, 81. Map: Rome, C2, p84.
Its brutalist 1970s architecture is
definitely a bit off-putting from
the outside. Inside, however, is a
very pleasant surprise, with a
fresh, modern reception area
with brightly coloured furniture
and stylish lighting. You can help
yourself to a bright red apple
from the reception desk while
checking in – very unusual in
Italy! The hotel has 242
good-sized modern rooms
and suites. There's a gym, and
Wi-Fi in communal areas and
some rooms. The terrace bar
on the seventh floor is especially
nice in summer, and is also open
to non-residents.

Franklin €€
*Via Rodi 29, T06-3903 0165,
franklinhotel.it.*
Metro: Ottaviano.
Map: Rome, A1, p84.
Music is the theme of this funky,
contemporary hotel. Each room
– 22 in total – has a four-poster
bed and drums as bedside
tables, but the real bonus is a
state-of-the-art Bang & Olufsen
stereo system on which you can
listen to over 400 CDs available
from the lobby. Different room
types are available (pop, rock,
jazz, etc) with services changing
accordingly. Free Wi-Fi.

Hotel Bramante €€
*Vicolo delle Palline 24/25,
T06-6880 6426,
hotelbramante.com.*
Bus: 40.
Map: Rome, B2, p84.
Hidden down a cobbled
alley near the Passetto wall,
this 16th-century building
was once home to architect
Domenico Fontana. The 16
rooms are simple and tastefully
furnished, and all come with
plasma TV and tea- and
coffee-making facilities.
Room 13 is one of the smallest
but probably the most delightful,
with the original high beamed
ceiling. The staff are friendly
and knowledgeable, and it's
an excellent address if you
are planning to stay in the
Vatican area.

Hotel Sant'Anna €€
*Borgo Pio 133, T06-6880 1602,
hotelsantanna.com.*
Metro: Ottaviano.
Map: Rome, B2, p84.
In a 16th-century building on a
pedestrianized street a stone's
throw from the Vatican, the hotel
has 21 large, spotless rooms. The
decor is a little old-fashioned, as
with many hotels in Rome, but
the staff are friendly and helpful.

Casa di Accoglienza Paolo VI €
*Viale Vaticano 92, T06-3909 1411,
casapaolosesto@pssf.it.*
Metro: Cipro-Musei Vaticani.
Map: Rome, A2, p84.
If you are on a tight budget,
this convent is probably your
best option, as long as you
don't mind the midnight curfew.
It offers basic but immaculate
rooms with en suite bathrooms
and air-conditioning; breakfast
isn't served. Given the price, early
booking is a must.

Eating & drinking

L'Arcangelo €€€€
Via Giuseppe Giocchino Belli 59/61, Prati, T06-321 0992, ristorantidiroma.com/arcangelo.
Mon-Fri 1300-1430, 2000-2330, Sat 2000-2330.
Bus: 70, 81. Map: Rome, C2, p84.
Sommelier and owner Arcangelo Dandini opened this elegant trattoria at the end of 2003. The menu reflects his origins – Rocca Priora, in the Castelli Romani area – with a seasonal menu and intensely flavoured meaty dishes. An interesting foie gras menu is sometimes available, and Roman specialities include tripe with mint and pecorino cheese, chickpeas and clams, and classic pasta dishes such as *tonnarelli cacio e pepe* (with pecorino and pepper) or *mezzi paccheri alla carbonara* (large pasta tubes). The very elegant decor has a 1950s feel, with wood panelling and classy retro lighting. Jazz music in the background is the icing on the cake.

Piero e Francesco €€€€
Via Fabio Massimo 75/77, Prati, T06-320 0444.
Mon-Fri 1230-1500, 1930-2330, Sat 1930-2330.
Metro: Ottaviano.
Map: Rome, B2, p84.
At this award-winning fish restaurant the best Mediterranean traditions are transformed by the imagination of chef Marco Coppola. Try their tasting menu at €70 (€60 without wine).

Velando €€€€
Borgo Vittorio 26, T06-6880 9955, ristorantevelando.com.
Mon-Sat 1200-1500, 1900-2300.
Metro: Ottaviano.
Map: Rome, B2, p84.
A favourite with clergymen of high rank, even Pope Benedict XVI used to eat here in his cardinal days, appreciating its Lombard cuisine from the Valcamonica region.

Maxelà €€€
Borgo Vittorio 92; T06-6880 4299, maxela.it.
Tue-Sun 1230-1500, 1930-2300.
Metro: Ottaviano.
Map: Rome, B2, p84.
Intentionally rough, it looks like an old-style butcher's shop, with marble tables and tea towels used as tablecloths. Beef, lamb, pork and veal can be chosen directly from the counter and cooked to your taste.

Osteria Leonardesca €€€
Via Sforza Pallavicini 19/21, Prati, T06-6813 9095.
Mon-Sat 1215-1530, 1830-2330.
Metro: Ottaviano.
Map: Rome, B2, p84.
Opened in 2007, this is one of the newest additions to the culinary scene in Prati. Award-winning chef Danilo dell'Otto (a pupil of Rome's star chef Heinz Beck) has designed a Mediterranean menu with an excellent selection of meat dishes. Reservation advised.

Borgo Antico €€
Borgo Pio 21, T06-686 5967.
Mon-Sat 2000-0000.
Metro: Ottaviano.
Map: Rome, B2, p84.
One of the few restaurants in the area that does not boast an English menu – a good sign among the tourist traps around the Vatican – in this tiny wood-beamed *taverna* the accent is on regional cuisine from Lazio. The fresh, homemade pasta changes every day. Try the *fettucine alla papalina* (with eggs and ham), or *patate cotte al vapore* (steamed potatoes) with *fonduta valdostana*, mushrooms and truffles. There are several types of tiramisù on the dessert list.

Del Frate €€
Via degli Scipioni 118, Prati, T06-323 6437.
Mon-Fri 1230-1500, 1830-2330, Sat 1830-2330.
Metro: Ottaviano.
Map: Rome, B1, p84.
Opened as a wine shop in 1922, the third generation of the Del Frate family expanded it into a restaurant in 2000. The rooms are lovely, with bare bricks, wine racks and soft lighting, and it's perfect for a good-value lunch after struggling with the tourist mob at the Vatican. For a healthy choice, try *zuppa di farro e fagioli* (barley and bean soup) or one of the many salads. In the evening it's a good place for *aperitivo*, with a €5 buffet. The

dinner menu offers, among other things, a wide choice of mostly Italian cheeses.

Osteria dell'Angelo €€

Via Giovanni Bettolo 32, Prati, T06-372 9470.
Mon-Fri 1200-1430, 2000-2300, Sat 2000-2300.
Metro: Ottaviano.
Map: Rome, A1, p84.
A Roman trattoria, unusually decorated with an array of rugby and boxing photos and memorabilia. Angelo's *tonnarelli cacio e pepe* (with cheese and pepper) are considered among the best in town.

Sicilia in Bocca €€

Via Emilio Faa' di Bruno 26, Prati, T06-3735 8400, siciliainboccaweb.com.
Mon-Sat 1300-1430, 2000-2330.
Metro: Ottaviano.
Map: Rome, A1, p84.
A slice of Sicily in Rome. The accent is on fish – try their tuna *carpaccio* as a starter – but there's plenty to keep meat eaters happy too. Their good selection of Sicilian wines will wash it all down.

Angeli a Borgo €

Borgo Angelico 28/30, T06-686 9674; angeliaborgo.com.
1200-1500, 1930-2330, Closed on Wed supper and Sat and Sun lunch.
Metro: Ottaviano.
Map: Rome, B2, p84.
Run by cousins Paolo and Camillo, who contribute to the friendly atmosphere of this excellent little gem. Locals come here to eat pizza made with high-quality ingredients. For an alternative to the traditional version, try their *nuvolette degli angeli*, warm pizza dough served with different dips. There's a good selection of healthy salads and an excellent dessert list – their tiramisù is definitely one tier above.

Cafés & bars

Fabrica

Via Girolamo Savonarola 8, Prati, T06-3972 5514, fabricadicalisto.com.
Tue-Sun 0730-0100.
Metro: Cipro-Musei Vaticani.
A tea house with a north European feel, over 120 different brews to choose from, and a lovely winter garden.

Old Bridge

Via dei Bastioni di Michelangelo 5, T06-3972 3026.
Metro: Ottaviano.
Just opposite the Vatican walls, near piazza del Risorgimento, this tiny place is the best for good, inexpensive ice cream. The small *cono* is only €1.30, which is great for your pocket in the Vatican area. However, be prepared to queue as it can get extremely busy, especially in the evening.

Zen 0

Via Santamaura 60, Prati, T06-3975 0827, zen-0.it.
Wed-Sun 1700-0100.
Metro: Ottaviano.
At this welcoming place you can sample anything from chocolate, tea and coffee to Zen beer (non-alcoholic and ginger-flavoured), Trappist beer and rare rums. Live music, jam sessions and art exhibitions are bonuses.

Entertainment

Alexanderplatz
Via Ostia 9, Prati, T06-5833 5781, alexanderplatz.it.
Daily from 2000, concerts start at 2200.
Metro: Ottaviano.
Rome's finest and oldest jazz venue, Alexanderplatz is just as you would imagine a jazz club to be: small, dark and intimate, with walls covered in autographs of the artists who have performed there. However, you will need to take out a membership (€10 for a month, €30 for a year).

Fonclea
Via Crescenzio 82a, Prati, T06-689 6302, fonclea.it.
Daily 2000-0200.
Metro: Ottaviano.
Another great place for live acts, Fonclea has been an institution for the past 30 years. Many famous Italian singers started their career here. They do a 'sound check appetizer', which consists of *aperitivo* and nibbles for €6. Food could be improved and it is certainly a little pricey for a pub, so not the best place for dinner, but a hip spot for a few drinks while listening to some good live music.

The Place
Via Alberico II 27-29, Prati, T06-6830 7137, theplace.it.
Oct-May, Tue-Sat 1900-0300.
Metro: Ottaviano.
A vibrant club with live acts. You can also have dinner there (from 1900) during the sound check.

The atmosphere is informal, with the stage just a step away from the audience. They have 70s and 80s retro nights at weekends.

Shopping

In Prati, **via Cola di Rienzo** is one of Rome's most popular commercial streets, with high-street names such as Luisa Spagnoli, La Cicogna, Benetton, Stefanel and Spatafora. At number 241, check out the tiny **Sabon**, packed with all sorts of cosmetics, all made with natural ingredients. **Via Ottaviano** is another shopping street, with less famous brands and lower prices.

Angelo Colapicchioni
Via Properzio 23, Prati, T06-6880 1310, colapicchioni.it.
Metro: Ottaviano.
Superb bakery, which also sells typical regional products. Among their specialities is *pangiallo*, a typical Roman sweet made with dried fruit and nuts. They have another branch in Prati, at via Tacito 76/78.

Antico Forno
Borgo Pio 8, T06-6813 4424.
Metro: Ottaviano.
They've been baking for the Romans for the last 500 years, and sell an excellent selection of bread and pizza by the slice, perfect for lunch on the go.

Castroni
Via Cola di Rienzo 196, Prati, T06-687 4383, castroni.com.
Metro: Ottaviano.
A gourmet paradise since 1932, it stocks plenty of Italian delicacies (from truffle-based products to olive oil and wine) as well as food from all over the world. The coffee itself makes the visit worthwhile.

Franchi
Via Cola di Rienzo 204, Prati, T06-687 4651, franchi.it.
Metro: Ottaviano.
Another institution for foodies, just next door to Castroni, specializing in cold cuts, cheese and takeaway foods.

Mercato Coperto di piazza dell'Unità
Corner of via Cola di Rienzo and piazza dell'Unità, Prati.
Daily, most stalls in morning only.
Metro: Ottaviano.
Housed in a beautiful Liberty-style building, this is Rome's first covered market, opened in 1913 for the inauguration of via Cola di Rienzo. It sells mostly fruit and veg but also fish and other food.

Tip...

Near the Vatican your shopping opportunities will be limited to tacky, overpriced religious souvenirs. Something more unusual can be found at the kiosk on piazza Citta' Leonina, beside the Passetto, where you can purchase lollipops decorated with the face of Benedict XVI!

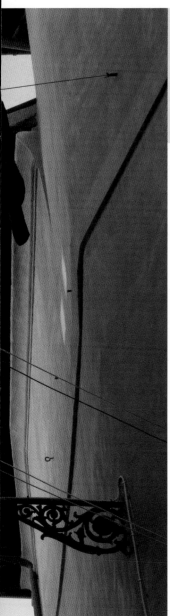

Contents

Washing hanging out to dry, Trastevere.

Trastevere & around

Introduction

What to see in...

...one day
Get a feel of the calmer pace of life in **piazza Santa Maria in Trastevere** and have a look at the mosaics in the **church** of the same name before browsing round the market in nearby **piazza San Cosimato**. Walk off lunch in the **Orto Botanico** and call in on **San Pietro in Montorio** on your way to see the views from the **Gianicolo hill**. Head back down for *aperitivi*, food and partying on or around **via della Scala** or **via del Fienaroli**.

...a weekend or more
As well as the above, see the fantastical Renaissance art in **Villa Farnesina** or some photography in the **Museo di Roma in Trastevere**. Take time to explore the less frequented streets of the eastern half of Trastevere, coinciding if you can with the narrow window for seeing the Cavallini frescoes in **Santa Cecilia**. Also in this area, seek out Trastevere's best biscuits and excellent **restaurants** and **cafés**. Cross the bridge to the **Isola Tiberina** and check out the ancient **Rotto** and **Fabricio** bridges, coming back for a laid-back prosecco.

Trastevere's otherness is embedded in its very name, which means 'across the Tiber'. Its inhabitants, calling themselves *noantri* ('we others'), are proud of their supposed slave origins, and even in ancient Roman times the area was very distinct from the centre of the city across the river. It was an Etruscan stronghold for a time, before becoming a place inhabited by craftspeople. These days its bohemian nature as a centre for immigrants and artists has largely given way to high-priced apartments and bars and restaurants that depend, at least in part, on tourist euros. Trastevere remains one of the city's most picturesque quarters, however, with creeper-draped cobbled streets, festooned with lines of washing, where the paint seems to peel a little more artistically than across the river.

There are a handful of interesting churches, a lively market and the Gianicolo hill, which has parks, statues and the botanical gardens. Most of the pleasure in Trastevere, however, is to be found by wandering its streets and piazzas, taking plenty of time to linger in its boutique shops, eateries and drinking holes. At night the area really comes into its own, filling up with young Romans as well as tourists, all drawn by the funky nightlife and good, traditional food.

Bar San Calisto, Trastevere.

Piazza Santa Maria in Trastevere

Bus: H, 23, 115, 125, 780. Map: Rome, C5, p84.

In the piazza at the heart of Trastevere, there are usually lovers, drunks, young travellers and well-to-do tourists sitting around the fountain even in winter. Buskers and street performers entertain the crowds, and cafés spill out on to the cobbles on two sides, opposite the eponymous church. The octagonal fountain dates from ancient Rome and has stood here since at least the 15th century; it was restored and embellished by the appropriately named Carlo Fontana at the end of the 17th century.

Basilica di Santa Maria in Trastevere

Piazza Santa Maria in Trastevere.
Daily 0700-2100, free.
Bus: H, 23, 115, 125, 780. Map: Rome, C5, p84.

Pope Julius I built the first church here in the fourth century, which makes it one of Rome's oldest, though there was a Christian place of worship on this spot even earlier, founded around 220 by Pope Callixtus I, who is buried under the altar. Innocent II rebuilt the church in 1138, using materials taken largely from the **Baths of Caracalla** (see page 82), including the capitals that top the columns in the nave. It is predominantly this structure that survives, in restored form, today.

On the façade, a 13th-century mosaic depicting Mary breastfeeding the baby Jesus overlooks the piazza. Inside, the extraordinary mosaics of the life of the Virgin around the lower part of the apse are by Pietro Cavallini, one of the greatest artists of the 13th century; they were added in 1291. A story that dates back to at least the third century tells of how oil gushed from the ground here before the birth of Jesus. An ancient sign near the altar, reading *"Fons olei"*, marks the spot. The Cosmatesque floor is a 19th-century copy of the original.

Above: Fountain in piazza Santa Maria. Opposite page: Bamboo growing in the Botanical Gardens.

Museo di Roma in Trastevere

Piazza Sant'Egidio 1b, T06-581 6563,
museodiromaintrastevere.it.
Tue-Sun 1000-2000, €3/1.50 concession
(price may rise during exhibitions),
free EU citizens under 18 and over 65.
Bus: H, 23, 125, 780. Map: Rome, C5, p84.

Photographic exhibitions are mostly the order of
the day in what was once Rome's folk museum,
and before that a convent. These can be excellent,
and are internationally focused – recent ones have
included a major Lisette Model show and sporting
images from around the world. The museum also
retains some of its original exhibits, including some
rather dull watercolours and a room featuring an
eccentric collection of art and trinkets from the
ex-folk museum, including material related to the
Roman dialect poet Trilussa: stand in the middle
of the room to activate a video installation
projecting images on to the four walls. Other
temporary exhibitions are held on the ground
floor, around the edges of the cloister.

Orto Botanico

Largo Cristina di Svezia 24, via Corsini, T06-686 4193.
Mon-Sat, summer 0900-1830, winter 0900-1730,
greenhouses 0930-1230, €4/2 concession.
Bus: 23, 125, 280. Map: Rome, B5, p84.

On the slopes of the Gianicolo hill, Rome's botanical
gardens, run by the city's Sapienza University, are
a green oasis and a peaceful respite from the heat
and clamour of the city below, over which they give
good views between the trees. The greenhouses
contain a rich collection of tropical plants, at their
best in spring and summer when they are a wealth
of flowers. There are tall palms, fountains, an oriental
garden with around 70 species of bamboo, an area
that recreates the native flora of the hill with species
such as holm oaks, a beautiful rose garden and a
fern garden. There are plenty of wilder, unkempt
corners as well as the more formal areas. In all, there's
plenty to fill a couple of hours of wandering – and it
also makes a great spot for a picnic.

Trastevere poets

Gioacchino Belli (1791-1863), considered *Il Poeta di
Roma*, wrote over 2,200 sonnets in the colourful
romanesco dialect, poking fun at the rich and
powerful (and very often the Church). There's a
monument to him in piazza Belli at the beginning of
viale Trastevere. In the same tradition, Carlo Alberto
Salustri, aka Trilussa (1871-1950), wrote social and
political satire. His anti-fascist poem *All'Ombra* ('In
the Shadow') is engraved on a plaque under his
statue in piazza Trilussa.

Villa Farnesina

Via della Lungara 230, T06-6802 7268,
positivamente.lincei.it.
Mon-Sat 0900-1300, €5/4 concession.
Bus: 23, 125, 280. Map: Rome, C4, p84.

Stories vary as to the degree to which Raphael
was personally involved in the decoration of this
early 16th-century Trastevere villa, originally
owned by the outstandingly wealthy Sienese
banker Agostino Chigi. Probably most of the work
here was overseen by Raphael but carried out by
assistants while, according to some, the great artist
cavorted with his mistress nearby.

The principal scene in the first room, the
marvellous **Loggia di Galatea**, was carried out
entirely by Raphael himself. A fantastical and
colourful seascape, complete with toothy dolphins,
cupids, centaurs and a merman, it has echoes of
Botticelli's *Birth of Venus*.

Above: Sunrise over Rome from the Gianicolo. Opposite page: Puppet show, piazza Garibaldi.

Still on the ground floor, the **Loggia di Psiche** is extravagantly frescoed; slightly diverse styles point to the involvement of many hands, but Raphael's overall vision is clearly present in the expert composition. On the ceiling, the marriage of Psyche and Cupid is depicted on the left, the council of the gods on the right. Fruit and greenery decorate the ribs. Fake windows, matching the real ones, are also painted – stand in the very centre of the room to fully appreciate the clever perspective of the arches.

Upstairs, the **Marriage room**, frescoed from floor to ceiling, is primitively carried out by comparison, but full of movement and action.

Galleria Corsini

Via della Lungara 10, T06-6880 2323, galleriaborghese.it.
Tue-Sun 0830-1930, €4/2 concession, free EU citizens under 18 and over 65. Bus: 23, 125, 280. Map: Rome, C4, p84.

Originally designed by Bramante, and home to the notorious Queen Christina of Sweden in the 17th century, the Palazzo Corsini now holds the 18th-century art collection of Cardinal Neri Maria Corsini, nephew of Pope Clement XII.

Christina, having embraced Catholicism and abdicated the Swedish throne, was at first welcomed to Rome with open arms and was an influential figure with various popes. She put Rome's Jews under her protection and built up one of the city's best art collections. Later, having taken various lovers – both men and women – and had a member of her entourage murdered, she became less popular, though she is one of only three women buried in St Peter's.

When Cardinal Corsini acquired the huge palace he had it remodelled by Ferdinando Fuga between 1732 and 1736. The gallery is on the first floor, in eight grand, marble-lined rooms hung from floor to ceiling with Italian and European art, especially of the 17th and 18th centuries. In room II, Rubens' *Head of an Old Man* was later used as a model for a larger painting, and there are two paintings by Van Dyck. In **room III**, Caravaggio's *St John the Baptist* is typically dark, if rather uncharacteristically soft-focused. In the same room are many works by Caravaggio's followers, notably the anonymous *Denial of St Peter* and Orazio Gentileschi's *Madonna and Child*, tenderly motherly without ever seeming religious. There's a Bruegel still life in **room IV**, and **room V** (Queen Christina's bedroom) has elaborate ceiling frescoes. Those with a weak stomach may want to avoid Salvator Rosa's horrific depiction of Prometheus having his guts ripped out in **room VIII**.

The gallery's misnamed 'painting of the month' (often more than one painting, exhibited for several months) is given spotlit pride of place in a room with lots of explanation and context.

Gianicolo

Bus: 23, 125, 280. Map: Rome, B5, p84.

It's worth the climb up the Janiculum Hill for the great views over Rome to the east and St Peter's to the north – sunrise from here is especially magical. The simplest route to the top is to follow vicolo del Cedro west from via della Scala and climb the steps to San Pietro in Montorio, bearing right to piazzale Giuseppe Garibaldi.

The summit is an area of villas and embassies: the Finnish one, in the handsome Renaissance Villa Lante, has a particularly coveted view. There are various war memorials here too, and it is from here that a cannon is fired every day at noon. This tradition was started in 1847 by Pope Pius IX in order to synchronize the city's church bells, and modern Romans continue to set their watches by it.

At the edge of piazzale Garibaldi there's a puppet theatre that puts on shows of **Pulcinella** (the Neapolitan original of Punch and Judy) on Saturdays and Sundays. To the north are busts of Garibaldi's troops, who fought a battle here against the French in 1849. Garibaldi himself sits atop a horse in the middle of the piazza; his wife Anita (see box), also on horseback, has her own piazza just to the north,

Anita Garibaldi

Uneducated and born into a poor family in Laguna in Brazil, Anita Ribeiro is one of the more unlikely of Italian heroes. Having already been married once, she met the young Italian revolutionary Giuseppe Garibaldi in 1839. He was fighting for a separatist republic in southern Brazil; she was just 18. A skilled horsewoman, within a month she had already fought alongside him in two battles. They married in 1842 and had four children before returning to Italy to fight against the Austrian Empire in 1848. In 1849 they fought together in the defence of Rome against French troops on the Gianicolo hill, before fleeing with the Garibaldian Legion. Pregnant again, and sick, she died in her husband's arms five weeks later. In 1860, when Garibaldi greeted Vittorio Emanuele II as king of a newly united Italy, he did so with Anita's scarf tied over his South American poncho.

where she is buried. To the west, the large park of **Villa Doria Pamphilj** (Apr-Sep 0700-2100, Oct-Mar 0700-2100), with shaded paths, ancient aqueducts, a theatre museum and a grand villa and gardens, is a good place for a wander, a run or a picnic.

Chiesa di San Pietro in Montorio

Piazza San Pietro in Montorio 2, T06-581 3940, sanpietroinmontorio.it. Jun-Sep 0930-1230, 1600-1800, Oct-May 0930-1230, 1400-1600, free. Bus: 44, 75, 115, 710, 870.

According to tradition, this church, high above Rome on the Gianicolo hill, stands on the spot where St Peter was killed. Not wishing to be compared to Jesus, so the story goes, he asked to be crucified upside-down. The highlight of the church is Bramante's 1502 **Tempietto**, a much fêted Renaissance structure in the courtyard, supposedly marking the actual site of Peter's martyrdom. The building has classical Roman influences, its perfect proportions and elegant Doric columns marking it out as a masterpiece.

The main church was commissioned by Ferdinand and Isabella of Spain, and it retains Spanish links today. The first chapel on the right has Sebastiano del Piombo's *Flagellation and Transfiguration* (c1516), and the fourth chapel on the same side may be the burial spot of Beatrice Cenci, who was beheaded in 1599 for the murder of her abusive father. Further up the hill, and with more good views over the city, is the grand

Fontana dell'Acqua Paola, built in the 17th century to celebrate the restoration of Trajan's aqueduct, which supplies it with water all the way from Lago di Bracciano.

Santa Cecilia in Trastevere

Piazza di Santa Cecilia 2, T06-589 9289. Mon-Sat 0930-1230, 1600-1830, Sun 1130-1230, 1600-1830, church free, archeological remains and crypt €2.50; Cavallini frescoes Mon-Sat 1015-1200, Sun 1115-1215, €2.50. Bus: H, 23, 44, 75, 125, 780. Map: Rome, D5, p84.

The patron saint of musicians, Cecilia was martyred around AD 230. The story goes that after trying unsuccessfully to scald or suffocate her to death by locking her in a hot bath, Roman officials tried to behead her, but that after three blows of the sword she still took three days to die, during which time she continued to sing. She was buried in the Catacomb of St Callixtus, and transferred here in 817. When her tomb was opened in 1599, her body was apparently uncorrupted, and Stefano Maderno's marble statue on the altar, sculpted when he was just 23, was based on sketches of her corpse. This Baroque masterpiece is a powerful work, with her face turned away in pain and defeat but seeming defiance. St Cecilia has featured in many other works of art since, and recently appeared on the British £20 note.

Downstairs, there are remains of a Roman house that may have once belonged to Cecilia, and been the place of her death. There are some fragments of

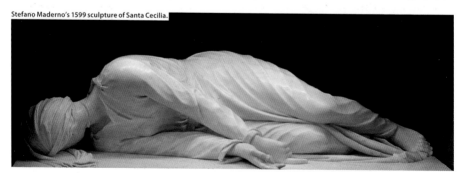

Stefano Maderno's 1599 sculpture of Santa Cecilia.

beautiful mosaic floor, with a swastika motif alternating with squares – a design popular in Rome and Pompeii. Carved stone Roman sarcophagi feature designs including the successful hunt of a giant wild boar. The crypt, which holds Cecilia's tomb, is an atmospheric spot, with tall, elegant columns and a richly decorated ceiling. The sparkling mosaic in the apse, from the ninth century, shows Christ, Cecilia and other saints.

Upstairs in the modern nuns' choir is one of the city's hidden masterpieces, an extraordinary fresco of the *Last Judgement* by Pietro Cavallini. Painted in 1293 all along one wall, it is slightly fragmented, and some of it is hidden below the current level of the floor. But it's a very beautiful painting, strikingly ahead of its time and foreshadowing much that was to come in Renaissance art, including the beginnings of an understanding of perspective and a human aspect that was absent from much of the other Byzantine-influenced work of the time.

Isola Tiberina

Bus: H, 23, 63, 280, 780. Map: Rome, D5, p84.

Rome was probably first settled next to this little island in the middle of the Tiber because it created a way to cross to the other side. Legends tell how a boat sank in the middle of the river and silt built up around it, creating an island, but in fact the island is composed of hard stone. In the third century BC, a temple to Aesculapius, god of medicine, was built here, and the medical connection has remained ever since. Today it is home to a hospital, a church, an expensive restaurant and little else, though it's well worth the short stroll around its perimeter for the views of the river and its bridges.

Ponte Fabricio, connecting the island to the main city, is the original Roman structure, built in 62 BC. These days it is restricted to pedestrian traffic. Just downstream, a single arch of the Pons Aemilius, now known as the **Ponte Rotto** ('broken bridge'), is all that remains of the first stone bridge built across the river, dating back to 179 BC. Three of its arches collapsed in storms in 1598, and a further two were demolished in 1885.

What the locals say

I love Rome in late spring, when it gets warmer. I like strolling through the *centro storico*, climbing up the Spanish Steps and admiring the skyline from the Pincio – if I feel particularly active, I also enjoy skating along the riverbanks or in Villa Borghese. For ice creams, I love Giolitti, near the Pantheon. My favourite views of the city are from the terrace of Bar Zodiaco in Monte Mario – also, looking at St Peter's dome through the Knights of Malta keyhole on the Aventine Hill still leaves me breathless. In the evening I like the market in Trastevere – there is a great atmosphere plus you can find many good bargains, from rare books to handmade jewellery. For some quiet time I go to Bibli café-bookshop on via dei Fienaroli, which is also a great place to have a cup of tea with friends. If I am staying out late, I love the healthy Roman habit of eating a warm *cornetto* in the middle of the night – my favourite address is Bar Professionisti on via Colonna.

Simona.

Chiesa di San Francesco a Ripa

Piazza di San Francesco d'Assisi, T06-581 9020. Bus: 23, 44, 280. Map: Rome, D6, p84.

Standing at the end of the street named after it, this church is notable for Gian Lorenzo Bernini's 17th-century Baroque monument to **Ludovica Albertoni**, demonstrating such orgasmic levels of religious pleasure that it may make you blush. Some may tell you that the blessed Ludovica is actually in agony, unlike the subject of his more famous sculpture of *L'Estasi di Santa Teresa* in the church of **Santa Maria della Vittoria** (see page 231); you may struggle to detect the thin line separating pleasure from pain. St Francis stayed here when he visited Rome in 1229, using a stone for a pillow, which can still be seen.

Sleeping

There was a time when Trastevere was considered Rome's accommodation desert. Recently, however, things have improved a lot, with a couple of excellent hotels opening and a handful of good guesthouses.

Buonanotte Garibaldi €€€
Via Garibaldi 83, T06-5833 0733, buonanottegaribaldi.com.
Bus: 23, 125, 280.
Map: Rome, C5, p84.
Just three rooms are arranged around the verdant courtyard of silk artist Luisa Longo; the first floor room has a private terrace. The guesthouse is decorated with the artist's work.

Donna Camilla Savelli €€€
Via Garibaldi 27, T06-588861, hotelsavelli.com.
Bus: 115, 125.
Map: Rome, C5, p84.
Up the hill from Trastevere's central buzz, this quiet ex-convent opened as a hotel in 2007. Designed in the 17th century by Borromini, it's now an elegant, sophisticated place, with a beautiful garden courtyard. Rooms are mostly spacious, even those that were once nuns' cells, with large,

comfortable beds, luxurious drapes and muted colours. Bathrooms are immaculately sparkly and flowers add style. For €650 a night, the imperial suite has a generous private terrace with good views over the city.

Residenza Arco de' Tolomei €€€
Via dell'Arco de Tolomei 27, T06-5832 0819, bbarcodetomomei.com.
Bus: H, 125, 780.
Map: Rome, D5, p84.
A homely little guesthouse with welcoming owners, tucked away on a quiet street on Trastevere's relatively undiscovered east side. Lots of old wood, faded floral wallpaper, books and portraits give the place antique character, and breakfast is served on a large table in the elegant dining room. Some of the six rooms overlook a tiny piazza filled with olive trees; others have their own small terraces.

Ripa €€€
Via degli Orti di Trastevere 3, T06-58611, ripahotel.com.
Bus: H, 115, 125, 780.
Map: Rome, C6, p84.
On the outside it may be an ugly, crumbling tower block, but inside, Ripa is sleek. A relatively early exponent of the design hotel, it has the feel of an old-fashioned view of the future – a take on the futuristic designs in 1970s science fiction movies. Curvy minimalism and muted

colours are used throughout the 170 rooms. The downside is that it's rather out of the way on the western side of Trastevere.

Arco del Lauro €€
Via dell'Arco de' Tolomei 27, T06-9784 0350, arcodellauro.it.
Bus: H, 125, 780.
Map: Rome, D5, p84.
In the same block as Residenza Arco de' Tolomei, Arco del Lauro has reasonably stylish modern rooms with muted colours and shiny wooden floors. The owners are friendly and multilingual.

Casa di Santa Francesca Romana €€
Via dei Vascellari 61, T06-581 2125, sfromana.it.
Bus: 23, 44, 125, 280.
Map: Rome, D5, p84.
St Frances of Rome lived here in the 15th century and it remains a holy place, complete with a chapel and a large crucifix. Whether or not the religious aspect appeals, it's very good value – simple but comfortable, efficient and immaculately clean, with 37 rooms around a beautiful central courtyard with umbrellas and orange trees.

Hotel Santa Maria €€
Vicolo del Piede 2, T06-589 4626, hotelsantamaria.info.
Bus: H, 23, 115, 125, 780.
Map: Rome, C5, p84.
Eighteen rooms, all on the ground floor, are arranged around a central courtyard with

orange trees, where breakfast is served in summer. It's a quiet spot, and guests are well looked after, with lots of free extras such as bikes to borrow, internet and Wi-Fi and an *aperitivo* buffet. Rooms are comfortable, with baths, safes and a yellow and cream colour scheme.

Residenza Santa Maria €€
Via dell'Arco di San Calisto 20,
T06-5833 5103,
residenzasantamaria.com.
Bus: H, 23, 115, 125, 780.
Map: Rome, C5, p84.
Opened in 2007, and run by the same friendly team as Hotel Santa Maria, this quiet little place has just six rooms, some of which are large enough for families. Old wooden beamed ceilings and antique stone carvings give the place some style; the barrel-vaulted breakfast room downstairs used to be a cistern. Free services offered by the hotel are available to guests staying here, making it excellent value.

San Francesco €€
Via Jacopa de' Settesoli 7,
T06-5830 0051,
hotelsanfrancesco.net.
Bus: 75. Map: Rome, D6, p84.
Sleek and modern, San Francesco is a stylish option. There's a rooftop bar with cacti and some rather uncomfortable chairs, and a grand piano and big contemporary art in the reception area. After this, bedrooms are slightly safe but perfectly comfortable.

Villa della Fonte €€
Via della Fonte dell'Olio 8,
T06-580 3797, villafonte.com.
Bus: H, 23, 115, 125, 780.
Map: Rome, C5, p84.
With only five plain, en suite rooms and a garden terrace, Villa della Fonte is a welcoming, if not especially spacious place. On a pedestrianized street just off piazza Santa Maria in Trastevere, simple, tiled rooms look out on to greenery-draped walls. Some rooms have sloping beamed ceilings, and there's free Wi-Fi throughout.

Eating & drinking

Asinocotto €€€
Via dei Vascellari 48,
T06-589 8985, asinocotto.com.
Tue-Sat 1200-1430, 1900-2300,
Sun 1900-2300.
Bus: 23, 125, 280.
Map: Rome, D5, p84.
Smart and creative, Asinocotto's
attention to detail is obvious.
Beautifully presented dishes
include stuffed courgette
flowers with goats' milk ricotta
and nettles, cocoa pasta with
goat and pistachio, and duck
with licorice and figs. It's a small
place, with an open kitchen, a
dark wood ceiling and a chilled
soundtrack, which, like the food,
plays with discordance.
Refreshing and satisfying.

Glass Hostaria €€€
Vicolo del Cinque 58,
T06-5833 5903, glass-hostaria.it.
Tue-Sun 2000-2330,
wine bar till 0200.
Bus: H, 23, 115, 125, 780.
Map: Rome, C5, p84.
A strikingly modern and slick
wine bar, Glass Hostaria serves
ambitiously creative dishes, such
as pigeon, orange and porcini
mushroom risotto or oxtail with
tamarind.

La Gensola €€€
Piazza della Gensola 15,
T06-581 6312.
Bus: 23, 125, 280.
Map: Rome, C5, p84.
The first mention of an osteria
here was in the 15th century, and
the road was named after the

restaurant rather than vice versa.
Small and smart, with excellent
fish dishes, Gensola is an
upmarket, efficient place.
Contemporary art helps relieve
a slight tendency towards
stuffiness, and the tuna with
sweet balsamic dressing is
excellent, as is the octopus
with oil and lemon.

Ripa 12 €€€
Via di San Francesco a Ripa 12,
T06-580 9093, ripa12.com.
Mon-Sat 1200-1500, 1930-2330.
Bus: H, 115, 125, 780.
Map: Rome, C5, p84.
Whether or not carpaccio of sea
bass was first served here, as
some claim, it makes an elegant
spot for a plate of seafood,
cooked or otherwise. You might
also try the octopus salad, a
risotto with prawns, courgettes
and saffron, or the grilled king
prawns with cognac.

Il Ciak €€
Vicolo del Cinque 21, T06-589 4774.
Daily 2015-2400.
Bus: H, 23, 115, 125, 780.
Map: Rome, C5, p84.
Steadfastly traditional, Ciak
serves hearty Tuscan cuisine
and has a rustic feel. It's not a
place for vegetarians: meat is
the mainstay, with an open grill
behind the hunks of meat in the
window. But if top quality wild
boar steak is your thing, then
you'll find few places better.
Wine comes in flagons – you
pay just for what you drink.

Le Mani in Pasta €€
Via dei Genovesi 37, T06-581 6017,
lemaniinpasta.com.
Tue-Sun 1230-1500, 1930-2330,
closed 3 weeks in Aug.
Bus: H, 23, 280, 780.
Map: Rome, D5, p84.
Deep in the less frequented
eastern half of Trastevere, this is

an intimate little place, specializing in seafood and popular with locals and a sprinkling of ex-pats. Portions are very generous and the homemade pasta is delicious, especially the tagliolini with clams or *alla gricia* (with bacon and cheese).

Quirino €€
Vicolo della Scala 3,
T06-5830 1885.
Daily 2000 till late.
Bus: 125. Map: Rome, C5, p84.
A fresh new, creative trattoria in an area where most restaurants have been around for decades, Quirino is a breath of fresh air. Fish is the speciality, and dishes such as brown flour fettucine with mussels, clams, cherry tomatoes and sea bass are exquisitely tasty. A blackboard menu has a good range of *secondi*, depending on the daily catch, and the homemade desserts are delicious too. A mixed but mainly Italian crowd fills the single bright, stone-ceilinged room.

Trattoria degli Amici €€
Piazza Sant'Egidio 6, T06-580 6033, santegidio.org.
Mon-Sat 1930-2330.
Bus: H, 23, 125, 780.
Map: Rome, C5, p84.
Contemporary art decorates the walls, jazz plays and the food is good traditional Roman. Try some of the deep-fried starters followed by creamy lasagne or

perfectly cooked gnocchi with pesto, then the beef carpaccio with artichoke and grana padana. Homemade desserts include a chocolate tart with pistachio sauce. Run by a cooperative of disabled people, degli Amici may be a good cause but it just feels like an excellent restaurant in a great setting on Trastevere's most picturesque piazza.

bir & fud €
Via Benedetta 23, T06-589 4016, birefud.blogspot.com.
Sun-Thu 1930-2400,
Fri-Sat 1930-0200.
Bus: 23, 125, 280.
Map: Rome, C5, p84.
This new kid on Trastevere's pizza block serves fantastic Italian beer on tap, from three artisan producers, including the sumptuous Re Ale – try one while you (almost inevitably)

wait for a table. The pizzas are exceptionally good, using carefully sourced ingredients and proper buffalo mozzarella. The *supplì* are also unusually good, with creative takes on the standard fried rice balls, such as purple cabbage and ricotta. Unusually for a pizzeria, it's possible (and advisable) to book.

Da Augusto €
Piazza de' Renzi 15, T06-580 3798.
Mon-Sat 1230-1500, 2000-2300.
Bus: 23, 125, 280.
Map: Rome, C5, p84.
A Trastevere institution, frill-free Da Augusto has famously low prices, and its tightly packed Formica tables are almost always full. The food is traditional Roman at its best – choices change daily – and tables outside on the piazza in summer make the inevitable queuing well worth it.

Da Enzo €
Via dei Vascellari 29, T06-581 8355.
Mon-Sat lunch and dinner.
Bus: 23, 125, 280.
Map: Rome, D5, p84.

It wouldn't win any prizes for its decor, but the bright, yellow-walled Da Enzo does the basics of traditional Roman food very well. Starters include a good range of deep-fried goodies, including artichokes and generously stuffed courgette flowers, and very good *pasta amatriciana*. It's popular with Romans and usually noisy, especially at weekends.

Da Lucia €
Vicolo del Mattonato 2, T06-580 3601.
Tue-Sun 1230-1530, 1930-2400.
Bus: 23, 125, 280.
Map: Rome, C5, p84.

A popular, old-fashioned place tucked away on a side street. The food is traditional Roman – they do a great *spaghetti con cacio e pepe* (with pecorino cheese and pepper) and succulent anchovies with lemon, plus a fair sprinkling of offal. On sunny days you may have to fight for an outside table.

Da Olindo €
Vicolo della Scala 8, T06-581 8835.
Mon-Sat lunch and dinner.
Bus: 23, 125, 280.
Map: Rome, C5, p84.

A properly traditional Roman trattoria, dining at little Da Olindo can feel a little like eating at the house of an elderly relative. The cooking is excellent, with fine examples of Roman dishes that haven't changed in years: the *cacio e pepe* is extremely cheesy and peppery, and the chicken with cherry tomatoes and black olives is perfectly cooked. There are good homemade desserts and a wonderful art collection that mixes contemporary nudes, hunting paintings, old photographs, still lifes and a signed AS Roma shirt.

Dar Poeta €
Vicolo del Bologna 46, T06-588 0516.
Daily 1930-2400.
Bus: 23, 125, 280.
Map: Rome, C5, p84.

On a cobbled side street, you'll spot Dar Poeta by the large crowds of people waiting outside. Inside it's even more packed, with barely enough room to squeeze your way to a table, but it's worth it for the tasty pizzas, delivered speedily by the young waiting staff. Save some room for a chocolate calzone.

Miraggio €
Via della Lungara 16a, T06-687 5319.
1230 onwards, 1930 onwards.
Bus: 23, 125, 280.
Map: Rome, C4, p84.

Upriver from most of Trastevere's hotspots, the traditional osteria of Miraggio attracts a healthy mix of American priests, Italian families and groups of young gay men. Tablecloths are checked and onions hang from a beam. The menu is extensive to the point of having too much choice, but all the options are excellent and very good value.

Ivo €
Via di San Francesco a Ripa 158, T06-581 7082.
Wed-Mon 1930-0100.
Bus: H, 23, 115, 125, 780.
Map: Rome, C5, p84.

One of Trastevere's best loved pizzerias, Ivo's serves up traditional thin-crust pizzas without too many smiles but with a certain panache. White pizzas (without tomato) outnumber the red ones, and there's rather sweet red beer or more standard lager on tap. Pizzas come in two sizes – go for large, which is not much bigger than standard elsewhere. There's a sense that nothing here has changed in a long time, nor probably will for years to come, and the locals like it that way.

Pizzeria ai Marmi €
Viale di Trastevere 53/59, T06-580 0919.
Thu-Tue evenings only.
Bus: 23, 125, 780.
Map: Rome, D5, p84.

Exceptionally popular, and known commonly as *l'Obitorio* ('the morgue') due to its tightly packed marble tables, the experience here is as much about theatricality as the exemplary thin-crust pizzas.

Five of the best

Picnic spots in Trastevere

❶ **Orto Botanico** sit among palm trees and rare plants.

❷ **Isola Tiberina** with views of the Ponte Rotto from its southern tip.

❸ **Villa Doria Pamphilj** an extensive, calm green space.

❹ **Piazza Santa Maria in Trastevere** watch the world go by from the steps of the fountain.

❺ **Piazzale Garibaldi** up on the Gianicolo hill overlooking Rome.

On a Friday or Saturday night you can expect a long wait for a table – give a name to the man on the door when you arrive. Good fried antipasti arrive in an instant. If you can, get a table next to the pizza oven to watch the action.

Cafés & bars

Via della Scala has several bars catering mainly to tourists, but offering excellent people-watching opportunities from their street-side tables. Try **Antilia** or **Caffè della Scala**.

b>gallery

Piazza Santa Cecilia 16, T06-5833 4365, b-gallery.it.
1000-2030, events until 2400.
Bus: H, 23, 44, 75, 125, 780.
This slick, bright, modern venue incorporates a downstairs gallery, a design and

photography bookshop, and a café where one of the best cappuccinos around comes with chocolate-covered coffee beans on the side.

Bar San Calisto

Piazza di San Calisto 3, T06-583 5869.
Mon-Sat 0530-0200.
Bus: H, 23, 115, 125, 780.
While the tourists pack one of the rather boring and expensive cafés on piazza Santa Maria in Trastevere, a much more mixed crowd of locals heads here. They serve good coffee and hot chocolate and keep the beer-in-the-street crowd happy until late.

Bibli Caffè

Via dei Fienaroli 28, T06-581 4534, bibli.it.
Mon 1730-2400,
Tue-Sun 1100-2400.
Bus: H, 23, 115, 125, 780.
One block east of piazza Calisto, this bookshop café is a hidden gem. At weekends tables are set out all through the shop, and a young literary crowd packs the place for a mouth-watering, mainly vegetarian buffet brunch (1230-1530). The café does a daily *aperitivo* buffet (1900-2030) and hosts occasional live music and cultural events.

Cantina Paradiso Wine Bar
Via San Francesco a Ripa 73,
T06-589 9799, cantinaparadiso.it.
Mon-Sat 1200-0200, Sun
brunch 1230-1600.
Bus: H, 115, 125, 780.
A bright red chandelier sets the
tone for this jazzy café, wine and
cocktail bar. The menu has a
good choice of grappas, as well
as cocktails.

Checco er Carettiere
Via Benedetta 7, T06-581 1413,
checcoercarettiere.it.
Daily 0630-0100.
Bus: 23, 125, 280.
Checco is a little Trastevere empire,
with a restaurant, an osteria and a
grocer, all firmly in the family. It is
this unassuming little café that sits
most firmly at the centre of local
life. Open nearly 24/7, it's the
perfect spot for a morning
cappuccino, decorated with either
a flower or a musical stave,
depending on your gender.

Da Saverio al Numero 1
Vicolo della Scala 1.
Bus: 23, 125, 280.
Homemade ice cream, funkily
designed patterned plastic chairs
and a clientele generally made up
more of locals and in-the-know
ex-pats than tourists.

Fior di Luna
Via della Lungaretta 96,
T06-6456 1314, fiordiluna.com.
Tue-Sun 1200-0100.
Bus: H, 23, 125, 280, 780.
Some of the best ice cream
around, including delicious
seasonal flavours such as pear,
chestnut, blackcurrant yoghurt
and crème caramel. Organic and
Fairtrade ingredients are carefully
chosen and they also do
sumptuously rich hot chocolate,
other great desserts, homemade
chocolates, coffee and teas.

Freni e Frizoni
Via del Politeanna 4/6,
T06-5833 4210, freniefrizioni.com.
1000-0200, buffet brunch
Sat-Sun 1200-1600.
Bus: 23, 125, 280.
The name means 'brakes and
clutches' – the venue used to be
a garage – and it does
metropolitan industrial chic with
more insouciance than
anywhere else this side of the
Tiber. There's a good *aperitivo*
buffet, the retro-cool style is
bolstered by fresh flowers and
chandeliers, and everyone here,
including the staff, is infallibly
young and beautiful.

Good Caffè
Via di Santa Dorotea 8/9,
T06-9727 7979, goodcaffe.com.
Daily 0700-0200.
Bus: 23, 125, 280.
Its strapline, "Food, drink and
wireless", gives a clue to its
anglophone clientele, especially

Five of the best

Trastevere *aperitivo* buffets

❶ **Freni e Frizioni** hip.
❷ **Bibli** literary.
❸ **Libreria del Cinema** cinematic.
❹ **La Mescita** smart.
❺ **Artù** abundant.

American students from the
nearby university, who come for
the relaxed atmosphere, free
Wi-Fi, generous breakfasts and
late-night live music and DJs.
The atmosphere remains Italian,
however, with a greenery-
entwined street-side terrace,
an *aperitivo* buffet and an
atmospheric interior.

L'Artù
Largo Fumasoni Biondi 5,
T06-588 0398.
Tue-Sun 1800-0200.
Bus: H, 23, 125, 780.
This wine bar, which serves full
meals as well as snacks, is in the
17th-century ex-presbytery of
Santa Maria in Trastevere and has
a great outdoor seating area.
Inside it's much funkier, with a
Mondrian-influenced bar,
coloured lights and eclectic
comfy seats.

La Mescita

Piazza Trilussa 41, T06-5833 3920, enotecaferrara.it.
Daily 1800-0200.
Bus: 23, 125, 780.
Part of the Ferrara mini-empire, which stretches along the street and now includes an expensive restaurant, a delectable shop and an osteria (**Ferrarina**) doing fixed-price meals. It's all good, but the classy wine bar is perhaps the best bit, though you pay for the quality. The *aperitivo* snacks are some of the best around.

Libreria del Cinema

Via del Fienaroli 31d, T06-581 7724.
Mon 1500-2200, Tue-Fri and Sun 1100-2200, Sat 1100-2300.
Bus: H, 125, 780.
With an *aperitivo* buffet from 1800-2100 and a great selection of cinema books and DVDs to peruse, this literary and cinematic café is a great spot for an evening glass of wine or a daytime coffee.

Ma che siete venuti a fà!

Via Benedetta 25, T06-9727 5218, football-pub.com.
Daily 1500-0200.
Bus: 23, 125, 280.
Some say it's the best place to find good beer in the whole of Italy. This little bar crams a dozen taps of well-kept artisan beer into a very small space, hung with football scarves. At any one time you'll find Danish, German and Italian beers available – if you're not sure where to start, try the fantastic, hoppy BiBock.

Ombre Rosse Caffè

Piazza Sant'Egidio 12, T06-588 4155, ombrerossecaffe.it.
Daily 0800-0200.
Bus: H, 23, 125, 780.
On Trastevere's most picturesque piazza, tables outside Ombre Rosse make a good people-watching spot. Inside there's lots of worn wood and old posters. It comes into its own in the evening for *aperitivo*, when it can get very crowded. Free Wi-Fi and occasional live music.

Entertainment

Cinema

Trastevere has two cinemas that show films in their original language on Mondays. In July and August there are also outdoor screenings on **Isola Tiberina** (isoladelcinema.com).

Alcazar
Via Cardinale Merry del Val 14, T06-588 0099, mymovies.it.
Bus: H, 780.

Nuovo Sacher
Largo Ascianghi 1, T06-581 8116, sacherfilm.eu.
Bus: H, 115, 125, 780.
Owned by Roman film director Nanni Moretti, this shows Italian and other European arthouse films.

Tip...

Frengo's Music (65 Via della Lungaretta 65, T06-5833 2402), which stocks a good selection of Italian as well as international recordings, is a good spot to pick up freebie listings magazines and flyers for what's on around town.

Music

Big Mama
Vicolo San Francesco a Ripa 18, T06-581 2551, bigmama.it.
2100-0130, shows begin 2230.
Bus: H, 44, 75, 115, 125, 780.
There are over 200 blues and other live gigs every year in this intimate and well-respected cellar club. A monthly membership card (€8) gets you free entrance to most shows. You can book a table up to 22 hours in advance.

Lettere Caffè Club
Via San Francesco di Ripa 100, T06-9727 0991, letterecaffe.org.
Mon-Sat 1500-0200, Sun 1100-1630, 1700-0200.
Bus: H, 44, 75, 115, 125, 780.
Despite the name and the books, the emphasis in Lettere Caffè is heavily on music. There are regular live performances by predominantly jazz, funk and electronica acts, as well as late-night DJs in a vaguely grungy venue decorated with contemporary art.

Shopping

Books

Open Door Bookshop
Via della Lungaretta 23, T06-589 6478, books-in-italy.com.
Mon 1600-2000, Tue-Sat 1030-1430, 1600-2000.
Bus: H, 23, 125, 280, 780.
A fabulous second-hand bookshop selling mainly English-language titles, including a good section on Rome, and plenty of holiday reading. The kind of place you could get lost in for hours.

The Almost Corner Bookshop
Via del Moro 45, T06 583 6942.
Mon-Sat 1000-1330, 1530-2000, Sun 1100-1330, 1530-2000; closed Sun in Aug.
Bus: 23, 125, 280.
An English-language bookshop with an excellent selection of new titles: fiction, guidebooks and, especially, Roman and Italian history.

Clothes

Jessica Harris
Vicolo de Leopardo 38, T06-4543 5476, jessicaharris.net.
Mon 1100-1900, Wed 1000-1400, Tue, Thu-Fri 1000-1900, Sat-Sun 1200-2000.
Bus: 23, 125, 280.
A young American fashion designer, Jessica Harris creates her stylish, feminine and very reasonably priced pieces in this little hidden-away atelier. Lace-trimmed and with floral touches, her influences range from ballet and art to Cyndi Lauper.

Joseph Debach

Vicolo del Cinque 19, T06-556 2756, josephdebach.com.
Bus: H, 23, 115, 125, 780.
Colourful and imaginative men's and women's shoes, with perhaps an abacus or a scroll where you might expect a stiletto.

Food & drink

Antica Caciara

Via San Francesco a Ripa 140, T06-581 2815, anticacaciara.it.
Mon-Sat 0700-1400, 1600-2000.
Bus: H, 44, 75, 115, 125, 780.
For Roman cheese this deli is hard to beat, whether it's wonderfully crumbly and tasty *pecorino romano* chiselled off the huge whole cheeses by the door, *formaggio di fossa* (matured in caves) or the sheep's milk ricotta delivered daily.

Dolce Idea

Via San Francesco a Ripa 27, T06-5833 4043, dolceidea.com.
Mon-Thu 1000-1930, Fri-Sat 1000-2030.
Bus: H, 44, 75, 115, 125, 780.
Naples' best artisan chocolate is sold from this delectable little outlet – specialities include dark chocolate with chilli.

Drogheria Innocenzi

Piazza San Cosimato 66 (corner of via Natale del Grande), T06-581 2725.
Mon-Sat 0700-1400, 1630-2000.
Bus: H, 44, 75, 115, 125, 780.
An Aladdin's cave piled high with sweets, biscuits, nougat, honey

and even hard-to-find international goods for homesick ex-pats, such as Marmite.

Forno La Renella

Via del Moro 15, T06-581 7265.
Officially 0900-2100, but often stays open much later.
Bus: 23, 125, 280.
An excellent baker and *pizzaiolo*, usually busy with people stopping by for a thick, moist

slice of focaccia or some tasty pizza. The bread and pastries are excellent too. You can eat at stools around the edge as well as take away. La Renella also has one of the best noticeboards around.

Frutteria Er Cimotto

*Piazza San Giovanni di Malva,
T06-581-5331.*
Mon-Sat 0700-2200, Sun
0800-1300, 1600-2000.
Bus: 23, 125, 280.
An excellent little grocer's that
somehow squeezes every kind
of fruit and veg you've ever seen,
and several you probably
haven't, into a tiny space. They
also do freshly baked bread from
a wood-fired oven and other
fantastic picnic options, as well
as freshly squeezed orange juice
for €1.50.

Innocenti Biscottificio Artigiano

Via della Luce 21, T06-580 3926.
Mon-Sat 0800-2000, Sun
0930-1400.
Bus: H, 23, 125, 280, 780.
Great homemade biscuits,
and, at Christmas time, their
chocolate panettone is one of
the best you'll find.

Valzani

Via del Moro 37, T06-580 3792.
Mon-Tue 1200-2030, Wed-Sun
1000-2030.
Bus: 23, 125, 780.
An old-fashioned Roman
pasticceria that opened in 1925

and hasn't changed much since.
Seasonal specialities include
handmade Easter eggs and the
little almond cookies called *fave
dei morti* – beans of the dead –
in November.

Markets

Piazza San Cosimato

Mon-Sat mornings.
Bus: H, 44, 75, 115, 125, 780.
Excellent, good-value fruit and
veg, as well as fish, honey and
other local produce.

Porta Portese

Sun 0700-1300.
Bus: 23, 44, 75, 280.
Rome's most famous flea market has been cleaned up a little these days. The tat stalls far outnumber those selling more interesting or legally questionable things, but there are still some gems along the enormously long stretch of stalls, such as old magazines and prints, seeds, old bits of carved stone and some remarkably cheap Italian leather shoes.

Souvenirs

Trad.Eco

Via dei Genovesi 11c,
T06-5833 0871, trad-eco.it.
Mon-Fri 0930-1300, 1530-1930.
Bus: H, 125, 780.
As well as their trademark hand-painted Pinocchio dolls, they do good baskets, bags, salt lamps and cinnamon-wood picture frames.

Associazione Culturale Random

Via della Scala 16, T06-686 5162.
Bus: 23, 125, 280.
In the midst of Via della Scala's hip hangouts, Random comes as a pleasantly eccentric surprise. A mini arts centre, it runs loosely structured printing, papermaking and art courses for kids, and, once a week, for grown-ups too. Colourful fabrics and abstract art abounds. For a great Trastevere souvenir, there are also some prints for sale. Courses for kids from €15, adults from €10 an hour.

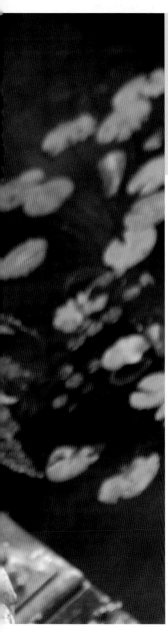

Contents

Villa Borghese & Tridente

A detail of the Nimphaeum inside Villa Giulia.

Introduction

While Rome couldn't be called Europe's most verdant capital, the landscape garden of Villa Borghese is certainly the exception. The city centre's largest green lung offers an unsurpassable romantic backdrop as well as plenty of art and culture, with highlights such as the Galleria Borghese (one of Rome's greatest art repositories) and the Etruscan museum of Villa Giulia.

Leaving the park brings you into the heart of the city and the elegant atmosphere of piazza di Spagna and via Veneto. This is the glitzy part of Rome, best captured in Fellini's *La Dolce Vita*, although there is little left of the really magical atmosphere of its heyday in the 1950s and 60s. It was once the hangout of the rich and famous, but this scene has since moved elsewhere. However, via Veneto is still an elegant place and the address of some of Rome's most luxurious hotels and exclusive shops. Soak up the glamour by dropping into the charming cafés or fall for the temptations of designer shopping.

What to see in...

...one day
Start at the **Spanish Steps**, then check the antique shops along **via del Babuino** and soak up the atmosphere of **via Margutta**. Head to **piazza del Popolo** and marvel at the Caravaggios in **Santa Maria del Popolo**. Dedicate the afternoon to the **Galleria Borghese**, before heading to the bars and restaurants along **via Veneto**.

...a weekend or more
Start your day in **piazza del Popolo** and visit **Santa Maria del Popolo** and the twin churches of **Santa Maria di Montesanto** and **Santa Maria dei Miracoli**. Explore **via Margutta** and **via del Babuino** before heading to **piazza di Spagna** and the **Keats-Shelley House**.
    The following day, begin at **Palazzo Barberini** and then walk along **via Veneto** to **Villa Borghese** (don't forget to pop into the spooky crypt of the **Chiesa dei Cappuccini**). Visit the **Galleria Borghese**, recharge with a light bite at the **Casina del Cinema**, then head to the terrace of the **Pincio** for some of the most romantic views of the city.

Aviary house.

Villa Borghese & around

As its name suggests, the Villa Borghese was designed for Cardinal Scipione Borghese Caffarelli in the early 1600s. The park was completely remodelled in later centuries in the naturalistic English landscape style, and owes its current aspect to Luigi Canina, who in 1827 also designed the spectacular entrance on piazzale Flaminio. The formal parterres around the villa have recently been restored to their 17th-century designs.

Romans were seeking shade under the trees here long before the arrival of Cardinal Borghese. The area to the north and northeast of the city has been occupied by villas and green spaces since the days of the Caesars: the Pincio area was once part of Augustus' imperial gardens, and nearby were the fabled gardens of the Villa Lucullus, laid out in the first century BC by the philosopher-general Lucullus on his return from conquering Anatolia, where he had seen gardens in the Persian style, which he reproduced in Rome. The Villa Medici (now home to the French Academy) was later built on the site – it served as a gilded cage for Galileo during his Inquisition trial.

Villa Borghese

villaborghese.it.
Metro: Flaminio or Spagna. Bus: 116.
Map: Rome, E1, p84.

Measuring 6 km around its perimeter,
Villa Borghese is central Rome's biggest park,
and also the loveliest. You will come across shady
woods, atmospheric avenues, a riding track (the
Galoppatoio) and – a fancy name for a rather
dated zoo – the **Bioparco** (Piazzale del Giardino
Zoologico, T06-360 8211, bioparco.it; daily Nov-Mar
0930-1700, Apr-Oct 0930-1800, €10/8 concession).
One of the park's nicest spots is the small artificial
lake dominated by the temple of Aesculapius
(the god of medicine), created in Ionian style in
the 18th century and containing a statue of the
deity. The lake has rowing boats available for hire
(€3 per person for 20 mins).

Culture in the park is vibrant: it's a sort of
green museum-land, scattered with a variety
of collections and academies. In addition,
there is a house dedicated to cinema (see page
217) and a Shakespearean theatre (see page 217).
And in spite of its romantic appearance, Villa
Borghese is keeping pace with modern times:
the park offers Wi-Fi access, allowing you to surf
the internet in the shade of an umbrella pine
(for a maximum of 1 hr per day).

Giardini del Pincio

Metro: Flaminio. Map: Rome, E1, p84.

The Pincio Gardens are on the western edge of
Villa Borghese, technically separated from it by the
Aurelian Wall and the busy road that runs beside it.
The wall is known as the *Muro Torto* ('crooked wall')
because of a section that collapsed in the sixth
century. According to a 16th-century legend, this
could have been the burial site of Nero (with the
emperor's ghost predictably making periodic visits).
Prostitutes used to be buried in the area – hence the

Out for a stroll.

other colloquial name, *Muro Malo* ('evil wall'), given to this part of the Aurelian Wall in the past.

The gardens owe their present appearance to Giuseppe Valadier, who redesigned them between 1810 and 1818 and also planned nearby piazza del Popolo, working under the orders of Napoleon. They were the first public gardens in the capital, and are scattered with 224 busts of famous people (which are often unfortunately targeted by vandals). Look out for the sculpture of the astronomer Angelo Secchi: at its base you will notice a small hole, which is where the Rome meridian passes through. The sloping park also contains the lovely **Casina Valadier** (now an elegant café and restaurant), a **water clock** dating from 1867 and an **obelisk** created in Rome for Emperor Hadrian (who dedicated it to his favourite, Antinous). Don't miss the **terrace**, from which there are breathtaking views over the city and the Vatican.

Museo e Galleria Borghese

Piazzale del Museo Borghese 5, T06-841 3979, galleriaborghese.it.
Tue-Sun 0830-1930 (admission in 2-hr time slots, last entrance 1700), advance booking essential (T06-32810 or ticketeria.it), €8.50/5.25/2 concession.
Metro: Flaminio or Spagna. Map: Rome, F1, p84.

Two of the most celebrated art collections in the world are housed in the 17th-century Casino Borghese. Both were started by Cardinal Scipione Borghese, an unrivalled patron and collector, who brought together the work of the greatest artists of his time; first and foremost among them was Gian Lorenzo Bernini.

Museo Bernini is represented in the museum section by some of the true masterpieces of Baroque statuary, all three commissioned by Cardinal Scipione: *David* (1623-1624, room II), whose face is modelled on that of the artist, and the mythology-inspired *Apollo and Daphne* (1624) in room III and *Rape of Proserpina* (1622) in the

Galleria degli Imperatori. Also here is Bernini's portrait of the cardinal himself. In fact, there are two almost identical busts, one beside the other: while carving the first one the artist realized that the block of marble he was working on was defective, and in order to avoid disappointing his patron he hastily produced a second version within a fortnight.

In 1807 Prince Camillo Borghese sold the collection to his brother-in-law, Napoleon Bonaparte. Many of its artworks were taken to France, where they still make up the core of the classical antiquity section of the Louvre. Two years earlier, Antonio Canova had portrayed Camillo's wife Pauline as *Venus Victrix* (room I); the sculpture was so graceful that the artist devised a mechanism that allowed it to rotate, to the amazement and thrill of the villa's guests.

Galleria Cardinal Scipione Borghese also assembled an impressive collection of paintings. Caravaggio is represented by some of his most extraordinary works (all in the Sileno room): *Boy with a Basket of Fruit* (c 1593-1595), *Madonna and Child with St Anne* (1605), *Young Sick Bacchus* (1592-1595), *St Jerome* (1605-1606) and *David with the Head of Goliath*, in which the giant's head is famously the last dramatic self-portrait the artist painted before his premature death. Other masterpieces include, in the Hercules room, Correggio's *Danäe* (1530-1531) and Titian's *Sacred and Profane Love* (c1514) in room XX.

Interestingly, the cardinal used any means necessary to secure these treasures for himself. He had Raphael's priceless *Deposition* (1507, Didone room) stolen by night from the Church of San Francesco in Perugia, causing a citizens' revolt. He went on to confiscate 107 paintings from Cavalier d'Arpino and even had the artist Domenichino jailed because he refused to hand over the splendid *Diana the Huntress* (1616-1617, room XIX), which had been commissioned by another client.

Museo e Galleria Borghese.

Galleria Nazionale d'Arte Moderna

Viale delle Belle Arti 131, T06-322981,
gnam.beniculturali.it.
Tue-Sun 0830-1930, gallery €6.50/3.25
concession, gallery and exhibitions €9/7, free EU
citizens under 18 and over 65.
Metro: Flaminio.

Housed in the Palazzo delle Belle Arti,
the collection mainly represents the most
important Italian artists of the 19th and 20th
centuries, divided into four chronologically
arranged sections.

The southwest wing starts with Neoclassicism
(the most notable works being those of Antonio
Canova and his school) and Romanticism,
including works by Francisco Hayez. The
quintessentially Italian movement of the
Macchiaioli is represented by artists such as
Giovanni Fattori, Silvestro Lega and Adriano
Cecioni; in the same section there are paintings
with a distinctly realist cast by the Neapolitan
school of the mid-19th century.

The southeast wing is dedicated to Italian art
of the later 19th century, with big commemorative
paintings of battles of the Risorgimento: Giovanni
Fattori's *Battaglia di Custoza* and Michele
Cammarano's *Battaglia di San Martino* stand
out. There is also a good selection of works by
foreign masters such as Courbet, Van Gogh,
Monet and Degas.

The early 20th-century collection in the
northeast wing features the so-called historical
avant-garde movements, from Symbolism to
Futurism (with works by Giacomo Balla, Umberto
Boccioni and Gino Severini) and Abstractionism,
from Cubism to the Metaphysical paintings of de
Chirico and Carlo Carrà.

More recent artistic styles are represented in
the northwest wing, with works by the likes of
Jackson Pollock, Antoni Tàpies and Cy Twombly,
as well as Italians including Alberto Burri, Gastone

Novelli and Lucio Fontana. Among the sculptors, Arnaldo and Giò Pomodoro, Umberto Mastroianni, Pietro Consagra and Lorenzo Guerrini are the most significant.

Museo Nazionale Etrusco di Villa Giulia

Piazzale di Villa Giulia 9, T06-8207 7304, villaborghese.it.
Tue-Sun 0830-1930 (last admission 1830), €4/2 concession.
Metro: Flaminio.

There are two compelling reasons to visit this museum: first, it's one of the best places to become familiar with the Etruscans, second only to Tarquinia's archaeological site (see page 260); second, but equally important, is Villa Giulia itself, built between 1551 and 1555 for Pope Julius III. It is a magnificent example of Renaissance architecture, with contributions by artists such as Giorgio Vasari, Bartolomeo Ammannati and Jacopo Barozzi da

Vignola. Conceived as inseparable from its garden, the centre of the complex is the **nymphaeum**, a multi-level structure with two series of overlaid loggias. It reintroduced an ancient Roman architectural feature: originally sacred to water nymphs, such monuments had come to be used by the Romans as picturesque settings for al fresco dining. Below it is Ammannati's **Fontana dell'Acqua Vergine**, decorated with caryatids and two statues representing the rivers Tiber and Arno. Julius III had the fountain built above the Acqua Vergine aqueduct (which also supplies the Trevi Fountain), piercing it – illegally – to create Rome's first 'water theatre'.

Museo Etrusco Opened to the public in 1889, Villa Giulia is the world's most important museum of Etruscan civilization. The finds on display come mostly from the territories of northern Lazio and are arranged according to where they were discovered. The most famous exhibit is the

Sarcophagus of the Married Couple, an almost life-size terracotta monument from Cerveteri (see page 260), dating from the sixth century BC, on which the couple recline together, looking as if they are chatting over dinner. It is one of the most evocative pieces illustrating the cult of the dead in Etruscan society. Other attractions include the *Apollo* from Veio (also from the sixth century BC), in polychrome terracotta, and the golden leaves from Pyrgi, inscribed with texts written in both Etruscan and Phoenician in the fifth century BC.

There is an interesting section about Etruscan women, who seem to have played a rather important role in the society (considered a scandal by many Greek writers of the time). On display are many everyday objects such as combs and small containers for perfumes, unguents and cosmetics.

Worth a visit in itself is the impressive display of jewellery from the **Castellani Collection,** which includes ornaments dating from the seventh century BC to the second century AD, as well as reproductions of the ancient treasures created by the Castellani family of jewellers in the 19th century.

Museo Carlo Bilotti

Viale Fiorello la Guardia, T06-8205 9127, museocarlobilotti.it.
Tue-Sat 0900-1900, €4.50/2.50 concession, free EU citizens under 18 and over 65.
Metro: Flaminio. Map: Rome, E1, p84.

A new cultural foundation housed in the ambitiously restored 16th-century Orangery, this is another part of the project to transform Villa Borghese into a 'culture park'. The museum houses a permanent collection of 22 works donated by Italian-American businessman Carlo Bilotti. At its core are 18 works by Giorgio de Chirico, and there are also works by Andy Warhol, Larry Rivers and Gino Severini. A large bronze, *Cardinale* by Giacomo Manzù, is displayed outside.

Opposite page: The Etruscan Museum of Villa Giulia.

North of Villa Borghese

Auditorium Parco della Musica

Viale Pietro de Coubertin 30, T06-8024 1281, auditorium.com.
Mon-Sat 1100-1800, Sun 1000-1800, guided architectural tours (available in English if booked in advance) Sat-Sun 1130-1630, €9/7 concession, €5 under 26.
Metro: Flaminio, then tram 2. Bus: M, 217, 910.

Designed by renowned architect Renzo Piano and opened in 2002, the 'park of music' is the biggest concert-hall complex of its kind in Europe. It comprises three large halls (variously likened to giant beetles, turtles and computer mice), positioned around an open-air amphitheatre. Each space has different features to suit different types of music, but they can be regulated to adjust the acoustics and capture the nature of a particular performance. Walls can be moved, for instance, and in **Sala Sinopoli** both stage and audience can be shifted. The largest hall, **Sala Santa Cecilia**, was created with symphonic concerts and large orchestras in mind, and seats over 2700 people. The outdoor amphitheatre in the heart of the Auditorium has a similar capacity.

The construction of the new complex exposed the remains of a large suburban villa. The structure – 4 m below the current street level – was in use from the second half of the sixth century BC to the second century AD, when it was probably abandoned after repeated flooding from the nearby Tiber. Thanks to an alteration in the original construction plans, the Roman villa has been successfully incorporated into the Auditorium itself.

Tip...

The best way to experience one of Renzo Piano's amazing spaces is to go to a concert. Check out the programme on the website or in local listings. The 'M' bus between Termini and the Auditorium runs daily every 15 minutes from 1700 until the end of the last event.

Auditorium Parco della Musica.

MACRO – Museo d'Arte Contemporaneo di Roma

Via Reggio Emilia 54, T06-6710 70400, macro.roma.museum.
Tue-Sun 0900-1900, €1 (may rise during exhibitions), free EU citizens under 18 and over 65.
Bus: 38, 60, 62, 80, 84, 88, 90.

Housed in the ex-Peroni brewery building, MACRO opened in 1999 and has become an important point of reference for international contemporary art. A huge extension by French architect Odile Decq is currently being built, and the museum will eventually cover an area of over 10,000 sq m. At the time of writing, only the foyer is open for temporary exhibitions. MACRO is scheduled to reopen in autumn 2009.

MAXXI – Museo Nazionale delle Arti del XXI Secolo

Via Guido Reni 2f, T06-321 0181, maxxi.darc. beniculturali.it.
Metro: Flaminio, then tram 2. Bus: C3, M, 233, 910.

Conceived as a centre for 21st-century art, MAXXI is scheduled to open at the end of 2009, and will be housed in an innovative building by Zaha Hadid, currently under construction.

South of Villa Borghese

Piazza Barberini

Metro: Barberini. Map: Rome, F2, p84.

It's all about the Barberini family and yet again Bernini, whose **Fontana del Tritone** (1642-1643) dominates the now traffic-congested piazza. His rather unusual composition, famous for its apparent lack of architectural support, represents a triton sitting on an open scallop shell, held up by four dolphins as he blows into a conch, symbolically proclaiming the glory of the Barberini family to the world.

Further glorification of the Barberinis comes in the shape of another Bernini fountain added in

Palazzo Barberini. The bees (top picture) are the symbol of the Barberini family.

Around the city

1644 – the small but lovely **Fontana delle Api** (Fountain of the Bees) in the northeast corner of the square. The three insects were the heraldic emblems of the Barberini family, and the fountain was installed to celebrate the 22nd anniversary of the papacy of Urban VIII. The sculpture was completed before the actual date of the anniversary, which was interpreted as a bad omen as the pontiff passed away eight days before the celebrations.

Until the 18th century the square was the site of a rather macabre practice: the foot of the Triton Fountain was the place where anonymous corpses found in the city were brought for identification.

Galleria Nazionale d'Arte Antica di Palazzo Barberini

Via delle Quattro Fontane 13, T06-32810, galleriaborghese.it.
Tue-Sun 0830-1930, €5/2.50 concession, free EU citizens under 18 and over 65.
Metro: Barberini. Map: Rome, F3, p84.

This grand palazzo was built to glorify the Barberini family following the election of Urban VIII to the papal throne in 1623. An exceptional team of artists – Bernini, Borromini, Maderno and Pietro da Cortona – worked on it, and the original decor sometimes steals the thunder from the paintings on display. Pietro da Cortona's Baroque frescoes of 1632-1639, *Triumph of Divine Providence*, on the ceiling of the Gran Salone, are a prime example.

The collection's absolute masterpiece, however, is in room 1: Raphael's recently restored *La Fornarina* (c1519). The large-eyed, distant-looking woman is probably Margherita Luti, the daughter of a baker in Trastevere and Raphael's lifelong lover and muse.

In room 4 look out for Marco Bigio's *Le Parche* (c1541), an interesting allegory of life and death that mingles classical mythology and Christian tradition. Room 6 has works by Titian and Tintoretto, while room 7 features Hans Holbein's portrait of Henry VIII of England at the age of 49, one of the best known of all royal portraits.

The Fontana del Tritone in piazza Barberini.

Tip...

Due to ongoing restoration, only the 13 rooms on the first floor (showing 16th- and 17th-century works) are currently open, and described here. The other floors should reopen by the end of 2010.

Caravaggio's powerful *Judith and Holophernes* (1597-1600) is in room 9; in room 10 look for Guercino's *Et in Arcadia Ego*, which reflects with macabre realism the misery of the human condition – even in serene Arcadia men are doomed to die. Guercino's work, painted between 1618 and 1622, was the first pictorial representation of the theme.

Galleria Comunale d'Arte Moderna e Contemporanea

Via Francesco Crispi 24; T06-474 2848, comune.roma.it/avi.
Currently closed: call for updates on future reopening.
Metro: Barberini.

The collection comprises over 4000 artworks, mostly by Italian artists of the 19th and 20th centuries. Highlights include Giorgio de Chirico's *Contest of the Gladiators* (1933-1934), a self-portrait by Renato Guttuso, and Mario Sironi's *The Family* (1927). Among the many sculptures also on display are *Bust of a Lady* (1907) and *Tête au nez cassé* (1913) by Auguste Rodin, plus the big *Horse* (1920-1926) in wood by Vincenzo Gemito.

Via Veneto

Metro: Barberini. Map: Rome, F2, p84.

The image most people have of this part of the city is still the one immortalized by Federico Fellini in *La Dolce Vita*. The name of the street alone (officially via Vittorio Veneto) is enough to evoke the glamour of the 1950s and 60s, when Hollywood celebrities crowded its elegant cafés – hoping to be spotted by the ever-present paparazzi. Today the fashionable crowd has moved on, and the café tables on the tree-lined pavements attract mainly tourists.

The entire district was created towards the end of the 19th century, as a result of some unscrupulous real-estate speculation by the Boncompagni Ludovisi princes, who parcelled out the land of their 17th-century villa. Only one Baroque building survived the wholesale redevelopment, the **Casino dell'Aurora Ludovisi** (via Lombardia 46, open by appointment Fri 1100-1200, write to Amministrazione del Principe Boncompagni Ludovisi, F06-4201 0745). Originally part of the Villa Ludovisi, this pavilion contains frescoes by Guercino, Domenichino and possibly Caravaggio. It is hidden away behind the **Palazzo Boncompagni** (1886-1890) designed by Gaetano Koch for Prince Rodolfo Boncompagni Ludovisi, which now houses the US embassy: also known as the Palazzo Margherita, it was once the residence of Margherita of Savoy, Queen of Italy from 1878 to 1900.

Chiesa dei Frati Cappuccini

Via Vittorio Veneto 27, T06-487 1185, cappucciniviaveneto.it.
Fri-Wed 0900-1200, 1500-1800, free but donations welcomed.
Metro: Barberini.

The hidden treat on via Veneto is far removed from the sophisticated atmosphere that still permeates the area: it is the Church of the Capuchins, officially known as the **Chiesa della Santissima Concezione**, built between 1626 and 1630. Its most striking feature is undoubtedly the ossuary in the crypt – a burial place that the friars' patient work throughout the centuries has transformed into a unique work of art. Four of its five chapels have been intricately decorated with the bones and grinning skulls of some 4000 Capuchins, who died between 1528 and 1870. The names of the chapels are self-explanatory: Crypt of the Skulls, Crypt of the Pelvises (with a large baldachin composed of pelvic bones and vertebrae), Crypt of the Tibia and Thighbones, and Crypt of the Three Skeletons.

Tridente

The formal layout of three long streets – via del Corso, via di Ripetta and via del Babuino – radiating away from the huge space of the piazza dell Popolo, provided the name for this elegant district. The three prongs of the Trident were planned in the 16th century, enabling the carriages of the wealthy to escape the old city's congested lanes. From the city's main northern gate, the Porta del Popolo, via del Corso carried traffic to piazza Venezia and the Capitoline; via di Ripetta ran in the direction of the Vatican; and via del Babuino led to the piazza di Spagna and the Quirinale. Today's visitors don't want to rattle through the area, though; they come for serious shopping (or window-shopping) in Rome's most glamorous stores.

Below: Glove shop in the Tridente. Opposite page: Piazza del Popolo.

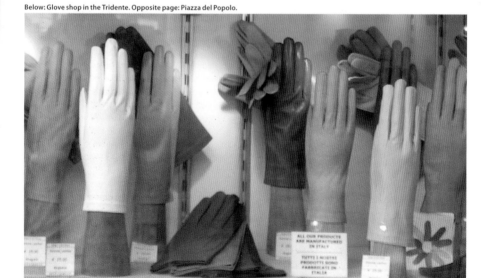

Piazza del Popolo

Metro: Flaminio. Map: Rome, D1, p84.

One of the finest examples of neoclassical architecture in Rome, this splendid piazza was designed by Giuseppe Valadier in 1793. Its central and most important feature is the 25-m **Flaminian obelisk**, which dates from 1200 BC and was originally erected by Rameses II in Heliopolis. It was the first Egyptian obelisk to be transferred to Rome by Emperor Augustus, who placed it in the Circus Maximus. Its current position dates back to 1589 and is the result of the indefatigable town-planning work of Pope Sixtus V and his architect Domenico Fontana.

At opposite ends of the piazza are two fountains. Both created by Giovanni Ceccarini in 1818-1821, they represent, on the west side, *Neptune between the Tritons* and, on the east, *Rome between the Tiber and the Aniene*. The other sculptures in the square – the sphinxes and the statues of the four seasons – are the work of different artists: Ceccarini, Filippo Guaccarini (*Spring*), Francesco Laboureur (*Summer*), Achille Stocchi (*Autumn*) and Felice Baini (*Winter*).

The piazza takes its name from the church on its northern side, **Santa Maria del Popolo**. The current building is the result of over six centuries of work in progress. The first church was built in 1099, financed by the people of Rome (hence the name). It was completely rebuilt in the 15th century, probably by Braccio Pontelli and Andrea Bregno, and was later modified by Bramante and Raphael – the latter designed the **Chigi Chapel** around 1516 for his patron, the Sienese banker Agostino Chigi, and supplied the designs for the mosaic panels in the dome, illustrating *The Creation of the World*. In the 17th century more alterations followed, this time in the shape of Bernini's Baroque interior.

Wonderful frescoes by Pinturicchio from 1508-1510 – *Coronation of the Virgin*, *Four Evangelists*, *Four Sybils* and *Four Doctors of the Church* – decorate the retro-choir, while the high altar boasts an early 13th-century panel in Byzantine style, the *Madonna del Popolo*, which tradition attributes to

It's a fact...

The Flaminian Obelisk was a source of fun for 19th-century Romans, who used to blindfold a playmate at its base and challenge them to walk as far as via del Corso. Very few managed it, because of the subtly irregular layout of the piazza.

the hand of St Luke. The real stars, however, are two spectacular paintings by Caravaggio, in the first chapel of the left transept: the *Conversion of Saint Paul* (right) and the *Crucifixion of Saint Peter* (left). Both were painted in 1600-1601, and Caravaggio's use of chiaroscuro (the dramatic contrast between light and dark), together with the austere realism of his treatment, marked a turning point in the history of art. Needless to say, his revolutionary genius was strongly criticized. A few years after their creation, when the two paintings were hung inside Santa Maria del Popolo, Poussin famously accused Caravaggio of having ruined Italian art.

Across the piazza, at the top of via del Corso, stand the 'twin' churches of **Santa Maria di Montesanto** (left) and **Santa Maria dei Miracoli** (right), two small masterpieces built by Bernini, together with Carlo Fontana, in the second half of the 17th century.

Above: Crowds in piazza di Spagna. Opposite page: The church of Trinita' del Monti, at the top of the Spanish Steps.

Casa di Goethe

Via del Corso 18, T06-3265 0412, casadigoethe.it.
Tue-Sun 1000-1800, €4/3 concession.
Metro: Flaminio. Map: Rome, D1, p84.

This is the house where painter Johann Heinrich Wilhelm Tischbein welcomed his friend Goethe from 1786 to 1788. It contains a large collection of letters, books, notes and copies of drawings related to the poet's journey to Italy, along with works by Tischbein himself, who painted Goethe during his stay. Temporary exhibitions and other cultural events are regularly held here.

Piazza di Spagna

Metro: Spagna. Map: Rome, E2, p84.

Bustling with Romans and tourists alike, all crowding the travertine staircase leading up to Trinità dei Monti, piazza di Spagna really is the outdoor theatre of Rome. It's been a magnet for artists and writers since the 16th century: the mysterious Cagliostro held his masonic meetings in a nearby inn, Giacomo Casanova wrote about the square in his *Memoirs*, and John Keats lived and died in the Casina Rossa at number 26 (now a museum dedicated to him and Shelley, see page 208).

The piazza is some 270 m long, narrowing in the middle; thus it's divided into two parts, almost resembling a butterfly's wings. It takes its name from the **Palazzo di Spagna**, which has been the seat of the Spanish Ambassador to the Holy See since the 17th century. Other notable buildings overlooking it include the **Palazzo del Collegio di Propaganda Fide** (a missionary training college), with one façade by Bernini (1664) and a more elaborate one by his rival Borromini (1667), and Borromini's **Cappella dei Re Magi** (1660-1664).

Opposite the Palazzo di Propaganda Fide is the **Colonna dell'Immacolata**, one of the last monuments of papal Rome. An ancient Roman column discovered in 1777 in the monastery of Santa Maria della Concezione, it was brought here by Pope Pius IX to celebrate the proclamation of the Dogma of the Immaculate Conception of Mary in 1854. Every year on 8 December, the city's firefighters, in the presence of the pope, pay tribute to the Virgin by placing a floral wreath on her statue at the top of the column.

The square's ideal fulcrum is the **Fontana della Barcaccia** (1627-1629) perhaps the best work of Pietro Bernini, who was probably helped by his more famous son Gian Lorenzo. According to tradition, the inspiration for this representation of a sinking boat came from Pope Urban VIII Barberini, who wanted to commemorate a boat that had been stranded in the square after the great flood of 1598. There is, however, another theory that the idea was Bernini's, and that he found an ingenious way to disguise the technical problem of inadequate water pressure by creating a fountain below ground level.

Scalinata di Trinità dei Monti

Metro: Spagna. Map: Rome, E2, p84.

The world's most spectacular outdoor staircase, the Spanish Steps were built entirely in travertine by Francesco de Sanctis in 1723-1726. The staircase consists of 138 steps, divided into 12 flights, which widen and narrow in varied stages, in accordance with the style of Rococo architecture. Built using French funds, it was designed to link the embassy of Bourbon Spain in the Palazzo di Spagna with the church at the top, which was under the patronage of the Bourbon kings of France.

The staircase was immediately a great success. Romans got into the habit of spending their evenings on the steps, improvising dances and concerts. In the 1800s, countrywomen from the Ciociaria region to the south of Rome used to come here to sell flowers and pose for the painters and sculptors who lived in the area.

Around the city

Chiesa della Santissima Trinità dei Monti

Metro: Spagna. Map: Rome, E2, p84.

Begun in 1502 by Louis XII and remodelled in the following centuries, Trinità dei Monti is one of the most impressive Franciscan churches in Rome. When it was built it must have looked very different – a little eerie, perhaps, as it was surrounded by a wood (which was often the scene of crimes) and isolated from the rest of the city. It would have been a perfect place for meditation, far from today's bustling atmosphere.

Valuable frescoes grace the single-nave interior. *Scenes from the Life of St John the Baptist* in the first chapel on the right are by Giambattista Naldini. The third chapel on the right contains an *Assumption* by Daniele da Volterra, the follower of Michelangelo who was commissioned to paint draperies over the nudes in the *Last Judgement* in the Sistine Chapel. Da Volterra's most famous work, dating from 1545, is the recently restored *Deposition* (in the second chapel on the left), which was based on drawings by Michelangelo.

The **Sallustian Obelisk** in front of the church is an ancient Roman monument in Egyptian style, found in the nearby gardens of Sallust, between the Pincio and Quirinale, and erected here by Pius VI in 1789. The hieroglyphics are a Roman imitation of those on the Flaminian obelisk in piazza del Popolo.

Keats-Shelley House

Piazza di Spagna 26, T06-678 4235, keats-shelley-house.org.
Mon-Fri 1000-1300, 1400-1800, Sat 1100-1400, 1500-1800, €4/3 concession, free under 6.
Metro: Spagna. Map: Rome, E2, p84.

When John Keats, seriously ill with tuberculosis, travelled to Italy, he was hoping that the warmer climate would improve his health. Unfortunately, he died a few months after reaching Rome, on 23 February 1821, in this house at the bottom of the Spanish Steps. He was 25. He is buried in the Non-Catholic Cemetery in Testaccio (see page 81). Percy Bysshe Shelley, hounded out of England by his creditors and society's disapproval of his atheism, had settled permanently in Italy in 1818, producing much of his major poetry here. He drowned at sea, aged 29, in mysterious circumstances, and his body was washed up at Viareggio on the Tuscan coast. His ashes are also in the Non-Catholic cemetery.

In 1903, a group of English and American admirers of the two poets started to raise the funds necessary to purchase the building in which Keats had lodged, and the Keats-Shelley Memorial House was opened in 1909 by King Vittorio Emanuele III. It contains relics associated with the lives of the two poets, from manuscripts, letters and artworks to a lock of Keats' own hair. Equally important is a library of Romantic literature that contains approximately 10,000 books and manuscripts, including material documenting the fervid cultural relations between England and Italy during the Romantic period.

Casa Museo Giorgio de Chirico

Piazza di Spagna 31, T06-679 6546.
Visits by appointment only, Tue-Sat and 1st Sun of each month, 1000, 1045, 1130, 1215, €5/3 concession.
Metro: Spagna. Map: Rome, E2, p84.

Located in the 17th-century Borgognoni palace, where de Chirico lived and worked from 1948 onwards, this memorial museum houses paintings, sculptures and graphic works from the artist's private collection. *Portrait of Isa with yellow mantle* and *Self-portrait in the garden* deserve a special mention. The artist's studio has also been preserved.

Tip...

If you want to live like a Romantic poet for a few days, a flat in the Keats-Shelley House is available to rent (see page 214).

A portraitist's easel just by the Sallustian obelisk, at the top of the Spanish Steps.

A walk around Tridente

From piazza di Spagna, walk down via Condotti. This elegant street, which links the piazza with the commercial hub of via del Corso, is Rome's Fifth Avenue, with the city's highest concentration of designer shops. It owes its name to the underground conduits of the Acqua Vergine aqueduct. At number 86 is the Antico Caffè Greco, a famous meeting place for numerous 19th-century artists, writers and composers, including Liszt, Gounod, Stendhal, Heine, Wagner, Schopenhauer, Twain, Gogol, Trilussa and d'Annunzio. Founded in 1760 by Nicola della Maddalena, a Greek, this luxurious café allowed its regulars to receive their correspondence here: letters were delivered to a wooden box situated near the entrance.

Via del Babuino, famous for its antique shops, is named after a small fountain by the Church of San **Atanasio dei Greci** (number 149, T06-3600 1260). The statue overlooking the granite basin is supposed to represent a reclining Silenus (the mythological companion of Bacchus, portrayed as half man, half goat), but it was so ugly that the Romans nicknamed it 'the Baboon'. Tradition has it that an ageing cardinal used to kneel down respectfully before the statue every time he passed by, mistaking it for a portrait of St Jerome. The Baboon was one of Rome's 'speaking statues' (see page 74) but all the satirical graffiti have recently been removed. The 16th-century church, with its brick façade and two belfries, was commissioned by Pope Gregory XIII to become a spiritual and cultural centre for

Greek Catholics. During his stay in Rome, Goethe apparently loved to take part in the magnificent Byzantine liturgy.

Next door to the church is the **Museo Atelier Canova Tadolini** (150, T06-3211 0702, museoateliercanovatadolini.it, Mon-Sat 0800-2030), a small two-storey construction where Antonio Canova used to work with Adamo Tadolini, his most talented protégé. Recently reopened as a café, it is the perfect place to have a drink surrounded by marble sculptures, as well as plaster casts of some of Canova's most famous works.

Also worth a look is the red-brick neo-Gothic complex of the **Anglican Church of All Saints** (1882-87). It is by George Edmund Street, one of the leading British architects of the Gothic revival.

Parallel with via del Babuino runs **via Margutta**, dotted with artists' workshops. The pretty **Fontana delle Arti** near number 54 was created by Pietro Lombardi in 1927, and honours the local artists in its depiction of easels, stands, paintbrushes and other tools. The street retains some of its old artisan charm, thanks to the presence of workshops such as **La Bottega del Marmoraro** (53b, T06-320 7660, Mon-Sat 0800-1930), where marble is still worked using traditional techniques. Last but not least, don't forget to peep into the courtyards of the old apartment buildings – in one of them (110) Federico Fellini lived with his wife Giulietta Masina.

Sleeping

Grand Hotel Parco dei Principi €€€€
Via Gerolamo Frescobaldi 5, T06-854421, parcodeiprincipi.com.
Bus: 52, 217, 910.
Map: Rome, G1, p85.
A stone's throw from Villa Borghese, the hotel is in a peaceful situation in a lovely park. Rooms are large and opulent, with elegant (if not stuffy) decor. It has an outdoor Olympic-size swimming pool, which is also available to non-residents (€35 per day Mon-Fri, €60 Sat-Sun). The rooms overlooking the swimming pool have great views across Villa Borghese towards the Vatican.

Rose Garden €€€€
Via Boncompagni 19, T06-421741, rosegardenpalace.com.
Metro: Barberini.
Map: Rome, F2, p85.
Spacious, beautifully appointed rooms, a fitness centre with sauna and an indoor swimming pool with jacuzzi are the highlights of this recently opened hotel, housed in an early 20th-century palazzo. Free Wi-Fi, and free minibar once a day.

Aleph €€€
Via di San Basilio 15, T06-422901, aleph.boscolohotels.com.
Metro: Barberini.
Map: Rome, F2, p85.
Architect Adam D. Tihany conceived this hotel as a Dantesque journey through the contrasting concepts of Heaven and Hell. The result is one of Rome's most sophisticated hotels, from the blessed delights of its Paradise Spa (also open to non-residents) to the temptations of the flame-red Maremoto Restaurant. Its 96 elegant – though not very large – rooms mix Italian art deco with minimalist chic.
The staff are helpful and friendly, and the location is excellent: a perfect fashionista's address.

Hassler €€€€
Piazza Trinità dei Monti 6, T06-699340, hotelhassler.it.
Metro: Spagna.
Map: Rome, E2, p84.
The prima donna of Rome's fanciest hotels, right at the top of the Spanish Steps. Each of the 95 rooms is uniquely decorated. Think vast expanses of marble, Baroque furniture and sumptuous chandeliers. Service is impeccable, as you would expect.

Hotel Art €€€€
Via Margutta 56, T06-328711, hotelart.it.
Metro: Spagna.
Map: Rome, E2, p84.
Opened in 2002, this is a great mix of old and contemporary, combining a 19th-century palazzo with sleek, funky design. The check-in and concierge area are two white pods in the lobby, under beautiful vaulted ceilings, while the Crystal Bar occupies a space that used to be a chapel. Upstairs, corridors are in funky shades – the most sought-after is apparently the relaxing blue on the top floor – but the 46 rooms are pleasantly minimalistic, with creamy bed linen and dark wood furniture. Ask for one with a view over the lovely courtyard. There's also a small gym with sauna and Turkish bath, and their business centre is open 24/7.

Hotel de Russie €€€€
Via del Babuino 9, T06-328881, hotelderussie.it.
Metro: Flaminio.
Map: Rome, D1, p84.
Exclusive yet understated elegance: Mapplethorpe floral prints and bathrooms with mosaic artworks are the most memorable features. Some standard rooms are rather small,

though – it's advisable to pay the supplement for a more spacious executive double. There is also a great 'wellness zone', with a sauna, Turkish bath and saltwater whirlpool bath, where you can be pampered at the end of a long shopping day.

Portrait Suites €€€€
Via Bocca di Leone 23, T06-6938 0742, lungarnohotels.com.
Metro: Spagna.
Map: Rome, E2, p84.
Salvatore Ferragamo's luxury 'town house' is exactly how you would expect a fashion designer's hotel to be. The 14 suites and studios each have their own stylish, fully equipped kitchenette,

cashmere blankets and DVD player. The greatest care goes into the smallest details – you can even leave your laptop to recharge inside the safe. Breakfast is served in your room or, even better, on the rooftop terrace, from where you can enjoy a fantastic view of the city.

Hotel d'Inghilterra €€€
Via Bocca di Leone 14, T06-699811, royaldemeure.com.
Metro: Spagna.
Map: Centro Storico, F2, p96.
One of the 'big names' of the capital, offering luxury right in the heart of the shopping district. Full of character, housed in the palazzo that previously

belonged to the Torlonia princes, it still oozes charm, although it could well do with some updating. Each of the 97 individually appointed rooms has a classical theme – think chandeliers, damasks and silks, Baroque mirrors and Chinese porcelain.

Il Palazzetto €€€
Vicolo del Bottino 8, T06-6993 41000, ilpalazzettoroma.com.
Metro: Spagna.
Map: Centro Storico, F1, p96.
They call themselves *affittacamere* (rooms to rent), but they're very exclusive indeed: four rooms only, three of them with breathtaking views over the

although the hotel has been recently restored, the rooms have retained that old-fashioned style that still characterizes many Rome hotels, with wallpaper and Venetian stucco.

Self-catering

The Landmark Trust
Piazza di Spagna 26,
T+44(0)1628-825925 (UK),
landmarktrust.org.uk.
Metro: Spagna.
Leased by British conservation charity the Landmark Trust, this is undoubtedly the most special apartment on offer in the whole city. It is located inside the Casina Rossa, on the floor above the rooms where John Keats died in 1821, and identical in form and layout. Keats would probably feel quite at home here, as everything has been restored to its original condition (though with a very welcome concession to double glazing), with tiled floors, tall windows and fantastic views of the Spanish Steps. A must for anybody looking for inspiration, it sleeps up to four people (from €490 per night, min stay 3 nights).

Spanish Steps. This is sister to the Hassler, and a cheaper alternative; you can also use the hotel's facilities. Il Palazzetto restaurant and wine bar is downstairs (see page 215).

Residenza A €€€

Via Veneto 183, T06-486700,
hotelviaveneto.com.
Metro: Spagna.
Map: Rome, F2, p84.
On the first floor of a via Veneto palazzo, this calls itself 'The Boutique Art Hotel' and it definitely ticks all the boxes: luxuriously finished rooms with great bonuses such as Apple flatscreen computers, DVD players and free internet. Breakfast is either at Caffè Strega (opposite the hotel) or en suite at no extra charge. They'll even throw in a daily newspaper for free. Advance booking is a must to snap up one of the seven rooms on offer.

Hotel Forte €€

Via Margutta 61, T06-320 7625,
hotelforte.com.
Metro: Spagna.
Map: Centro Storico, F1, p96.
Located on the first floor of a 17th-century palazzo in peaceful via Margutta, with a wrought-iron lift, the hotel has 19 rooms. The singles are rather small and,

Eating & drinking

Papà Baccus €€€
Via Toscana 36, T06-4274 2808,
papabaccus.com.
Mon-Fri 1230-1500, 1930-2330,
Sat 1930-2330.
Bus: 52, 88, 910.
Map: Rome, F2, p84.
The specialities of this family-run
Tuscan place are salami and
sausages from the Cinta Senese
pig, an ancient breed that
originated in the countryside
around Siena and feeds on
acorns, chestnuts and tubers.
The pork comes from the family's
own farm in the Foreste
Casentinesi National Park.

Tuna €€
Via Veneto 11, T06-4201 6531,
tunaroma.com.
Mon-Fri 1200-1500, 1930-2400,
Sat-Sun 1930-2400.
Metro: Barberini.
Map: Centro Storico, H2, p97.
This is one of the newest
additions to the string of elegant
places in the via Veneto area.
They call themselves a *pescheria*
(fishmonger) – but a very posh
one indeed. The menu is strictly
fish-based, amid elegant
minimal-chic-meets-Baroque
white decor, with friendly service.

Cafés & bars
Laboratorio Pasticceria
Lambiase Antonio
Via Cernaia 49/a, T06-494 1363.
Metro: Castro Pretorio.
The place that Roman night owls

visit before calling it a night – an
underground bakery open all
night long. Locals cram in to buy
a *sorchetta*, a mouth-watering
pastry topped with cream and
chocolate. The queue is endless
but it's well worth the wait, and
you'll feel you've been initiated
into the real Rome of the
Romans.

Lotti
Via Sardegna 19-21, T06-482 1902.
Sun-Fri 0700-2230.
Metro: Barberini.
Just off the upper part of via
Veneto, Lotti has been in
business since 1917 and serves
spectacular pastries, of which
the *tortino* with ricotta is one
of the most delicious.

Dal Bolognese €€€
Piazza del Popolo 1/2,
T06-361 1426.
Tue-Sun 1245-1500, 2015-2315.
Metro: Flaminio.
Map: Rome, D1, p84.
The best of Emilia Romagna
cuisine – think tortellini and
other regional delicacies. Eat at
one of the outside tables, right
on the grand piazza, brushing
shoulders with the politicians,
diplomats and TV celebrities
who are habitués of this place.
Book in advance.

Il Palazzetto €€€
Vicolo del Bottino 8, T06-6993
41000, ilpalazzettoroma.com.
Tue-Sun 1200-1530, 1930-2230.
Metro: Spagna.
Map: Rome, E2, p84.
Chef Vincenzo di Tuoro cooks
Italian recipes revisited with a
contemporary twist. Aside from
the beautifully presented food,
the other highlight of the place is
its enviable location, just behind
the Spanish Steps. Its scenic
terrace in Trinità dei Monti offers
an amazing vista and is a real
bonus, especially on a bright
sunny day. Cheaper light lunch
options are available.

Nino €€€
Via Borgognona 11, T06-679 5676.
Mon-Sat 1230-1500, 1930-2300.
Metro: Spagna.
Map: Centro Storico, F2, p84.
Opened in 1934, this restaurant
is still pretty much a family
business. Tuscan-born owner
Alberto Antonucci serves tasty
dishes true to his region.
Specialities include game
dishes and Tuscan classics
such as *bistecca alla fiorentina*
(T-bone steak).

Osteria Margutta €€€
Via Margutta 82, T06-323 1025,
osteriamargutta.it.
Mon-Sat 1200-1500, 1930-2400.
Metro: Spagna.
Map: Rome, E1, p84.
The accent is on Roman food,
with a fresh fish menu three
times a week (Tue, Fri, Sat).

The red and blue decor has a distinctly Parisian feel. Booking recommended.

Margutta RistorArte €€
Via Margutta 118, T06-3265 0577, ilmargutta.it.
Daily 1230-1530, 1930-2330.
Metro: Spagna.
Map: Rome, D1, p84.
This place has been serving a fully vegetarian menu since 1979, which is a pleasant surprise considering Italy is not exactly a vegetarian-friendly country. In addition to the traditional menu, you can enjoy a 'Green Brunch' from €12. They do yummy – though pricey – chocolate desserts.

Palatium – Enoteca Regionale €€
Via Frattina 94, T06-6920 2132, enotecapalatium.it.
Mon-Sat 1100-2400.
Metro: Spagna.
Map: Centro Storico, F2, p96.
A multi-sensory journey though the aromas and flavours of the region of Lazio. They offer 181 different wines, to be matched with over 1,000 typical products – all of them strictly regional. The menu also features a kosher section, in homage to the Judeo-Roman culinary tradition.

Di Fronte A €
Via della Croce 38; T06-678 0355.
Tue-Sun 1230-2330.
Metro: Spagna.
Map: Centro Storico, E1, p96.
On a quiet pedestrianized street, this funky restaurant is popular with a young crowd. The decor is pleasantly bright, with yellow and red walls and bare bricks. The kitchen is open all day so you can pop in for a pizza whenever you feel hunger pangs.

Cafés & bars
Antico Caffè Greco
Via Condotti 86, T06-679 1700, anticocaffegreco.eu.
Sun-Mon 1030-1900;
Tue-Sat 0900-1930.
Metro: Spagna.
A hotspot for writers and artists since it opened in 1760, it still retains its 19th-century appeal and is the perfect place to drink coffee in style while resting your eyes from the temptations of via Condotti's shop windows.

Babington's Tea Room
Piazza di Spagna 23, T06-678 6027, babingtons.com.
Daily 0900-2015.
Metro: Spagna.
They've been serving tea and scones *all'inglese* to nostalgic Anglo-Saxons and Romans alike since the Misses Babington and Cargill first put the kettle on in 1893. Famously, not even the Second World War drove them out of business and they

continued to make tea even during the German occupation. A proper Victorian atmosphere in Rome does not come cheap, though.

Caffè Rosati
Piazza del Popolo 4/5a, T06-322 5859, rosatibar.it.
Metro: Flaminio.
An institution since 1922, it's very popular with Roman intellectuals, no doubt attracted by its good selection of cakes. The elegant atmosphere comes at a price, though – coffees start at €4.50.

Museo Atelier Canova Tadolini
Via del Babuino 150a/b, T06-3211 0702, museoateliercanovatadolini.it.
Mon-Sat 0800-2030.
Metro: Spagna.
One of Rome's most atmospheric cafés, located in Antonio Canova's workshop: you can drink your espresso surrounded by impressive neoclassical sculptures. Unmissable.

Entertainment

Cinema

Casa del Cinema
Largo Marcello Mastroianni 1,
Villa Borghese, T06-423601,
casadelcinema.it.
Daily, times vary.
Metro: Spagna.
Opened in 2004 in the
Casina delle Rose, the 'House
of Cinema' has two projection
halls, a bookshop, café and
exhibition area. Films are shown
in their original language with
subtitles. Screenings are free
and can be popular, so arrive
early. There's also a **DVD room**
(Tue-Sun 1600-2000, dvdonline@
palaexpo.it) with over 2500
movies to watch on computer,
also free: download the
catalogue from the website.

Clubs

Gilda
Via Mario de' Fiori 97,
T06-678 4838, gildabar.it.
Wed-Sun 2300-0400.
Metro: Spagna.
An evergreen nightclub since
1987, it's a favourite with writers,
politicians and actors. Jacket
required.

Music

Auditorium Parco della Musica
Viale Pietro de Coubertin 30,
T06-370 0106, auditorium.com.
Box office daily 1100-2000.
Metro: Flaminio, then tram 2.
Bus: M, 217, 910.
The Auditorium is the home of
the **Accademia Nazionale di
Santa Cecilia** (santacecilia.it),
which plays a full programme of
classical orchestral and chamber
concerts.

Gregory's Jazz

Via Gregoriana 54a;
T06-679 6386, gregorysjazz.com.
Tue-Sun 2100-0200.
Metro: Spagna.
This English pub is a little temple to
jazz music. The other highlight is
the very good selection of Scotch,
Irish and American whiskies.

Theatre

Silvano Toti Globe Theatre
Largo Aqua Felix, Villa Borghese,
T06-0608, globetheatreroma.com.
Jun-Sep Tue-Sun 2115, standing
€10/7 concession, balcony seats
from €7/5.
Metro: Flaminio. Bus: 116.
The open-air theatre faithfully
modelled on Shakespeare's
Globe in London was created in
2003, the idea of Roman actor
Gigi Proietti. It has a capacity of
1,250, with 450 standing in the
pit, as in the Elizabethan original.
Most of the productions,
naturally, are Shakespeare's
plays (mainly in Italian).

Shopping

Art & antiques

Via del Babuino is great for antiques, and via Margutta is the street of artists, with several art galleries to visit.

Alinari

Via Alibert 16a,
T06-679 2923, alinari.com.
Mon 1500-1900, Thu-Sat
0900-1300, 1500-1900.
Metro: Spagna.
The Rome shop of a famous Florentine family of photographers, where you can purchase beautiful prints.

Animalier & Oltre

Via Margutta 47, T06-320 8282,
animaliereoltre.com.
Mon 1530-1930, Tue-Sat
0930-1300, 1530-1930.
Metro: Spagna.
Interesting furniture, antiques and animal-themed curios.

Alberto di Castro

Via del Babuino 71, T06-361 3752,
dicastrostampe.com.
Mon 1530-1930, Tue-Sat
0930-1300, 1530-1930.
Metro: Spagna.
Lovely antique prints and engravings of the city.

Books & stationery

Cartotecnica Romana

Via Frattina 124, T06-679 0404,
cartotecnicaromana.it.
Mon 1530-1930, Tue-Fri
0930-1300, 1530-1930,
Sat 0930-1300.
Metro: Spagna.

This shop has sold exclusive fountain pens and elegant stationery since 1914.

Pineider

Via dei Due Macelli 68,
T06-679 5884, pineider.com.
Mon-Sat 1000-1900, Sun
1100-1400, 1500-1900.
Metro: Spagna.
A famous brand established in 1774, specializing in fine papers and stationery.

The Lion Bookshop

Via dei Greci 33/36, T06-3265 4007,
thelionbookshop.com.
Mon 1530-1930, Tue-Sat
1000-1930, Sun 1000-1930.
Metro: Flaminio or Spagna.
Just round the corner from via del Babuino, they specialize in English titles, with over 30,000 books to choose from.

Clothes

The area around piazza di Spagna and via Condotti is the prime location for designer shopping, and most names need no introduction. In piazza di Spagna you'll find the boutiques of **Missoni** (number 78), **Dolce e Gabbana** (94/95), **Dior** (73/75), **Sergio Rossi** (98), **Genny** (27), and **Krizia** (87). **Francesco Biasia**'s stylish bags are at 62a. Just off piazza di Spagna is a branch of **Dimensione Danza** (via San Sebastianello 5), great for dance and fitness wear.

Via Condotti is a fashionista's heaven: **Armani** (76), **Valentino**

(15), **Gucci** (8), **Ferragamo** (72), **Prada** (88-93), **Alberta Ferretti** (34), **Max Mara** (17-20) and **La Perla** (78-79) are all there, together with many others. For jewellery, **Cartier** (10) and **Bulgari** (82) face each other, and just next door is **Damiani** (84), with stylish contemporary jewels.

There are more designer stores along via Borgognona: **Gianfranco Ferrè** (7a/c), **Moschino** (33), **Pucci** (21) and **Laura Biagiotti** (43). Make sure you have a look in **Rene Caovilla**'s gorgeous store (9-10): the address for modern Cinderellas who are after simply fabulous evening shoes.

Via Frattina, parallel to via Condotti, has several shops that are particularly popular with a young crowd, including **Gente** (70) and **L'Altra Moda** (118). **Abitart** (via della Croce 46/47) is a little boutique packed with colourful and funky dresses by young Roman designer Vanessa Foglia. For more retail therapy along via Veneto, there's **Versace** (104) and **Luisa Spagnoli** (130).

Food & drink

You probably won't need the services of a butcher during your stay in Rome, but it's worth peeping through the window of **Macelleria Annibale** (via di Ripetta 236/237), one of the oldest in Rome, still with its original 19th-century fittings.

Fratelli Fabbi
Via della Croce 27/28,
T06-679 0612, fabbi.it.
Metro: Spagna.
An excellent deli, perfect for
foodies looking for Italian
delicacies, with a mouth-
watering display of cheese
and cold cuts.

Salsamenteria Croce
Via della Croce 78b, T06-678 3153.
Metro: Spagna.
Nice, minimalistic place to get
panini, salads or quiches. Eat in
or take away.

Homewares
Fornari & Fornari
Via Frattina 133, T06-678 0105,
fornariandfornari.com.
Mon-Sat 1000-1930.
Metro: Spagna.
Beautiful, stylish designer
kitchenware.

TAD
Via del Babuino 155a,
T06-3269 5131, taditaly.com.
Mon 1200-1930, Tue-Fri
1030-1930, Sat 1030-2000,
Sun 1200-2000.
Metro: Spagna.

One of the funkiest stores
in the area. The stock is very
eclectic, from the flowers at the
entrance to colourful fabrics
from all over the world, cool
designer furniture and ethnic
CDs. There is also a hairstylist
and a café.

Contents

Trevi, Quirinale, Monti & Esquilino

One of Rome's must-see sights, the Trevi Fountain marks
the spot where springwater, channelled down a 20-km
aqueduct, arrived in the city.

Introduction

I f ancient Rome set the pattern for the modern city, Suburra, in Monti, was the original suburb – the name of its swampy origins is even the source of the word. Monti has continued to be an originator. As in Centro Storico, a walk through its streets reveals ironmongers and carpenters hard at work, but here they're working alongside artisans producing bespoke jewellery and clothing collections.

While Monti retains its deliciously local vibe, and is still undiscovered by most visitors to Rome, on the other side of the Quirinale the city's best-known fountain, la Fontana di Trevi, continues to be a huge tourist attraction. So many coins are thrown into the fountain for luck, and to ensure a return visit, that around €10,000 is collected each week. Now there's fun to be had indoors in this area too, thanks to renovations over the last decade. They have resulted in two world-class exhibition spaces for temporary art shows – the Scuderie del Quirinale and the Palazzo delle Esposizioni – and the visit-worthy Palazzo Massimo alle Terme, where the ancient Roman statues that once filled the Terme di Diocleziano are now beautifully displayed.

What to see in...

...one day
Start off at the **Fontana di Trevi**, nip into **Palazzo delle Esposizioni** or the **Scuderie** if there's an exhibition that appeals, then go to **Palazzo Massimo alle Terme**. After that, best speed to **Monti**, independent shoppers' haven, also replete with galleries and crammed with off-the-beaten-track bars and restaurants.

...a weekend or more
On the first day you'll have time to visit **Galleria Colonna** before heading up to one of the temporary exhibitions at the **Palazzo delle Esposizione** or the **Scuderie**. Next day head to **Palazzo Massimo alle Terme** to stroll round some very well-presented ancient statues. If the **Domus Aurea** has reopened it's *the* excavation site to see the excesses of one emperor. If not, the mosaics in **Santa Maria Maggiore** are quite a showstopper. End the afternoon with a browse around the tiny workshops, boutiques and galleries in **Monti** before an *aperitivo* and dinner on one of the little piazzas you've passed en route.

Trevi & Quirinale

While the crest of the hill is dominated by the white façade of the Palazzo del Quirinale, the president's official residence, this area is most famous for the Trevi Fountain, tucked away in the maze of little streets. Although other fountains in Rome are grander and have more spacious settings, the much-visited, very central Trevi has been the focus of songs, poems and films. Also in the area are two of Rome's best temporary exhibition spaces, the Scuderie del Quirinale and the Palazzo delle Esposizioni, gleaming from renovations that have brought both to a world-class level. In sharp contrast is Galleria Colonna, where visitors can peep into the small but very opulent wing of a palazzo that is still a private home.

Mermen blow on conches in the elaborate sculpture that is the Fontana di Trevi.

La Fontana di Trevi

Piazza di Trevi.
Metro: Barberini. Map: Rome, E3, p84.

"Ti senti l'acqua?" Italians ask excitedly as they approach the Trevi Fountain, because you can hear it, along with the hum of the crowd that throngs it night and day, flicking so many coins into the water for luck or for a return visit that €500,000 is picked up annually. An easy walk from the Centro Storico, the Trevi is always surrounded by photo-taking tourists, dodging the sellers of tat to throw in their coins.

The Trevi Fountain is a very Rome-specific phenomenon. Yes, Anita Ekberg did splash very provocatively at Marcello Mastroianni while wearing a stunning strapless dress in Federico Fellini's 1960 film *La Dolce Vita*, and yes, the underwater lamps do make the rippling reflections very pretty at night. That said, it is a cascade, not a thunderous roar, of water; it rather strangely backs on to the façade of a building rather than being freestanding; it is not Rome's loveliest sculpture; and its very name gives away the fact that it's folded into a web of narrow lanes (*tre vie* means 'three streets'). Like the inexplicably massive popularity of the Spanish Steps, la Fontana di Trevi's must-see status seems to exceed what it is. There are bigger, more gracious fountains that celebrate the arrival of water that's travelled much farther to reach the city. There are less-awkward-looking central figures. La Fontana dell'Acqua Paola, for example, set on the crest of the hill at **Gianicolo** (see page 175), with its 180-degree view across Rome to the often snow-capped mountains beyond, is more romantic in setting and more sober in its sculptural backdrop.

The Trevi's reason for being can be traced back a couple of millennia. Even 2000 years ago the water from the Tiber wasn't the thinking man's choice for a drink. Instead, water was channelled down purpose-built aqueducts from as far away as Lake Bracciano (about 40 km northwest of Rome). After the successful completion of each aqueduct, it's believed that a spectacular fountain was constructed to mark the water's arrival for the citizens to use in their homes. These ancient celebratory fountains all disappeared. But echoing the work of the Roman emperors, various popes in the 16th and 17th centuries restored the long-broken-up aqueducts and rebuilt the fountains where they might once have stood.

The Trevi Fountain is the product of one of the earliest such projects. In 1570 Pope Pius V restored Emperor Agrippa's ancient aqueduct, the Acqua Vergine, bringing fresh water from a spring about 20 km east of the city. Although Gian Lorenzo Bernini was initially commissioned, in 1732 the somewhat less brilliant Niccolò Salvi and his team of sculptors started the much-delayed fountain for Pope Clement XII; it took 30 years to complete, but in the interim Salvi died, and his scheme was much altered, so it's not clear who we have to thank for the central, slightly knock-kneed figure standing in a shell, surrounded by mermen trumpeting on conches, with a plunging Pegasus on each side, all set on a deck of coral.

No matter how hot the day, the water is a no-go zone, and not just because of the whistle-blowing police that stand by but because of the high bleach content that keeps the water so tantalizingly green.

Tip...

Try to get to Trevi early in the morning so you can see the fountain without feeling you're walking into someone's photo, or they're walking into yours – or worse, you have to wait for a gap in the crowd to get to the railing.

Colossal statues of horse tamers Castor and Pollux embellish a fountain on the enormous piazza del Quirinale.

Galleria Colonna

Via della Pilotta 17, T06-678 4350, galleriacolonna.it.
Sat only 0900-1300, closed 25 Jul-29 Aug, €10/8
concession, free guided tour in English 1145.
Bus: H, 40, 60, 64, 70, 170. Map: Rome, E4, p84.

Although the Colonna Gallery is best known for a
central, glittering room, the fact that it is accessed
through a side door and up narrow back stairs
makes the visual richness quite unexpected. The
house is still the private home of the Colonna family,
which accounts for the restricted opening hours.

The main room is so abundantly full of
gilt-framed mirrors and paintings it's almost
dazzling. The honey-coloured marble was taken
from an ancient Roman temple nearby: the
'recycling' was permitted by the then Barberini
pope, Urban VIII – the very same who'd stripped
travertine from the Colosseum for St Peter's and
bronze from the Pantheon to make cannons.
A cannonball, incidentally, still sits on the marble

step where it smash-landed – a memento
of the 1848 crossfire between Garibaldi's
freedom fighters and the pro-pope supporters
at the Quirinale.

Frescoes overhead recount the tale of the
military glory of an early Colonna family member:
he's positioned next to Hercules in a big show of
strength. And if the statues seem out of proportion,
they are: as gardeners came across limbs, legs or
bases, they were pieced together, resulting in the
figures' slightly wonky appearances.

A collection of tiny bas-relief copies of famous
works of art are serious status-markers: most families
had one or two, but the Colonnas commissioned so
many that a large ebony dresser was specially made
to display them. Starting from *The Last Judgement*
centre stage, how many can you identify?

Much is made of Antonio Carracci's unattractive
Beaneater, significant because it heralds the arrival
of the Realism movement and the use of dull
colours that dried quickly.

Just before leaving, look at the series of works painted in 1565 by Michele di Ridolfo del Ghirlandaio; when they were cleaned in 2002, the fabric draped over the reclining ladies was removed, as it had been identified as having been added in the mid-1840s, when such nudity was considered overwhelming.

Piazza del Quirinale

Metro: Repubblica or Cavour.
Bus: H, 40, 60, 64, 70, 170. Map: Rome, E4, p84.

The Quirinale is a good spot to look out across the city towards the much higher Gianicolo hill. And the best place to admire the view is leaning on the parapet-like wall of piazza del Quirinale. The fountain on the piazza is, as usual, an assemblage of disparate elements but, unusually, all the pieces date from ancient Rome. The most beautiful part is the granite basin, which was brought here from the Forum. The colossal statues of the two horse tamers, Castor and Pollux, who are wrestling with enormous, shire-horse-sized beasts, are copies of even earlier Greek originals. The 15-m obelisk is a Roman copy of an Egyptian original, which Emperor Augustus had placed by his tomb (see page 123); later it was presumably pushed over and covered in silt, and subsequently unearthed and brought to this piazza.

Palazzo del Quirinale

Piazza del Quirinale, T06-46991, quirinale.it.
Sun only 0830-1200, closed mid-Jun-mid-Sep, €5, free under 18 and over 65; gardens open 2 Jun only, 1500-1900, free.
Metro: Repubblica or Cavour.
Bus: H, 40, 60, 64, 70, 170. Map: Rome, E3, p84.

Built in 1573 as a papal summer residence, the Quirinal Palace became the official royal residence after the unification of Italy in 1870. When the monarchy was abolished in 1946, it passed to the president of the Republic. It's paradoxical, given that complaining about politicians is practically a national pastime, that Italians line up in their

thousands to visit. Presumably a fascination for power is the attraction, because walking through the corridors is really all that visitors get to do.

The visit consists of a cordoned-off walkway through 20-odd rooms encircling a courtyard. As furniture is removed from the rooms before the arrival of the public, what's on show is limited to enormous Murano chandeliers, some paintings and tapestries. It's worth look up on entering the last room, the Great Hall of the Corazzieri, or cavalry: an entertaining trompe l'œil fresco has revellers hanging over the edge of a painted loggia that runs round the upper walls; it was painted by Agostino Tassi, Giovanni Lanfranco and Carlo Saraceni in 1616.

Capella Paolina, a chapel in the Palazzo del Quirinale complex, rivals the Sistine chapel in size and splendour.

Via del Quirinale, alongside the Quirinale Palace.

The palace has a chapel by Carlo Maderno, the Cappella Paolina, which rivals the Vatican's Sistine Chapel in size and splendour. It isn't open to the public, but concerts are regularly held there for live broadcast (Oct-Jun, Sun 1200): if you time your visit so that you reach it – at the end of the tour – around 1130 you can look in through the open door, and you may be able to get a seat in the audience if you want to stay for the music.

Scuderie del Quirinale

Via XXIV Maggio 16, T06-3996 7500, scuderiequirinale.it.
Tue-Thu and Sun 1000-2000, Fri-Sat 1000-2230, €10/7.50 concession, combined ticket with Palazzo delle Esposizioni (valid 3 days) €18/15 concession, free under 6.
Metro: Repubblica or Cavour.
Bus: H, 40, 60, 64, 70, 170. Map: Rome, E3, p84.

A showpiece exhibition site, and the former stable block of the Palazzo Quirinale across the square, the

> ## Tip...
> Scuderie exhibitions are popular, so don't plan on going at the weekend if you can avoid it. You can reserve tickets to avoid the queues (T06-3996 7500); there's a booking fee of €1.50.

Scuderie has become known for its must-see shows. The space is rented from the Quirinale, so although the Scuderie is managed by the same team who run the Palazzo delle Esposizioni (see page 229), the Scuderie's exhibition content tends to be more classical: recent shows have featured the work of Giovanni Bellini, Antonello da Messina and Albrecht Dürer. That said, while the subjects might be traditional, thanks to the talented display and lighting designers installing the exhibitions, the shows prove universally popular. It's not uncommon to see queues stretching down the street every weekend in the closing month of a show.

Like its big sister the Palazzo delle Esposizioni around the corner, the Scuderie has no permanent collection of its own, but because it is a much smaller space, it mounts only one exhibition at a time. Between the end of one show and the inauguration of the next, the Scuderie is closed for a full month. They tend to run from late September to early January and from February to early June, with a smaller exhibition through July and August, so check the upcoming schedule on the website to avoid disappointment. The summer exhibition always features photography, and to tie in with the theme accompanying films are screened on the Scuderie's terrace.

Palazzo delle Esposizioni

Via Nazionale 194, T06-3996 7500, palazzoesposizioni.it.
Tue-Thu and Sun 1000-2000, Fri-Sat 1000-2230, €12.50/10 concession, combined ticket with Scuderie del Quirinale (valid 3 days) €18/15 concession, free under 6.
Metro: Repubblica or Cavour. Bus: H, 64, 70, 71, 170, 640. Map: Rome, F3, p84.

Hosting up to three major temporary shows at a time, the newly reopened exhibition centre is one of Rome's top galleries. The immense spaces in the palazzo lend themselves to the often very physical events (which often have enormous models or enclosed DVD viewing rooms) staged by the competent in-house team and guest curators. Built in the 19th century, the palazzo was designed for this purpose and it is still gleaming after opening in autumn 2007 following a colossal, five-year makeover.

The world-class level of the palazzo's exhibits gives it the status to collaborate with major centres of fashion, art, photography and other disciplines, within Europe and beyond, to stage exhibitions that range from an acclaimed Rothko show to a collaboration with National Geographic focusing on 'Mother Earth', and the just-closed celebration of Darwin's work and expeditions coinciding with the 200th anniversary of his birth. Thanks to the trio of exhibition spaces, and their overlapping schedules, there's always something to see,

even though the palazzo has no permanent collection. Information panels are bilingual throughout, although some detailed labelling and DVD installations are in Italian only.

In the Palazzo delle Esposizioni's original 1880-1882 designs by Marcello Piacentini there was a top-floor flourish that was not realized. The plans were for a hall-like conservatory on the roof, with a glass curtain wall and a glass roof arching overhead. The architectonic space was finally constructed in 2007 when, as part of the renovation work, the original blueprints were dug out and the elegant glass warehouse was beautifully completed. Since the palazzo's grand reopening it has been home to **Open Colonna** (Scalinata di via Milano 9a, T06-4782 2641, opencolonna.it, Tue-Sat 1230-1500, 1930-2300), a bar and gourmet restaurant headed up by renowned Italian chef Antonello Colonna, which gains as much by being associated with the dynamic aesthetic of the palazzo as vice versa.

In addition, the palazzo has an excellent bookshop and a good café. In a well-thought-out move, each has been given an entry independent of the main exhibit desk, allowing the spaces to take on lives of their own.

Quattro Fontane

Junction of via delle Quattro Fontane and via del Quirinale/via 20 Settembre.
Metro: Barberini. Map: Rome, F3, p84.

Three of the Four Fountains, one on each corner of a busy crossroads, were designed by the aptly named Domenico Fontana in 1593; the smallest one, on the grille in the wall of Palazzo Barberini's gardens, is by Pietro da Cortona. Although sadly quite eroded, the lovely fountains present the personifications of two rivers, Rome's Tevere and Florence's Arno, and two goddesses, Diana and Juno, with a little half-moon basin in front of each.

Tip...

Slip into the tiny Baroque church at the crossroads, **San Carlo alle Quattro Fontane**, to gaze up at Borromini's exquisite oval dome, built above a circle of windows so that it appears to be floating.

Basilica di Santa Maria della Vittoria

Via XX Settembre 17, T06-4274 0571.
Metro: Repubblica.

While the Church of Victorious Saint Mary has seen a recent surge in popularity – with visits from fans of Dan Brown's *Angels and Demons*, in which the basilica is featured – a sculpture by Giovanni Lorenzo Bernini has long attracted attention to it. Called *L'Estasi di Santa Teresa*, it is considered a sculptural masterpiece, but its fame is also partly due to the ambiguity of the ecstastic moment it captures, especially when viewed alongside an entry in the autobiography of the saint, Teresa of Avila. Seeming to have collapsed back on to a marble support, the young nun is depicted as being almost oblivious of a boy angel hovering over her, who has just pierced her breast with an arrow: her expression of pleasure-pain and her pose suggest she's experiencing an ecstasy that is seen by many critics as being due to more than religious epiphany. She writes: "In [the angel's] hands I saw a long golden spear and at the end of the iron tip I seemed to see a point of fire. With this he seemed to pierce my heart several times so that it penetrated to my entrails. When he drew it out, I thought he was drawing them out with it and he left me completely afire with a great love for God. The pain was so sharp that it made me utter several moans; and so excessive was the sweetness caused me by this intense pain that one can never wish to lose it." Although it is unlikely that Bernini would have depicted a glimpse of glory as lust fulfilled, Teresa does appear to be in a state of divine joy.

Five of the best

Secret gardens

❶ The garden of lavender and roses rambling up to the **Terme di Diocleziano** (see page 235).

❷ The grassy courtyard enclosed by a cloister designed by Michelangelo at the **Terme di Diocleziano** (see page 235).

❸ The citrus-planted courtyard inside the ticketed area of **Palazzo Massimo alle Terme** (see page 234).

❹ The verdant, shady garden of **Villa Maria Pia** on via del Quirinale in summer; there are benches throughout.

❺ **Giardini del Quirinale**, the flat park near the piazza, perked up by palm trees and stone benches.

Right: The gardens at Terme di Diocleziano.
Opposite page: San Carlo alle Quatro Fontane.

Monti & Esquilino

Monti is only a little segment of the southwest side of Esquilino, but it has so much to offer, with galleries, bars and eateries that are innovative and exciting, and thankfully not yet on many visitors' radar. The entire district has a fantastically local atmosphere. As you stroll around, notice how often the word *bottega* ('workshop') features in the name of an independent business. You'll find envelope-pushing goldsmiths and young couturiers whose street-side studios double as their shops. Drop in: you'll interrupt their work but they'll be pleased to discuss a possible commission.

Monti is banded by via Nazionale, via Cavour and the imposing Santa Maria Maggiore Church; the larger area of Esquilino stretches from the ancient baths complex above Termini and along the railway tracks to scoop down to the Colosseum. Esquilino has become central Rome's most multicultural neighbourhood, with its own Chinatown. Predictably, the area around the station is plagued by litter, but great escapes can be found in the pretty garden of Terme di Diocleziano and the statuary in Palazzo Massimo alle Terme.

Basilica e Museo di Santa Maria Maggiore

Piazza Santa Maria Maggiore,
T06-483195, vatican.va.
Church daily 0700-1900, free, loggia (pre-booked guided tour only) €5; museum daily 0830-1830, €4/2 concession.
Metro: Termini. Map: Rome, G3, p84.

The Cappella Borghese contains a painting said to be by St Luke himself.

Although many artists, sculptors and architects contributed (at various times) to the harmony of the main elements of Santa Maria Maggiore, its mosaics are the big draw for visitors. Episodes from the Old Testament appear in glittering mosaic panels that run the full length of the nave, set above the colonnades. The panels date from the original fifth-century church, but even sharper are the mosaic scenes from the same period illustrating the life of Mary, including Herod interrogating the Magi, which completely cover the arch that crosses the nave. Not content to stop there, more mosaics clothe a half dome beyond the arch, completed by Jacopo Torriti in the 13th century when the original apse was knocked down and moved a few metres to make room for the choir: they show Mary being crowned by her grown-up son, and, in a smaller scene, on her deathbed.

The enormously flamboyant **Cappella Borghese** (finished in 1612) to the left of the arch, was conceived to be "unequalled in sumptuousness", according to the Borghese Pope Paul V, whose tomb is in the left wall. The focus of the chapel, at the centre of the gilded marble and bas-relief, is a painting set behind glass of the Madonna and Child. Italian Catholics are especially reverential towards it, as it is thought to have been painted by St Luke himself.

Back in the main nave, the unusual flat ceiling, composed of 100-odd square coffered panels, is said to have been gilded with the first gold brought back from the Americas; it was designed by Giuliano di Sangallo and finished by his brother Antonio. The decorative inlaid marble floor, meanwhile, was completed in the 1290s by members of the Cosmati family.

From the piazza outside the entrance you can see the original 13th-century mosaics on the façade, protected by an elaborate colonnaded porch, but to get a better look, book a visit up to the loggia.

The little **museum** (accessed via the shop, past the font, in the first chapel on the right) displays the papal garments (some dating from the 16th century), candelabra, jewel-encrusted gold communion goblets, jewelled rosaries and more that were previously hidden away in storage when not being used for important services such as Easter and Christmas.

Palazzo Massimo alle Terme

*Largo di Villa Peretti 1, T06-3996 7700,
archeoroma.beniculturali.it.*
Tue-Sun 0900-1945, combined ticket (valid 3
days) with Crypta Balbi, Palazzo Altemps and
Terme di Diocleziano, €7/3.50 concession, plus
€3 during exhibitions, or Archaeologia card,
free EU citizens under 18 and over 65.
Metro: Termini. Map: Rome, G3, p84.

The ancient Romans aspired to recreate the luxury
of the Greek courts in their own villas. So great was
the demand for sculptures of significant Greek
figures (philosophers, poets and illustrious men
and women) that enterprising sculptors set up
workshops in Rome as early as the first century
AD to create replicas for wealthy Romans keen to
notch up extra prestige. The ground floor of this
museum houses an excellent exhibition of ancient
Roman sculpture. The statues in **rooms VI** and **VII**
(and many more besides) are Roman copies of
Greek originals, but are such highly crafted works
that they are valued in themselves.

Up on the first floor, sculptures are grouped to
show the importance of military might as well as the
aspiration to the Greek ideal of aesthete as athlete.
The importance of theatre is also given prominence.
Two panels in **room III**, found near piazza di Pietra
(which you've quite likely walked through) are
probably part of **Hadrian's Temple** (see page119)
– a thought-provoking reminder of just how much
has been excavated from under the pavement, and
how much might still lie buried, waiting to be found.

Not to be missed on the second floor is a
serene wrap-around fresco of a garden, dating
from AD 20-30 – it was only uncovered in 1863 in
Villa Livia, and until it was cut up and moved to
make room for the US embassy, it was the oldest
known example of a continuous fresco. It depicts
flora and fauna in such detail that even before
restoration, when one of the panels fell and was
damaged, 20-odd botanical species, and more
than two dozen kinds of birds, had been identified.

Room VIII overlooks Termini Station, which
neatly links the hulking building to the delicate

What's a fresco?

A fresco is a like a mural, only more complicated.
The paint was applied to wet plaster, so that it was
drawn into the plaster as it dried and became part
of the fabric of the wall. The technique was highly
desirable because it produced a durable painting
that wouldn't be damaged by flaking and would be
less prone to fading.

Before frescoing, an artist plastered only as much
wall as could be painted in a day, using lime mortar.
While the plaster was wet, the painter climbed
up with a cartoon, prepared to ensure that the
proportions were adjusted to look right from below:
normal ratios would mean that, from the floor, feet
looked huge and heads tiny. The artist would take
powdered pigment and dust it over holes pierced
in the cartoon to transfer the outline. The acidity of
the lime in the plaster would melt the cartoon, so the
artist would have to take it down quickly, then get
back up and start painting before the plaster dried.
If they made a mistake, they would have to wait for
the plaster to dry completely, then smash it off, draw
a new cartoon, re-plaster and start again. The same
heartbreaking restart was the only option if an artist
worked too slowly and any part of the plaster dried
before it had been frescoed.

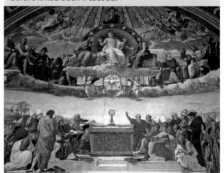

**Enterprising sculptors set up
workshops in Rome as early as
the first century AD to create
replicas for wealthy Romans
keen to notch up extra prestige.**

mosaics on display here, dating from AD 130-140, which were found during excavations to build the rail hub.

In **room XI** don't miss the inlaid marble *Pannello con testa* (or 'panel with head' – the English translations seem to fall away the further from the ground floor you go), a portrait in which the hair is delicately depicted in individually inlaid curls.

The **basement** houses a vast coin collection in a huge vault (note the thickness of the doors as you step in!). Using the keypads to zoom big magnifying glasses across the display cases to see the details on the coins is especially fun, and interesting, for kids.

Opened in 2000, this is a brightly lit and well-laid out space, with lots of comfortable stools throughout; outside, benches between the orange trees in the central courtyard make a very welcome spot for a break.

Terme di Diocleziano

Via Enrico de Nicola 79, T06-3996 7700, archeoroma.beniculturali.it.
Tue-Sun 0900-1945, combined ticket (valid 3 days) with Crypta Balbi, Palazzo Altemps and Palazzo Massimo, €7/3.50 concession, plus €3 during exhibitions, or Archaeologia card, free EU citizens under 18 and over 65.
Metro: Termini. Map: Rome, G2, p84.

Escape the scuzz of Termini Station by simply crossing the road in front of the piazza to the Baths of Diocletian. There's lots to see, although not a great deal of Diocletian's Baths, it must be said. There's a Michelangelo-designed cloister that's so big it's great for kids who need to run about. There's an enormous collection of inscribed tablets demonstrating how Romans communicated, ranging from pleas to the gods to graffiti; the exhibition runs to three floors and is quite well labelled in English. There's also a rather dry display of pre-Roman findings from the Lazio region.

But, although a big deal is (rightly) made of the former glory of Emperor Diocletian's baths, there's only one building related to the baths that's open to visitors, and it's nothing like as atmospheric

Tip...

The gardens alongside the baths are a welcome oasis in the Termini area, and as the ticket office is in the building at the far end, you can stroll in, picnic on a wall and toddle out and no-one minds.

as **Ostia Antica** (see page 256). Everything in the neighbourhood, though, including the cloister, has been built over the baths, which is the main reason there's so little to see today. Take a look at the exterior of the vast **Church of Santa Maria degli Angeli** next door: the beautiful outer structure that the church fills was originally part of the baths.

The part of the complex that is open is a single great barn of a building, but there's not much to convey the original appearance of the baths, which, in their heyday, covered some 13 ha, with pools, granite tubs (like those in piazza Farnese's fountains), gardens and halls incorporating *frigidarium* (cold), *tepidarium* (warm) and *caldarium* (cauldron-hot) enclosures. The brick building that is Sala X would have been covered in marble and floored throughout in mosaics. Astonishingly, the massive complex was completed just eight years after it was begun in AD 298.

The enormous pale-blue cloister dates from the late 1590s and is based on designs by Michelangelo, though he died before building started. Hundreds of statues and inscribed funerary tablets are set in rows across a rambling lawn and around hedges and palm trees.

San Pietro in Vincoli

Piazza di San Pietro in Vincoli 4a, T06-9784 4952.
Daily 0800-1200, 1500-1800.
Metro: Cavour. Map: Rome, F4, p84.

The Church of St Peter in Chains is named after the two sets of chains that bound Peter while he was in prison, in Jerusalem and in the Mamertine prison in the Forum in Rome. When they were placed alongside each other 1500-odd years ago, they miraculously fused together, and can be seen here hanging in a reliquary beneath the altar.

What looks like horns on Michelangelo's statue *Moses*, in San Pietro in Vincoli, are actually symbolical rays of light.

Emperor Nero's opulent villa Domus Aurea, the Golden House, was so huge that approximately 200 rooms are still to be uncovered.

An oval fresco in the ceiling, *The Miracle of the Chains*, dating from 1706, is Giovanni Battista Parodi's celebration of the event.

The basilica is also the home of Michelangelo's statue of *Moses*. Completed in 1515, it was intended as part of a planned funeral monument for the Rovere family's pope Julius II, who renovated the church and wanted a memorial to himself that included 45-plus statues. After Julius died, however, *Moses* was as far as the grand plan got. Somewhat strangely, Moses sports horns, although earlier audiences would have understood them as symbolically representing rays of light.

Domus Aurea

Via della Domus Aurea, T06-3996 7700, pierreci.it.
Tue-Fri 1000-1600, pre-booked guided tour only (in English), €4.50, but closed as this guide went to press.
Metro: Colosseo.Map: Rome, F5, p84.

On the hill above the Colosseum is the Golden House, Emperor Nero's three-storey villa, which

It's a fact...

The sundial in **Santa Maria degli Angeli** was used to regulate the city's clocks until 1846, when the custom began of sounding a midday cannon from Gianicolo.

was begun in AD 64 immediately after the great fire of Rome, and gives an inkling of his excesses. Its south façade was clad in gold and its interior opulently decorated with marble and frescoes, but the minute Nero died in AD 68, its materials were pillaged and it was earthed over and built on, as no contemporary wanted a reminder of the tyrant emperor.

After the villa was accidentally stumbled upon in 1480, its buried rooms were visited by Renaissance artists, who copied the frescoes on the vaulted ceilings by candlelight, some leaving their signatures scratched into the stone.

After decades of work, some 30 rooms have been excavated, but an approximate 200 have still to be uncovered. Unfortunately, whenever it rains heavily, as it did during the winter of 2008/2009, the Domus Aurea suffers flooding and closes for long periods, which in the past have lasted months.

Listings
Sleeping

Trevi & Quirinale

Boutique Hotel Trevi €€€
Via delle Muratte 90/92, T06-699 1192, boutiquehoteltrevi.com.
Metro: Barberini.
Map: Rome, E3, p84.
Although you can't see the Fontana di Trevi, when you open a window you can hear it. Located on a pedestrianized street, the hotel opened in 2008 and rooms are still gleaming from the makeover. Some bedrooms feature pretty fabric wall coverings, while others have a more classic decor (there's even an entirely wood-panelled room); period furnishings include beautiful walnut-blonde tables and chests of drawers.

Daphne Inn €€€
Via degli Avignonesi 20, T06-8745-0086, daphne-rome.com.
Metro: Barberini.
Map: Rome, F3, p85.
Small but luxurious, the nine rooms and suites that form Daphne Trevi are irresistible. Not only is each a thoughtful assembly of neutral tones, sleek furniture and well-chosen artwork, but the staff are super-helpful and breakfast a feast. There's Wi-Fi and tea and coffee making facilities, and they offer a cellphone to use during your stay (you just pay for your calls). Set up by an American and her Italian partner, Daphne Trevi is complemented by a further

eight, equally delightful rooms in the nearby Daphne Veneto.

Hotel White €€€
Via in Arcione 77, T06-699 1242, travelroma.com.
Metro: Barberini.
Map: Rome, E3, p84.
The revamped first and second floor rooms are recommended (avoid the unrenovated third floor). Rooms are small but well laid out, making the most of what's available. The single-hue colour scheme and pared-down glass and wood furnishings in the light bedrooms are a welcome relief for those tired of the classic look.

Trevi B&B €€€
Via del Lavatore 83, T06-6938 0944, bbtreviroma.it.
Metro: Barberini.
Map: Rome, E3, p84.
The sisters who opened this B&B, two minutes from the Trevi Fountain, brought in interior designers to help perfect their concept, and it really shows.

It's refreshing to see the original features of each room given a this-decade lift – wooden ceilings are pale, not dark, which subtly complements design-aware furnishings, and bathrooms are sleek, with giant shower heads. Exceptionally well thought-out and finished, the B&B now has 15 rooms, and plans for a self-contained flat.

Self-catering
Residence Barberini
Via delle Quattro Fontane 171/172, T06-420 3341, residencebarberini.com.
Metro: Barberini.
Map: Rome, F3, p85.
Each of the 12 luxury suites accommodates up to four, with a bedroom, living room with sofa bed, kitchen and bathroom (€375 per night). Offering the privacy of a small apartment, each is carefully furnished, with air-conditioning, TV/DVD and large showers. The fifth-floor penthouse (€550 per night) has a terrace either side.

Exedra €€€€

Piazza della Repubblica 47,
T06-489381, boscolohotels.com.
Metro: Repubblica.
Map: Rome, G3, p85.

This sumptuous hotel is
refreshingly design-conscious
with super-elegant spaces
galore, from the rooftop, bar-side
open-air pool, to a serene spa
and ground-floor brasserie.
Very comfortable rooms on
upper floors have balconies or,
on the fourth floor of the
Clementine wing (built on the
site of Diocletian's hot baths),
pretty terraces.

Radisson SAS es Hotel €€€

Via Filippo Turati 171, T06-
444841, rome.radissonsas.com.
Metro: Termini.
Map: Rome, H4, p85.

Rome's single best option for
serious design style, es (as in
'Esquilino') is vast. The ambitious
development is way ahead of its
time, because the surrounding
area hasn't caught up in terms of
regeneration. From the
Japanese-inspired marble/
concrete ground floor to the
glittering poolside restaurant
and bar crowning the seventh
floor, with its gritty view over
Termini's rail tracks, the hotel is
popular with the fashion and
cinema crowd. Younger clients
love the one-space bed-and-
bathrooms (with a little separate
room for the loo). There's Wi-Fi

throughout, a spa and gym,
and even the requisite Roman
remains, uncovered under
the lobby.

Canada Hotel €€

Via Vicenza 58, T06-445 7770,
hotelcanadaroma.com.
Metro: Castro Pretorio.
Map: Rome, H2, p85.

As if a canopied bed or
exquisitely painted ceiling
weren't reason enough, extras
like providing a pushchair on
request and gifts to celebrate
each Bank Holiday could account
for the number of returning
guests. The 70 spacious rooms,
with Wi-Fi and flatscreen TVs, are
complemented by an equally
generous bar and *salotto*, all
restored to the original 1870s
style. The Canadian-born Pucci
brothers who run it may have
learnt from the best (grandfather
Pucci trained at Hotel de Russie
before opening this) but resting
on their laurels they are not.

Hotel Antica Locanda €€

Via del Boschetto 84, T06-4788
1729, antica-locanda.com.
Metro: Cavour.
Map: Rome, F4, p84.

The rooms here are spread
through two old houses, so each
is different. One has its own
corridor, another has a little extra
dressing room and several have
that nice extra, a window in the
bathroom. Rooms are air-
conditioned, and many look out
on to pretty via del Boschetto.

Hotel Ivanhoe €€

Via Urbana 50, T06-486 813,
hotelivanhoe.it.
Metro: Cavour.
Map: Rome, F4, p84.

Handily located on a little piazza
just off one of the most buzzing
streets in Monti, this decent little
hotel offers a good basic standard.
Rooms are simply furnished but
clean as a pin; some corner
bedrooms have two windows, and
there's a roof terrace. Friendly staff
are more than willing to help with
visiting plans.

Nerva €€

Via Tor de' Conti 3,
T06-678 1835, hotelnerva.com.
Metro: Cavour or Colosseo.
Map: Rome, F4, p84.

Located on a quiet lane in Monti
not far from the Colosseum,
Nerva would benefit from a
revamp, but the owners and staff
are so friendly you can forgive the
cramped shower cubicles. More
modern than the 19 rooms on
site are three renovated rooms
nearby. There are also two rooms
for people with disabilities.

The Beehive €

Via Margherita 8, T06-4470 4553,
the-beehive.com.
Metro: Termini.
Map: Rome, H2, p85.

This stylish budget hotel
provides accommodation in
private rooms but also has a
pristine dorm (just €25 per
person). All rooms share
bathrooms. The American

Fawlty Towers Hostel €
Via Magenta 39, T06-445 0374,
fawltytowers.org.
Metro: Termini.
Map: Rome, H3, p85.
Despite the lame name, this hostel goes to the top of its class thanks to a big, bright, well-equipped kitchen in a rough-and-ready conservatory; right alongside is a rooftop terrace with tables and chairs and plenty of greenery. The shared dorms and bathrooms are basic but clean: dorms are mixed-sex, but small enough for girl-only to be arranged on request. No credit cards.

Il Covo €
Via del Boschetto 91,
T06-481 5871, bbilcovo.it.
Metro: Cavour.
Map: Rome, F4, p84.
Opened 10 years ago by the family behind La Bottega, minutes away on piazza Madonna dei Monti, where guests have breakfast. The rooms (all with private bathroom) are spacious and equipped with the basics, and via del Boschetto is one of Monti's most interesting streets, packed with independent shops. Reception is staffed until 2000, then guests have their own keys. No lift or telephone.

Locanda Monti B&B €
Via Madonna dei Monti 50,
T06-4890 5230,
locandamonti.com.
Metro: Colosseo.
Map: Rome, F4, p84.
There are only three double rooms in this B&B, but they are very spacious and each has its own ample bathroom, with air-con, fridge, TV and Wi-Fi. It's not modern, but a reasonably priced option for staying in Monti, just minutes from the Colosseum. Marble floors and cast-iron bed-frames add to the Rome atmosphere. Breakfast is a simple, help-yourself affair.

Self-catering
Palazzetto degli Artisti Suites
Via della Madonna dei Monti 108, T06-6992 4931,
palazzettodegliartisti.com.
Metro: Colosseo.
Map: Rome, F4, p84.
The 14 suites and studios are beautifully restored, with unfussy furnishings and blonde parquet throughout. Staying here is as close to a home-from-home as you can imagine, albeit with a great view from the upper floors, and it's really well positioned: just a short walk from the Colosseum but close to Monti's hub. Kitchens are very well equipped, and rates start at a reasonable €100 per night.

owners "like nice things" so there's an Apple on the internet station, and Philippe Starck furniture in the pretty garden. Their energy-friendly approach means ceiling fans, not air-con, organic, vegetarian meals and packed lunches. Not all guests are youngsters – just people who appreciate what's offered. There are also three self-catering apartments nearby, which can be booked as a whole (€210 per night for six people) or as individual rooms (€70 for a double), sharing kitchen, bathroom and communal areas.

Eating & drinking

Trevi & Quirinale

Colline Emiliane €€€€
Via degli Avignonesi 22,
T06-481 7538.
Tue-Sat 1245-1445, 1930-2245,
Sun 1245-1445.
Metro: Barberini.
Map: Rome, E3, p84.

Drop by on a Sunday morning
and see the pasta maker hard at
work, using techniques learnt
from her mum and grandma
who worked here before her. As
its name suggests ('hills of Emilia
Romagna'), the cuisine is based
on Bolognese tradition, with its
signature hearty winter fillers.
Summer sees the place packed
too, so reservations are
recommended.

Le Tamerici €€€€
Vicolo Scavolino 79,
T06-6920 0700, letamerici.com.
Mon-Sat 1230-1530, 1930-2330.
Metro: Barberini.
Map: Rome, E3, p84.

Fish is the focus here, and an
entire wall of wine is an
indication of the niche wines on
offer from small vineyards. The
clientele is mainly local,
savouring the Mediterranean
cuisine with a Pugliese flourish
(the fish comes in from Gallipoli
daily). Dishes are light, and the
changing menu might include
baby gnocchi with clams and
cherry tomatoes, or a sumptuous
pumpkin risotto with pecorino
cheese.

Il Chianti €€€
Via del Lavatore 81/82a, T06-678
7550, vineriailchianti.com.
Mon-Sat 1200-0200, hot food
served 1230-1530, 1900-2330.
Metro: Barberini.
Map: Rome, E3, p84.

The house speciality is all things
Tuscan. With an ivy-covered
façade and tables aplenty in the
little piazza on a lane winding
down to the Trevi Fountain, this
place meets visitors' expectations:
inside it's all solid, comfortable
wood furniture, wine in
abundance, and food that's better
than good, with lots of organic
ingredients from Colforito.

Cafés & bars
Fontana di Trevi
Piazza di Trevi 90, T06-679 7764.
Daily 0800-2400.
Metro: Barberini.

A gelateria and bar just across
from the fountain. Service can be
a little gruff, but it's buzzing with
locals coming for a quick coffee,
which gives it a reassuringly
authentic vibe.

Papyrus Café
Via de' Lucchesi 28,
T06-699 0949, papyruscafe.com.
Mon-Sat 0900-2300,
Sun 0900-2100.
Metro: Barberini.

Just minutes from the Trevi
Fountain but far from the touts
and tat, this café has an arthouse
feel; books (some in English) are
for sale alongside the bar.

Monti & Esquilino

La Taverna dei Fori Imperiali €€€
Via Madonna dei Monti 16,
T06-679 8643,
latavernadeiforiimperiali.com.
Wed-Mon 1230-1530, 1900-2300.
Metro: Colosseo.
Map: Rome, F4, p84.

The dad cooks, the mum and
daughter make *dolci* and wait
tables and the son is the maitre
d', although he can apparently
cook too. But don't let the
humble/honest air fool you,
because this is a family that
brings together a range of
dishes that are extra good.

Fafiuchè €€
Via Madonna dei Monti 28,
T06-699 0968, fafiuche.it.
Tue-Sun 1700-0100
(occasionally closed Sun),
aperitivo 1830-2100.
Metro: Colosseo.

The delicious concept behind
this foodie haven is that many of
the ingredients in the dishes are
also available for sale. Typical of
the sharp focus on fresh and
handmade is the ricotta, which
is delivered daily from Gaeta
(halfway to Naples), because if
it's not fresh, it's not good.

Listings

La Bottega del Caffè €€
Piazza Madonna dei Monti 5,
T06-474 1578.
Daily 0800-0200.
Metro: Cavour.
While it was Monti's best-kept secret, La Bottega was the most welcoming place; now it's better known some of the inside waiting staff have developed attitudes, so all the more reason to sit outside. Lunch and dinner menus offer a select range of light dishes; pastas and salads are both good.

La Cicala e la Formica €€
Via Leonina 17, T06-481 7490,
lacicalaelaformica.info.
Daily 1200-1530, 1830-2300.
Metro: Cavour.
Tables outside in a mini-piazza and two intimate rooms are presided over by a man passionate about food, taking influences from Tuscany, Milan and Puglia, which brings a nice variety to the staples. Bread and pasta is made in-house, as are the desserts, and the house wine is very good.

Urbana 47 €€
Via Urbana 47,
T06-4788 4006, urbana47.it.
Daily 1000-1600 (lunch 1300-1500), 1700-2400 (dinner 2030-2400).
Metro: Cavour.
A straightforward restaurant this is not – its sofas and raw metal furniture are lounge-cool and it does *aperitivi*-plus-snacks, but there's a commitment to organic and locally sourced produce and a serious kitchen set-up. Brunch (with plates charged by weight) and the owner's individual taste in decoration make the space almost unintentionally hip.

Alle Carrette €
Via della Madonna dei Monti 95,
T06-679 2770.
Daily 1900-2400.
Metro: Colosseo.
A cheap and cheerful pizzeria with a nice show of flexibility: if you don't want your pizza super-thin, you can ask for it to be *alta* (deep). Among the fried delicacies on offer for antipasti are really good *supplì*, with a crisply fried skinny crust and perfect rice packed around a knob of mozzarella.

Cafés & bars
Antico Caffè Santa Maria
Piazza di Santa Maria Maggiore 7a, T06-446 5863,
caffesantamaria.it.
Daily 0500-0200.
Metro: Termini.
Ice creams are as much a speciality at this smart café as the baked-on-site goodies supplying the *pasticceria*. In warmer weather the full lunch and dinner menu sees the tables on the pavement outside packed.

Er Baretto
Via del Boschetto 132,
T06-482 0444.
Mon-Thu 0700-2330, Fri-Sat 0700-0100, Sun 0700-2330.
Metro: Cavour.
The trademark of this chirpy little café is a leaf etched in the *schiuma* (foam) of a cappuccino. Several tables outside make it a good spot to take a break from shopping and soak up some sun. There's free Wi-Fi.

The Beehive Café
Via Marghera 8, T06-4470 4553,
the-beehive.com.
Mon-Fri 0730-1030, 1200-1500, 1830-2230, Sat 1830-2230, Sun 0730-1300 (brunch), 1830-2230.
Metro: Termini.
Organic, vegetarian dishes are served in this little café but here's the interesting element: the diner chooses how hungry she is (the portion), and how much to pay. In a city short of vegetarian restaurants, this is a great option.

Al Vino al Vino
Via dei Serpenti 19, T06-485803.
Sun-Thu 1100-1400, 1800-0030, Fri-Sat 1100-1400, 1800-0130.
Metro: Cavour.
There's no kitchen at this cheerful chiefly-wine-only bar, so tuck into plates of cheese, *salumi* and olives. The cosy room that incorporates the bar is the most convivial.

Entertainment

Agave
*Via di San Martino ai Monti 7a,
T06-488 2134, agavebookbar.
blogspot.com.*
Mon-Thu 1230-0030, Fri-Sat
1230-0130, Sun 1230-2300.
Metro: Cavour.
Wine and books plus cupcakes
and cocktails are on offer here.
It only opened mid-2008, but
already regularly hosts photo
exhibits and book launches, and
all in the most laid-back series of
interconnected spaces. There's
even a stack of board games for
a rainy afternoon.

Al 104
*Via Urbana 104,
T06-474 2772, al104.com.*
Tue-Sat 1230-2300.
Metro: Cavour.
A light, white space furnished
with Kartell chairs; lunch and
dinner are served but it's also a
great place to have a glass of
wine.

Dom
*Via degli Zingari 49, T06-4472
71005, domchampagneria.it.*
Tue-Sat 1900-0200, Sun brunch
from 1200 (reservations only).
Metro: Cavour.
As in Dom Perignon, naturally.
This *champagneria* is a long, slim,
very elegant space, with more
intimate lounge zones on the
lower floors. Come for *aperitivo*;
dinner is by reservation only.

Children
Time Elevator
*Via dei Santi Apostoli 20,
T06-9774 6243, time-elevator.it.*
Daily 1030-1930, €12.
A 45-minute cinematic
experience (in English) for ages
five and up that gallops through
the highlights of Rome's history
via the monuments you've seen
as you walked round the city.
Flight simulators (your chair
moves about), a surround-sound
system and some special effects
do the trick.

Cinema
Warner Village Moderno
*Piazza della Repubblica 44-45,
T892111, warnervillage.it.*
Metro: Repubblica.

Clubs
Ice Club Roma
*Via della Madonna dei Monti
18-19, T06-9784 5581,
iceclubroma.it.*
Daily 1800-0200, entry, cape,
gloves plus one drink €15.
Metro: Colosseo.
If the heat of the sun gets too
much, why not don a cape
and gloves (you'll need them)
and head into the -5°C ice bar
for a vodka cocktail in an
ice-cone cup.

Shopping

Art

The House of Love and Dissent
Via Leonina 85, T06-4890 3661, loveanddissent.com.
Tue-Sat 1100-2000.
Metro: Cavour.
The gallery stages shows by street artists, or collectives like Just Seeds, under themes of political or social messaging. The shop stocks organic cotton T-shirts illustrated by artists and jewellery made from found objects.

Fondaco
Via degli Zingari 28, T06-4543 4947, fondaconet.it.
Mon-Fri 1000-1900, Sat by appointment.
Metro: Cavour.
Sculptures, photographs, prints and illustrations by an artist who publishes in Rome's daily *La Repubblica*; the offerings are curated by the architect owners, whose ethos is "furnish with art". No credit cards.

Motel Salieri
Via Giovanni Lanza 162, T06-4898 9966, motelsalieri.org.
Mon-Sat 1100-1900.
Metro: Cavour.
The raw, industrial space is shared by art and fashion. Artists are invited to stage temporary shows, under the title Guest At, in the main space. The area beyond is dedicated to the fashion designers producing FQR, a capsule ready-to-wear collection and accessories.

Theatre Café
Via IV Novembre, 157a (Largo Magnanapoli), T06-6994 1462, theatrecaferoma.com. Mon-Sat 0600-0200, Sun 0700-0200.
Bus: 40, 60, 170.
Live Blues, soul, or jazz rocks this small but friendly bar on Thursday and Friday nights from 2200.

White
Via degli Avignonesi 73, T06-9727 8949, whitelrc.com.
Mon-Sat 1230-1530, 1930-2400, Sat DJ 2400-0400, Sun 1230-1530, 2000-2230 (aperitivo only), DJ till 0100.
Metro: Barberini.
Although White is a restaurant, it's the lounge-style club that is the big draw for hip 20- and 30-somethings. Open less than a year, its white banquettes are crowded with pretty people checking out the brave folks on the dance floor.

ZTL
Via di Sant' Eufemia 8, T06-6694 2041, ztlristoclub.com.
Mon 0800-1800, Tue-Sun 0800-0200, DJ Fri-Sun from 2000, €30 (includes 1 drink).
Bus: 40, 60, 64, 70.
One minute from Piazza Venezia, this handily positioned club opens its bar for breakfast and caters for lunch and dinner or an *aperitivo*, then transforms on weekend nights. The friendly staff and the mad wall graphics finish the space. Its name emphasizes its position – you can't get anywhere in the centre because of the traffic-barring *Zona a Traffico Limitato* but you can come here.

Books

Bookàbar
Via Milano 15-17,
T06-4891 3361, bookabar.it.
Tue-Thu 0930-2000, Fri-Sat
0930-2230, Sun 0930-2000.
Metro: Repubblica or Cavour.
Bus: H, 64, 70, 71, 170, 640.
The bookshop of the Palazzo
delle Esposizioni is an excellent
source for art, architecture,
design and photography, along
with cinema, dance, music and
theatre. The Bookàbar café is
round the corner.

Clothing

Anteprima
Via delle Quattro Fontane 38/40,
T06-482 8445.
Mon-Sat 0930-2000, Sun
1100-1400, 1500-2000.
Metro: Repubblica.
A team selects the women's
pieces from Italian and foreign
labels to create a look that's
more Paris than Rome, with
eye-catching, unusual
accessories.

Atelier Centoventisette
Via del Boschetto 127,
T06-482 3572,
paolo.santoro@fastwebnet.it.
Mon 1200-2000, Tue-Sat
1000-2000.
Metro: Cavour.
Exclusive women's collections
with French and Spanish labels
'known by those who know
them', like Deux Mille Vingt Six
and Iconoclast.

DOP
Via Urbana 25, T06-4890 6412.
Mon-Sat 1030-1930.
Metro: Cavour.
Stocking new designers like
Japanese label Mito, UrBahia
(which is French) and FTC
(Italian), this store is a fantastic
place to discover pieces by hot
new talent.

Galleria Alberto Sordi
Piazza Colonna, T06-6919 0769,
galleriaalbertosordi.it.
Daily 1000-2200.
Metro: Barberini.
Bus: 62, 71, 85, 175, 492.
This elegant Milan-like arcade is
home to a number of upmarket
brands, and a good café.

Kokoro
Via del Boschetto 75, T06-487
0657, kokororoma@gmail.com.
Mon-Sat 1100-2000.
Metro: Cavour.
With designers making garments
in the workshop to the rear of the
store, it's exciting to see pieces
coming together while you
browse. One-size, floaty
silhouettes and wrap-arounds are
key to the women-only collection.

Lol
Piazza degli Zingari 11,
T06-4814 160.
Mon-Sat 1000-2000.
Metro: Cavour.
Women's collections (Missoni,
Forte Forte and more) alongside
bags and really original jewellery
in this sumptuous store.

Misty Beethoven
Via degli Zingari 12,
T06-488 1878, mistybeethoven.it.
Mon 1600-2000, Tue-Sat
1100-2000.
Metro: Cavour.
The lingerie, cheeky accessories
and sexy shoes are described
as very Vivienne Westwood by
local devotees.

Paraphernalia
Via Leonina 6, T06-474 5888,
myspace.com/paraphernalia6.
Mon 1530-2000, Tue-Sat
1030-2000.
Metro: Cavour.
Clothing for guys and women
with a French vibe, although
also Berlin labels like Starstyling;
among some great accessories
are shoes for women by Les
Prairies de Paris. Individual
pieces are handpicked so there
are constant new appearances.

Patrizia Greco Couture
Via degli Zingari 51b,
T393-246 7571.
Mon 1500-2000,
Tue-Sat 1000-2000.
Metro: Cavour.
The shop of this talented
young designer is also her
atelier. In addition to couture
and hats, Greco reworks vintage
pieces to sumptuous effect.
She hosts aperitivi evenings
twice a month: ring to check
when the next one will be.

Super

*Via Leonina 42, T06-4544 8500,
super-space.com.*
Mon 1530-2000, Tue-Sat
1030-1400, 1530-2000.
Metro: Cavour.
Johnny Serra Caracciolo's men's
and women's collections are
sourced from the most
innovative emerging and
established designers; he also
has some retro design, vintage
accessories and perfume.

Tina Sondergaard

*Via del Boschetto 1d,
T334-385 0799.*
Mon 1500-1930, Tue-Sat
1030-1930.
Metro: Cavour.
An international group of
designers, headed up by Danish
Tina Sondergaard, work on site,
and the excitement as they
discuss fabrics and the latest
finished pieces is infectious. After
shopping for fabrics in Florence,
the trio make a maximum of six
of each design, using the leftover
material for hip one-off hats and
caps. No credit cards.

YU

*Via degli Zingari 54,
T06-474 2737.*
Mon 1530-1930, Tue-Sat
1000-1930.
Metro: Cavour.
Made-to-measure clothing, in
jersey, wool and cotton,
including a fantastic swimwear
range.

Food & drink

Antico Forno

*Via delle Muratte 8,
T06-679 2866, anticoforno.it.*
Mon-Sat 0700-2200, Sun
0700-2100.
Metro: Barberini.
More than just a bakery, this
marble-countered treasure trove
has been open 100 years and is
the place to come to set up a
sumptuous picnic. *Porchetta*
(freshly roasted seasoned pork)
sandwiches are the most
popular choice. For presents to
take home, there's also olive oil,
pasta, wine, prosciutto, salami
and more. Its bar next door
serves a very good cappuccino.

La Bottega del Cioccolato

*Via Leonina 82, T06-482 1473,
labottegadelcioccolato.it.*
Mon-Sat 0930-1930, closed
Jul-Aug.
Metro: Cavour.
The chocolate models of the
Pantheon and the Colosseum
aren't bad, but the 70-80
varieties of filled chocolates are
the big sellers, all freshly made in
the workshop at the back. The
summer closure reflects their
belief that chocolate shouldn't
be refrigerated.

Nuovo Mercato Esquilino

Via Lamarmora.
Mon-Sat 0500-1500.
Metro: Vittorio Emanuele.
The extensive covered market
has Rome's best ethnic produce,
with North African fruit and

vegetables along with Chinese
and Bangladeshi spices,
reflecting the diverse
backgrounds of the Esquiline
area's population.

Salumeria di Ciavatta

Via del Lavatore 31, T06-679 2935.
Mon-Sat 0715-1430, 1630-2000.
Metro: Barberini.
Stocked with artisan cheeses,
prosciutto, fresh pizza by the
slice and bread, this is a handy
stop to complete a picnic.
There's also *pizza bianca ripiena*
– plain pizza sliced open and
filled sandwich-style.

Tondi Forno

Via dei Serpenti 7, T06-4893 0145.
Mon-Sat 0730-2100,
Sun 1100-1600.
Metro: Cavour.
One of Monti's top pizza-by-the-
slice places; they also do *supplì*
(rice balls) for a tasty snack on the
go, and bread for picnics. For a
cheap, good lunch, there's a
tavola calda here too.

Homewares

Archivia

*Via del Boschetto 23,
T06-474 1503,
archiviacomplementi.com.*
Mon 1530-1930, Tue-Sat
1000-1930.
Metro: Cavour.
Lovely things with a focus
on artisan or exclusive
collections, like Italian
painted porcelain Taitù.

Activities & tours

Jewellery
Anà
Via del Boschetto 4, T06-4782 5539.
Mon 1600-1930, Tue-Sat
1100-1430, 1600-1930.
Metro: Cavour.
Handcrafted jewellery worked
with silver and jade, amethyst,
river pearls and more.

Diego Ruffolo – Orafo
Via Baccina 91, T06-678 1786,
diego.ruffolo@tiscali.it.
Mon-Fri 0930-1300, 1400-1900,
Sat 0930-1300.
Metro: Colosseo.
There are several goldsmiths
designing jewellery along via
Baccina but our favourite is
Swiss-trained Ruffolo, who works
with gold, silver, copper and
titanium. Commissions normally
take two weeks but he's flexible.
He and his team craft inventive
pieces that offset a modern cut
right through to classically
inspired designs.

Escat
Via dell'Angeletto 10,
T06-474 5721.
Mon 1600-2000, Tue-Sat
1000-1400, 1600-2000.
Metro: Cavour.
When shoe designer Elena
Scategni travels for work, she
buys non-stop: with her house
overflowing, she's opened a
store. Her jewellery choices, in

Plexiglas, rubber, silver and glass,
plus vintage and new bags,
decorations for the house and
more fill this little treasure trove
of a shop.

Per Lei
Via del Boschetto 35,
T06-4891 3862, perlei.co.uk.
Mon-Sat 1100-2000.
Metro: Cavour.
The gorgeous jewellery hand
crafted by a Peruvian designer is
made from silver, paper, glass
and stone. Necklaces are
asymmetrical and wrist cuffs
are delicate.

Wellbeing
Kami Spa
Via degli Avignonesi 11-12,
T06-4201 0039, kamispa.com.
Sun-Thu 1000-2200, Fri-Sat
1000-2400.
Metro: Barberini.
As soon as you step over the
threshold of the newly opened
and blissfully serene spa, the
lighting and the pool, guarded by
a pair of stone dragons, trigger a
deep feeling of relaxation.
A series of rooms represent
Japan, China, Indonesia, Thailand
and India, each dedicated to
treatments from that country.
The sole difficulty is deciding
between treatments as
tantalizingly named as the
Golden Petal scrub and the
Four Hands hot stone massage.

Contents

A fresco depicting the Spring by Pierleone Ghezzi inside Villa Falconieri in Frascati.

Day trips from Rome

Parco dell' Appia Antica

The Appian Way, which heads through the Aurelian Wall at Porta San Sebastiano and runs southeast from Rome, originally stretched as far as Brindisi on the Adriatic coast. One of the most famous of Roman routes, it was known as *regina viarum* ('queen of roads') and was a crucial line of trade and communication between Rome and the eastern Mediterranean. In 71 BC Marcus Licinius Crassus, the general who suppressed the rebellion of Spartacus, had the 6,000 slaves he captured crucified along the side of the road: they were left there to rot to deter future uprisings.

Since burials were not allowed within the city walls during Roman times, the Appian Way was a popular location for the rich and important to build their mausoleums, and many ancient remains dot the route. Early Christians also buried their dead here, in 300 km of catacombs tunnelled into the rock, several of which can be visited. Though there are some major sights on the road, a great part of the attraction is wandering along and discovering the many minor tombs and ancient remains.

On the way out into the countryside, a regional park – the Parco Regionale dell'Appia Antica (parcoappiaantica.org) – covers the first 16 km of road as well as the **Valle della Caffarella** and the remains of several Roman aqueducts. Most people visit the park for the Roman remains, but if countryside is what you're after, the Caffarella Valley has verdant peacefulness, and woods of oak and ilex. You can rent bikes and pick up maps from the park information office (via Appia Antica 42, T06-512 6314). Some of the road is still paved in original Roman stone, and traffic is restricted on Sundays. An excellent part of the park for cycling, the **Area degli Acquedotti** stretches southeast from Porta San Sebastiano, with paths running through a rural landscape where sheep graze under long stretches of ancient aqueducts that once brought water to Rome.

Catacombe di San Callisto

Via Appia Antica 110/126, T06-5130 1580, catacombe.roma.it.
Mar-Jan Thu-Tue, 0900-1200, 1400-1700, €6/3 concession.

The largest of the catacombs, there are around 20 km of tunnels in the Catacombs of St Callixtus, with half a million tombs on four levels. Guided tours (in English) of about 25 minutes lead visitors into the cool, damp, underground burial chambers. Here you can see fourth-century frescoes, the tombs of several early popes (their remains having long since been taken to churches in Rome), and a copy of Stefano Maderno's statue of Santa Cecilia (see page 176), who was also supposedly buried here. Although they are usually described as Christian in origin, the catacombs were created by merging pre-existing underground burial sites, some of which may have been pagan.

Catacombe di San Sebastiano

Via Appia Antica 136, T06-785 0350.
Mid-Dec-mid-Nov, Mon-Sat 0900-1200, 1400-1700, €6/3 concession.

The word 'catacomb' itself derives from the burial ground here, which was originally called *San Sebastiano ad catacumbas* – 'St Sebastian near the hollow'. St Sebastian is buried in the crypt. The site has also been connected to Sts Peter and Paul since the third century, and it may be that their bodies were brought here after their deaths. The fourth-century basilica was narrowed in the 17th century to just the central nave.

Circo e Villa di Massenzio

Via Appia Antica 153, T06-780 1324, villadimassenzio.it.
Tue-Sun 0900-1330, €3/1.50 concession.

The large circus of Maxentius, overgrown but still clearly discernible, is over 500 m long. One of

Day trips from Rome

the best-preserved Roman circuses, the starting gates are still visible at the end near the entrance. The rest of the villa, including the mausoleum of Maxentius's deified son Romulus, is rather less easy to make out, beyond high brick walls.

Tomba di Cecilia Metella

Via Appia Antica 161, T06-3996 7700, pierreci.it. Tue-Sun 0900 till 1 hr before sunset, combined ticket with Villa dei Quintili and Terme di Caracalla, valid 7 days, €6/3 concession, or Archaeologia Card, free EU citizens under 18 and over 65.

The Appian Way's most impressive tomb, the round mass of the Mausoleum of Cecilia Metella rises 11 m above the road below. The entombed Cecilia was the daughter of Metellus Creticus, Roman consul in 69 BC, and from the size and grandeur of her tomb, obviously a person of some importance. Ox skulls and garlands decorate the marble frieze. Inside there's less to see – entrance is probably not worth the price of the ticket unless you also intend to visit the other sights it covers.

Villa dei Quintili

Via Appia Nuova 1092, T06-3996 7700, pierreci.it. Tue-Sun 0900 till 1 hr before sunset, combined ticket with Terme di Caracalla and Tomba di Cecilia Metella, valid 7 days, €6/3 concession, or Archaeologia Card, free EU citizens under 18 and over 65; entrance also from via Appia Antica 290, Apr-Oct Sat-Sun only.

One of the biggest villas around Rome, this grand pile was once owned by the Quintilius brothers. They were Roman consuls in AD 151, but were accused of conspiracy and murdered by Emperor Commodus, who enjoyed living here himself.

Further down the road, on the right, the **Casal Rotondo**, from the age of Augustus, is the Appian Way's largest tomb, though little is known about its occupants.

Listings

Eating

L'Archeologia €€
Via Appia Antica 139, T06-788 0494, larcheologia.it. Wed-Mon 1230-1500, 2000-2300.
One of the best choices along the Appian Way, just beyond the catacombs of San Sebastiano, l'Archeologia offers traditional Roman food and an ancient wisteria-draped garden in summer, an open fire in winter.

Appia Antica Caffè €
175 Via Appia Antica, T338-346 5440, appiaanticacaffe.it. Tue-Sun summer 0730-2000, winter 0730-1800.
For something quick and simple, this café has a back garden further along and serves panini and hot pasta dishes. They also rent out bikes.

Activities

You can hire bikes for €3 per hour, or €10 for four hours, from the information office of the **Parco Appia** Antica (via Appia Antica 58/60, T06-513 5316, parcoappiaantica.org, daily summer 0930-1730, winter 0930-1630).

Transport

The road starts at the Porta San Sebastiano, just southeast of the Caracalla Baths. The open-top **Archeobus** (T06-684 0901, trambusopen. com, daily every 30 mins 0830-1630, €13) runs from Termini via piazza Venezia and the Colosseum and stops all along the route through the park. A ticket (€15/10 concession) permits users to get on and off as often as they want for a day, and also gives discounted entrance to the catacombs.

It's also possible to reach the park by public transport. Bus 118 runs along the first part of the route from the Circo Massimo metro; bus 660 runs from Colle Albani metro. Buy your return tickets in advance. Another good way to reach the park is to take the overground train to Ostiense and walk along one of the best-preserved stretches of the Aurelian Wall – it's half an hour or so to Porta San Sebastiano.

EUR

Envisaged by Mussolini as a glorious new symbol of a brave new Italian nation, the suburb of EUR ('e-uur') was built for the 1942 world fair, the Esposizione Universale Roma, an event that, because of the Second World War, never took place. These days it can seem rather soulless – a sterile, windswept area of huge roads and monolithic office blocks. But despite its lack of a human angle it's worth a visit for some of its architecture: a rationalist interpretation of ancient Roman style that is startlingly modern. Some of the buildings house the museums they were designed for, one of which in particular – the Museo della Civiltà Romana – is excellent.

Nearby, by way of contrast, a cluster of churches commemorates the place where St Paul was martyred.

Palazzo della Civiltà di Lavoro

Viale della Civiltà di Lavoro.

EUR's most impressive landmark building is often referred to as the *Colosseo Quadrato* ('square Colosseum'), and the influence of Roman architecture is clear. Refurbishments under way at the time of writing will create new office space inside and new café facilities on the ground floor. Clad with travertine marble, the 58-m tall building, designed as the centrepiece of EUR, was opened in 1940. The inscription at the top means 'A nation of poets, of artists, of heroes, of saints, of thinkers, of scientists, of navigators, of travellers'. Facing the

Palazzo della Civiltà di Lavoro.

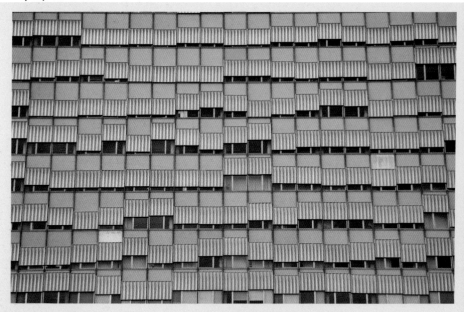

Palazzo at the other end of the street is the **Palazzo dei Congressi**, another iconic building, which is still used for conferences today.

Piazza Guglielmo Marconi

The huge, overblown centre of Mussolini's fascist vision was to have been surrounded by museums. Three survive: the **Museo dell'Alto Medioevo** (T06-5422 8199, Tue-Sun 0900-2000, €2/1 concession), which houses a collection of medieval art and crafts; the **Museo Preistorico Etnografico** (T06-549521, Tue-Sun 0900-1400, €4/2 concession) with prehistoric artefacts, and the **Museo delle Arti e Tradizionei Popolari** (T06-591 2669, Tue-Fri 0900-1800, Sat-Sun 0900-2000, €4/2 concession), which contains objects and costumes of traditional Italian culture.

Palazzo dello Sport

Piazzale dello Sport.

Built for the 1960 Olympics, but nowadays used more for music concerts than for sport, the circular auditorium at the south of EUR is on the edge of a park with a central lake. An innovative running system is being installed here, enabling you to check on your lap times and calories consumed – pick up a special chip at Punto Caffè Lago.

Museo della Civiltà Romana

Piazza Giovanni Agnelli 10, T06-0608, museociviltaromana.it.
Tue-Sat 0900-1400, Sun 0900-1330, €6.50/4.50 concession, free EU citizens under 18 and over 65, joint ticket with planetarium and Museo Astronomico €8.50/6.50.

In one of EUR's hulking great buildings, the Museum of Roman Civilization is old-fashioned but has some redeeming features that make it well worth the trip. Many of the exhibits are models of Rome and Roman statues made at the beginning of the 20th century; they're beginning to show their age, and it's worth skimming through some of the 59 sections to find the highlights – notably casts of the bas-reliefs from Trajan's Column (see page 72) and a huge scale model of ancient Rome at the time of Constantine. The reliefs are extraordinary – doubly so because they were made to decorate a column whose details are difficult to appreciate from the ground. The compositions illustrate Trajan's military victories against the Dacians, and seen close up they reveal a rare understanding of expression, movement, aggression and fear, and a stunning degree of detailing, from leaves on a tree to the weeds in the hair of the river god Danube.

The 21st-century **Museo Astronomico** in the same building has a comfortable, state-of-the-art, three-dimensional planetarium, but the shows are in Italian unless you book in advance with a group. The museum has good, large models of the moon and planets.

Abbazia delle Tre Fontane

Via di Acque Salvie, off via Laurentina,
T06-540 1655.
Daily, 0800-1300, 1500-1800.

At the place where St Paul was beheaded, around AD 67, on the orders of Emperor Nero, his severed

Listings

Eating
Futurarte Café €
Viale Civiltà del Lavoro 50/52,
T06-591 0843, futurartecafe.it.
This huge cafeteria, hung with reproductions of Futurist art, is popular with office workers, and is a good place for a quick lunch, very much in keeping with the EUR surroundings. It's also good value, with set menus of pasta, pizza and salads with bread, water and fruit from €8.

Transport
There are four EUR metro stops. EUR Palasport and EUR Fermi are the most central; Laurentina is the nearest to the Museo della Civiltà Romana and the Abbazia delle Tre Fontane.

head is supposed to have bounced three times on the ground: fountains miraculously sprang up at the places where it landed. Three late 16th-century churches, designed by Giacomo della Porta, stand on the site today, 10 minutes' walk east from the Museo della Civiltà Romana, and are a favourite with pilgrims.

In the **Church of San Paolo delle Tre Fontane**, supposedly built on the exact spot where Paul was executed, the stone pillar to which he was tied is preserved. More interesting as a building, however, is the **Church of Santa Maria in Scala Coeli,** built over an earlier structure that now forms its crypt. This includes a fifth-century altar dedicated to St Zeno and his 10,203 followers, all martyred here by Diocletian in 298. Best of the lot, however, is the gracefully simple Romanesque abbey itself, originally built in the seventh century.

Above: Model of ancient Rome, Museo della Civiltà Romana.
Opposite page: Office block in EUR.

Ostia Antica

Named from the word for 'mouth' or 'door', Ostia was ancient Rome's gateway to the sea, as well as the first line of defence against whoever might come from it. The port was founded at the mouth of the Tiber in the fourth century BC, or perhaps even earlier, and grew to become an economically important city of around 50,000 people, responsible for controlling the import of goods, especially grain, to Rome.

Today, despite its air of abandoned dilapidation, Ostia is one of Italy's most impressive ancient Roman sites, and is, for the most part, free of the hordes of tour groups that plague Pompeii. And while the wild flowers, herbs and moss that grow over much of the site may not be good for the remains themselves, they add an air of romance to the peaceful site. About 30 km southwest of Rome, it now lies 3 km from the sea – the Tiber silt that preserved the remains having also moved the coastline.

From the entrance at Porta Romana the paved main street, the Decumanus Maximus, stretches all the way to Porta Marinara, about 3 km away. Left and right are houses, temples and public buildings to explore. The whole site is easily big enough to fill a whole day, and even then there will be things you don't see. Joining a guided tour is not a bad idea, as the scale of the place can be a little overwhelming. The following are some of the highlights.

Terme di Nettuno

This large complex of baths to the right of the Decumanus Maximus was built in the second century AD by Emperor Hadrian and completed by Antoninus Pius. From a terrace up steps beside the road there are good views down over the spectacular mosaics that give the baths their name: Neptune, god of the sea, is shown with trident in one hand and the reins of galloping sea horses in the other, surrounded by dolphins and semi-aquatic mythical creatures. In the room next door, Neptune's wife Amphitrite is less complete,

Essentials

T06-5635 8099, itnw.roma.it/ostia/scavi. Apr-Oct 0830-1900, Nov-Mar 0830-1700, €6.50/3.25 concession, free EU citizens under 18 and over 65. Guided tours available Tue-Sun (advance booking required), audioguides available, map of site €2. There are usually guides touting for business along the Decumanus Maximus.

while beyond Neptune the mosaic in the frigidarium depicts the sea monster Scylla. The colonnaded area to the west would have been used for exercise.

Teatro

Ostia's beautiful theatre, just to the west of Neptune's baths, would have seated around 3,000 spectators when it was built by Agrippa at the time of Augustus. It was later restored and extended by Commodus in the second century. Though the arches facing the Decumanus Maximus were rebuilt in 1927, most of the rest of the structure is original. Wonderfully expressive marble heads face the stone seats, from where there are good views across the Piazzale delle Corporazioni.

Tip...

Crouch in the central niche at the back of the stage and speak to experience the strange acoustic sensation of your voice being amplified back at you.

Piazzale delle Corporazioni

Evidence of Ostia's importance in the world of Roman commerce can be found in the intriguing Square of the Corporations behind the theatre. Set around a central temple dedicated to Vulcan (the principle deity of Ostia), it is a huge space that was once surrounded by a portico. Stalls around three sides were the offices of everyone involved in shipping, from rope makers to Carthaginian ship owners. They can be identified by the maritime-themed mosaics, with accompanying Latin text, on the ground in front of each stall.

Mitreo delle Sette Sfere

Heading west again, the small Mithraeum of the Seven Spheres is hidden, as is typical of Mithraic

structures. Ostia was unusually obsessed with the mystery cult of the god Mithras, which reached Rome via Persia, and this is one of many temples dedicated to him in the city. The seven semicircles on the floor represent the seven planetary spheres, and personifications of these planets are depicted in mosaic, along with signs of the zodiac. At the back of the room is a bas-relief of Mithras killing the sacred bull.

Via di Diana

With well-preserved *insulae*, or blocks of flats, via di Diana gives a good insight into how the ordinary people of Ostia would have lived. It runs parallel to the Decumanus Maximus one block further north. Some rooms still have frescoed walls, and you can climb stairs to an upper level. On the left of the street, a remarkably well-preserved *thermopolium*, or hot snack bar, seems little different to the simple eateries of modern Rome. There is a basin for washing up, a counter with a stove, and a courtyard at the back with benches and a fountain. On the wall, a fresco depicts fruit and vegetables.

Forum
Built under Emperor Hadrian in the second century, Ostia's forum was a relatively late addition to the city, as it became necessary only once the city grew and took on some of its own political responsibilities. At the north end of the forum, the **Capitolium** (a temple dedicated to Jupiter, Juno and Minerva) is one of the largest buildings on the site; its wide steps face the **Temple of Rome and Augustus** at the other end.

Terme di Sette Sapienti
Via della Foce, branching off to the right beyond the forum, is a pretty, winding street that predates Ostia and once led to the mouth of the river. On the left, halfway along, the **House of Serapis** leads to more impressive mosaics in the **Baths of the Seven Sages**, this time in a large bowl. Here too are frescoes of people bathing. Next door, the **House of the Charioteers** has more frescoes.

Museo
At the northern edge of the site, the museum is a well-managed collection of statues from the site and the surrounding area. The kissing **Psyche and Amor** is an iconic statue, but equally impressive is a life-sized statue of Trajan and another of Perseus carrying Medusa's head. Best of all, however, is the room of sarcophagi, especially the extraordinary tomb of Patroclus, decorated with scenes from the myth of Meleager.

Listings

Eating
There is a cafeteria on site, serving dull sandwiches and reheated pasta. It's a good idea to bring a picnic.

Transport
Roma-Lido trains leave every 15 minutes or so from Porta San Paolo station, next to Piramide metro. Ordinary €1 tickets are valid all the way to Ostia Antica, and the journey takes about 25 minutes. On arrival, cross the bridge over the road outside the station and walk straight on for about 300 m.

Right: Decumanus Maximus, Ostia Antica.
Opposite page: Terme di Nettuno, Ostia Antica

Tarquinia & Cerveteri

Once upon a time there were the Etruscans. Long before the Romans came along, the coastal stretch north of the yet-to-be-founded city was the most powerful and densely populated part of Etruria, their ancient country.

The Etruscan necropolises of Tarquinia and Cerveteri (both UNESCO World Heritage Sites) are a true archaeologist's paradise, full of the mystery of days long gone. Tarquinia's exceptional painted tombs – masterpieces of ancient creative genius – realistically depict the Etruscans' lives and beliefs, shedding light on their customs and society. Cerveteri, on the other hand, with its labyrinth of enormous mushroom-like tombs, is a sort of 'city of the dead', seemingly modelled on what Etruscan towns were actually like. It's the perfect place to get lost in history.

Tarquinia

The ancient Tarxuna is now a lovely fortified medieval town overlooking the sea. Although the necropolis and the Etruscan museum are the two main attractions, the 12th-century **Santa Maria di Castello**, in the oldest part of town, and the alleys of the medieval quarter are worth a visit in their own right.

Museo Archeologico Nazionale di Tarquinia

Piazza Cavour, T0766-856036.
Tue-Sun 0830-1930, €6/3 concession,
free EU citizens under 18 and over 65.

Housed in the Renaissance Palazzo Vitelleschi, the museum features most of the finds from the ancient town and its necropolis: sarcophagi, funerary sculptures, Greek and Etruscan vases. The star exhibit is an almost life-size pair of **winged horses**, dating from the fourth or third century BC, from the pediment of the Temple of the Queen. The relief is one of the most important Etruscan artworks ever brought to light – the horses are made of terracotta and therefore very fragile, which explains why so few of such decorations have survived.

Tip...

If you are intending to visit the museum and the necropolis on the same day, you can buy a combined ticket for €8/4 concession.

A detail of the fountain on Piazza del Comune, right in the heart of Tarquinia's old town.

The recurring images of wealthy Etruscans reclining on couches at banquets while watching dancers and entertainers convey the impression of a civilized, hedonistic society. Many of the paintings also bring out the Etruscans' rampant sexuality, from the erotic flogging of the **Tomba della Fustigazione** (490 BC) to the orgiastic dance in the **Tomba delle Baccanti** (510-500 BC).

Cerveteri

Just like nearby Tarquinia, the old city of Kysry (Caere in Latin) was a rich maritime power, and its history can be traced back as far as the ninth century BC. Here too, an extensive necropolis and a small but interesting museum are the highlights.

Museo Nazionale Cerite

Piazza Santa Maria Maggiore, T06-994 1354.
Tue-Sun 0830-1930, €6/3 concession, or combined ticket with necropolis €8/4.

Housed within the mighty walls of Castello Ruspoli, the museum features luxury goods imported from Greece, which show the strong influence of Hellenistic culture on Etruscan civilization. The second floor houses sarcophagi and objects found in the nearby necropolis.

Necropoli della Banditaccia

Piazza della Necropoli, T06-994 0001.
Tue-Sun, summer 0830-1930, winter 0830-1630, €6/3 concession, free EU citizens under 18 and over 65, or combined ticket with museum €8/4.

Cerveteri's city of the dead is very different from the necropolis in Tarquinia. First of all, it's laid out like a town, with streets and squares. Second, the tombs themselves imitate contemporary homes and are the only evidence of Etruscan residential architecture. Don't miss the **Tomba dei Rilievi** (fourth century BC), whose walls are covered with bas-reliefs of all those articles that the deceased would need in the afterlife, including weapons,

Necropoli Monterozzi

Strada Provinciale Monterozzi, T0766-856308.
Daily, summer 0830-1930, winter 0830-1400 (last admission 90 mins before closing), €6/3 concession, free EU citizens under 18 and over 65.

This is what is left of the once powerful Etruscan Tarxuna: a massive 6,000 tombs (many yet to be explored), of which some 200 are finely painted. About 20 are open to the public and they are all of exceptional artistic quality. The custom of painting tombs was quite common among the Etruscan aristocracy, but in Tarquinia it assumed vast importance over a long period of time – from the seventh to the third centuries BC. Had these tombs not been discovered, we would probably still know very little about the society of the Etruscans, as they left no written documents.

tools and even household pets. Equally important are the **Tomba della Capanna** (seventh century BC), one of the earliest monumental tombs on the site, and the more sophisticated and slightly later **Tomba dei Dolii** – its Camera degli Alari was discovered intact during excavations and it is one of the most important complexes of the time.

The site is huge, so study the map first and decide what you want to see before walking too far.

Right: La Cantina dell'Etrusco in Tarquinia.
Opposite page: An old-fashioned sign of a butcher's shop in Tarquinia's centro storico.

Listings

Eating
Antica Locanda le Ginestre €€€
Piazza Santa Maria 5, Cerveteri, T06-994 0672, le-ginestre.it.
Tue-Sun 1200-1500, 1930-2300.
This award-winning restaurant is rightly considered one of the best eateries in Lazio. Among the *primi*, try the *gnocchi di polenta con sugo di cinghiale* (semolina dumplings with wild boar ragù). Fish dishes are especially good. Service is impeccable and the atmosphere elegant.

Arcadia €€€
Via Mazzini 6, Tarquinia, T0766-855501, on-web.it/arcadia.
Tue-Sun 1230 onwards, 1800 onwards.
A multi-award-winning family affair, run by Ferdinando and his wife Trine, who opened it in 1997. Fish is the speciality, but they're also renowned for tasty traditional dishes. Everything is prepared with fresh, seasonal ingredients.

La Cantina dell'Etrusco €
Via Menotti Garibaldi 13, Tarquinia, T0766-858418, vinoetrusco.it.
Wed-Sun 1900-2400.
Earthy food in an atmospheric, vaulted 14th-century setting: the menu is not very varied but will especially please meat lovers. If you are not on a diet, try the *bruschetta tarquiniese* with *guanciale* (cured pork cheek). Wash it all down with one of over 100 Italian wines, or a glass of the local *vino etrusco*. Ask to see the ancient cellars downstairs, with rows of old barrels.

Transport
Trains to Tarquinia leave from Termini (about 50 mins, also stopping at Ostiense, Trastevere and San Pietro, trenitalia.com for timetables). The Necropolis is a 20-minute walk from the town centre, or you can get a bus from Barriera San Giusto to the Cimitero stop.

To reach Cerveteri, catch one of the half-hourly Cotral buses (cotralspa.it for timetables) from outside Cornelia metro.

Viterbo

Alittle gem in the north of the region, Viterbo charms visitors with its perfectly preserved medieval centre: impressive churches and palaces, narrow alleys and quiet piazzas. Echoes of the Dark Ages still resound everywhere – this is the only place in Italy where you can stroll along Cemetery Street, sit on a bench in peaceful Death Square, or admire the church of St Mary of the Plague.

Viterbo is the city of water – its many fountains grace almost every square and its sulphurous springs are hailed as a remedy for many conditions. Most importantly, this is also the *città dei papi*: during the 13th century at least a dozen popes were elected here, died in the town or spent some time within its thick city walls and in the comfort of a beautiful Gothic palace.

Palazzo dei Papi

Piazza San Lorenzo.
Salone del Conclave open by appointment: ask at Museo del Colle del Duomo (to the left of the cathedral, T338-133 6529).

Viterbo's Papal Palace, dating from 1255-1267, is an impressive building quite similar in style to a medieval city hall. Raniero Gatti, the city's Capitano del Popolo (an official something like a modern-day mayor) had it erected to provide the popes with an appropriate dwelling when they moved to Viterbo to escape Roman hostility and violence. They didn't always have a good time here, though. When the first resident – Clement IV – died in 1268, the cardinals could not agree on his successor.

Day trips from Rome

After three years of deliberations, the exasperated townspeople locked them up in a hall of the palace (history's first papal conclave), put them on a starvation diet and removed the roof. This quickly led to the election of Gregory X. The roof was fixed but collapsed six years later on the head of the then Holy Father, John XXI, who was quickly entombed in the cathedral next door. This was the last straw, and the prelates beat a hasty retreat to Rome.

Duomo

Piazza San Lorenzo, T0761-340048.
Daily, around 0900-1300, 1500-1800.

Next door to the Papal Palace, the simple Romanesque Cathedral of St Laurence was built between the 12th and 13th centuries. Its façade was finished in 1570, thanks to the then Bishop of Viterbo, Cardinal Gianfrancesco Gambara. Inside there are two notable early paintings, *Redentore Benedicente* (1472) by Girolamo da Cremona and a 12th-century *Madonna with Child*.

Santa Maria Nuova e Chiostro Longobardo

Piazza Santa Maria Nuova, T0761-340700.
Daily, around 0900-1300, 1500-1800, cloister (entrance at side of church) around 0900-1300 and 1600-sunset, free but donations welcomed.

The name is misleading, as this is Viterbo's oldest church, dating from 1080. Austerely Romanesque in style, it was originally a pagan temple, and its façade boasts an ancient image of Jupiter. St Thomas Aquinas preached from its tiny outdoor pulpit in 1266.
There is an eerie story about the **Lombard Cloister** and the **crypt**. Both served as paupers' graves for victims of the plague in the 1300s; they were rediscovered only last century when the floor of the sacristy above collapsed.

Austerely Romanesque in style, it was originally a pagan temple, and its façade boasts an ancient image of Jupiter.

Museo Civico

Piazza Crispi 2, T0761-348275.
Tue-Sun, summer 0900-1900, winter 0900-1800, €3.10.

Housed in the former convent next door to Santa Maria della Verità, the museum features an Etruscan and Roman section as well as a rich picture gallery. Sebastiano del Piombo's *Pietà* is the star of the collection. In the adjoining church, the **Mazzatosta Chapel** contains the *Marriage of the Virgin* (1469), frescoed by Lorenzo da Viterbo.

A walk through Viterbo's medieval squares

The starting point for a tour of the old town is **piazza del Plebiscito** with its medieval buildings: **Palazzo del Podestà** (with a 44-m high clock tower), **Palazzo del Capitano del Popolo** and **Palazzo dei Priori**. The last is now the city hall, but some rooms and the lovely courtyard, with a 16th-century fountain by Filippo Caparozzi, are open to the public (0900-1200, 1600-1900, free). Also on the square is the **Chiesa di Sant'Angelo in Spatha**, whose façade incorporates a sarcophagus (now replaced by a copy) known as Galiana's Tomb. According to tradition, Galiana was a renowned beauty killed by an unrequited lover.
Via di San Lorenzo will take you to **piazza del Gesù**. This was the city's political and social centre, dominated by the 11th-century church of the same name (closed). At the altar of this church in March 1271, not far from where the cardinals were still arguing over the identity of the next pope, Guy de Montfort brutally murdered Henry of Cornwall as a result of a family feud: he appears among the murderers in the river of blood in the seventh circle of Dante's *Inferno*.
Continuing along the same street, you reach **piazza della Morte**. Despite its name – Death Square – it is one of the nicest squares of the city, decorated with Viterbo's oldest fountain, erected in the 13th century. The piazza is named after the Confraternity of Prayer and Death, whose charitable task was to give a Christian burial to corpses abandoned in the countryside.

Tip...

The best time to visit the city is during the celebrations in honour of St Rosa (3 Sep), when the Macchina di Santa Rosa, a 30-m high illuminated tower of metal, wood and papier-mâché, is carried around the streets of the old town by 100 devoted men. Unmissable.

Last stop is the peaceful **piazza San Pellegrino** (follow the yellow signs to 'Quartiere Medievale' and 'S. Pellegrino'), right in the heart of the oldest district. This piazza comes to life at the beginning of each May during the San Pellegrino in Fiore festival, when local residents compete for the most beautiful flower-adorned balcony.

Around Viterbo

Terme dei Papi

Strada Bagni 12, T0761-3501, termedeipapi.it.
Thermal pool Wed-Mon 0900-1900, Sat also 2100-0100, weekdays €12, Sat €15, Sun €18.

Viterbo's sulphurous springs are 3 km west of the town. They have been popular since Etruscan and Roman times and even Michelangelo is known to have taken the waters there. Although virtually nothing is left of the old *thermae*, the springs still do their job and are reputed to be good for just about everything, from rheumatism to dermatitis. For a relaxing day, head to the monumental outdoor Thermal Pool: the naturally hot water is especially pleasant in winter. The spa also offers a range of beauty treatments.

Villa Lante

Bagnaia, T0761-288008.
Tue-Sun Nov-Feb 0830-1630, Mar 0830-1730, 1-15 Apr and 16 Sep-Oct 0830-1830; 16 Apr-15 Sep 0830-1930, €2.

The medieval village of Bagnaia, 4 km east of Viterbo, was once a famous summer resort for wealthy clergymen. Aside from the fascination of its small *centro storico*, the most striking attraction

is this Italian garden attributed to Giacomo Barrozzi di Vignola. Cardinal Gambara, a man with a modern taste for outdoor living, commissioned the project in the 1570s. Many of the fountains were designed by Siena-born Tommaso Ghinucci, who also worked on the more famous Villa d'Este in Tivoli.

Listings

Eating
L'Archetto €
Via San Cristoforo 1, T0761-325769.
Tue-Sat 1230-1430, 1930-2130, Sun 1230-1430.
This family-run trattoria tucked under an archway off via Saffi is the perfect place to sample traditional local cuisine. Tasty game dishes are their speciality, but you should also try *acquacotta* – a typical vegetable soup with bread and egg – or the equally delicious *minestra di ceci e castagne* (chickpea and chestnut soup).

Gran Caffè Schenardi
Corso Italia 11/13, T0761-345860.
This has been Viterbo's most elegant meeting place since 1818: you can sip your coffee in a neoclassical environment, surrounded by statues, stucco decorations and French mirrors.

Transport
There is a regular train service from Ostiense (also stopping at Trastevere and San Pietro) to Viterbo Porta Fiorentina (about 2 hrs). Alternatively, Cotral buses depart from Saxa Rubra station (first bus 0630, last bus from Viterbo Riello 2000).
Viterbo tourist information office is at via Ascenzi 4 (T0761-325992, Tue-Sun summer 1000-1300, 1500-1900, winter 1000-1300, 1500-1700).

Tivoli

About 30 km east of Rome, Tibur (modern-day Tivoli) grew up at the edge of the Sabine Hills, around the waterfalls of the Aniene River. Settled from at least the 13th century BC, it was home to the Tiburtine Sybil, one of the semi-mythical women who could foretell the future. In 90 BC the town's inhabitants were given Roman citizenship and it became an important stop on the via Tiburtina, across the Apennines to the east.

Appreciating the pastoral and watery charms of the area, Roman emperors built their grand summer houses in the hills here. The extensive ruins of Villa Adriano, Hadrian's enormous holiday complex, take some effort to get to, but are well worth it. More easily reached, and open to the public in the summer, are the Roman remains in the centre of Tivoli, on either side of a gorge with waterfalls.

During the Renaissance a new appreciation of the Roman remains made the town fashionable, and Villa d'Este was built in the 16th century, using some materials taken from the Villa Adriano. Today it is famous for its extraordinary fountains.

Villa d'Este

Piazza Trento, T0774-332920, villadestetivoli.info. Tue-Sun 0830-1 hr before sunset, €6.50/3.25 concession, free EU citizens under 18 and over 65.

Built for Cardinal Ippolito d'Este II, son of Lucrezia Borgia, who became governor of Tivoli in 1550, the villa has elaborate frescoes by Girolamo Muziano and Federico Zuccari, but is more famous for its fountain-filled formal gardens. The fountains are supplied with water from the Aniene, using about 300 litres a second.

From the entrance visitors enter a large central loggia (the cardinal's private rooms were on the first floor). Off this loggia is a sequence of richly frescoed rooms illustrating Old Testament scenes. The *Salone della Fontana* is notable for its virtuoso use of perspective on the ceiling – stand directly underneath for the full effect.

Outside, 17 elaborately complex fountains are scattered around a formal Renaissance garden, with carefully tended box hedges, trees and reflecting pools. Two of the highlights are not just spectacular but also musical. The so-called **Owl Fountain** uses hydraulic pressure to play a chorus of birdsong (every 2 hrs from 1000), though it tends to sound more like a cuckoo than an owl. The **Organ Fountain**, not finished until 1611 and Baroque in style, plays a tune on a real organ (every 2 hrs from 1030). Other fountains include the Ovate Fountain, representing Tivoli, the Rometta Fountain at the opposite end of the Hundred Fountains, and the many-breasted Goddess of Nature, spurting water from her nipples.

Villa Gregoriana

Entrances in piazza Tempio di Vesta and largo Sant'Angelo, T06-3996 7701, villagregoriana.it. Apr-15 Oct daily 1000-1830, 16 Oct-Nov and Mar Tue-Sat 1000-1430, Sun 1000-1600, €4/2.50 concession, free to National Trust members.

After a serious flood of the Aniene River in 1826, which destroyed much of the oldest part of the town, a plan was devised to dig a tunnel through Monte Catillo. This had the advantage not only of diverting the water but also of creating a 120-m high waterfall, which is now the centrepiece of the recently restored gardens of the villa. Other attractions include grottoes, paths winding through the 2,300 trees, and the ancient Roman temples of Vesta and Tiburno, the former circular, the latter – which may actually have been dedicated to the Sybil – square.

Villa Adriana

Via di Villa Adriana, T0774-382733, pierreci.it. Daily 0900-1 hr before sunset, €6.50/3.25 concession (€10/6.75 during exhibitions), free EU citizens under 18 and over 65.

One of the grandest sites of ancient Rome, to call Hadrian's construction outside Tivoli a villa is a little misleading. In fact it's a sprawling complex containing palaces, temples, libraries, theatres, baths, pools and piazzas. Hadrian had his rural escape built in the second century, moving into it entirely for just the last three years of his reign.

Contemporary visitors enter at the northern end, near the Teatro Greco, and a path leads up to a small building housing a model of the complex – useful for getting your bearings. Boards around the site give information in English, but it's worth getting a map from the bookshop at the entrance.

Highlights include the so-called **Teatro Marittimo**, which is not a theatre at all, but a small villa surrounded by a moat – probably a peaceful bolt-hole for Hadrian. To the east the **Hospitalia** are living quarters with beautiful geometric mosaic floors. Just to the south is the **Palazzo Imperiale**, the original hub of the complex. Much of the design drew on, and represented, places the emperor had travelled to – to the west, bath complexes stretch south towards an example of this, the **Canopo**, a large bath of water representing an Egyptian city, possibly Alexandria.

Listings

Eating
Ristorante Sibilla €€
Via della Sibilla 50, T0774-335281, ristorantesibilla.com. Tue-Sun lunch and dinner.
Backing on to the Roman temples of Sybil and Vesta, a smart restaurant that serves up traditional pasta dishes and a good selection of meat cooked on an open grill. There's a great greenery-draped terrace overlooking the gorge, and, in winter, an open fire.

Gholò
Via Rosolina 66, T0774-531640.
Near the entrance to Villa Adriana, this upmarket little café and gelateria does excellent panini as well as handmade chocolates, biscuits and cakes.

Transport
There are frequent buses to Tivoli from Ponte Mammolo metro (€2, around 50 mins), passing within 1 km of Villa Adriana. Alternatively, trains run every hour or so (€2.30, around 1 hr) from Tiburtina. Turn right out of the station and follow the signs for 15 minutes to the town centre and Villa Gregoriana. Orange local buses run once or twice an hour from piazza Garibaldi to near the Villa Adriana (€1).

Tivoli's helpful tourist information kiosk is just off piazza Garibaldi (T0774-313536, Tue-Sun 1000-1400).

Castelli Romani

The Roman Castles are a series of towns in the Alban Hills, southeast of the capital, which can be thought of as a sort of 'Rome before Rome'. Albano, for instance, is named after the ancient Alba Longa, the 'mother city' of Rome, and the legendary birthplace of Romulus and Remus. They are also a 'Rome outside Rome' – a favourite day trip for those living in the capital, providing plenty of unbeatable food, good wine and amazing landscapes. The proverbial hospitality of their inhabitants is the icing on the cake.

Frascati is the best known of the Castelli. It name derives from *frasche*, the branches used in the construction of ancient timber houses. Today, leafy branches still decorate the entrances of the local osterie (traditionally called *fraschette*), the best places to enjoy the local wine. Although the town was severely bombed during the Second World War it still retains its charm, and on clear days it offers superb views of the Tyrrhenian Sea and Rome. Its string of villas reflects its importance as the chosen holiday retreat for Rome's noble families from the 16th century onwards. The

View of Monte Porzio Catone, one of the towns of the Castelli Romani area.

public park of **Villa Torlonia** features a Baroque *teatro delle acque* ('water theatre') by Carlo Maderno; the grounds of the 17th-century **Villa Aldobrandini** have fine views over the capital; and Borromini's **Villa Falconieri** (open to the public only occasionally) is decorated with amazing frescoes by Pier Leone Ghezzi.

Just southwest of Frascati, **Grottaferrata** was built around the abbey founded by St Nilus in 1004, which is still run by Greek Catholic monks. Its **Basilica di Santa Maria** (daily, around 1000-1230, 1600-1730) is possibly the finest church of the entire area, a fusion of Byzantine elements and medieval Italian art. The highlight is in the chapel on the right: a superb fresco cycle by Domenichino (1610), depicting episodes from the life of Sts Nilus and Bartholomew.

Like Frascati, **Marino** is well known for its wine. During its grape festival, the *Sagra dell'Uva* (first Sun in Oct), wine flows freely from the town's main fountain.

Passing volcanic **Lake Albano** you come to the dramatically located **Rocca di Papa**, one of the area's best-preserved medieval towns. Its citadel is known as the 'Bavarian quarter' because Emperor Ludwig's militiamen were stationed here in the 14th century.

Significantly nicknamed 'Vatican II' by the late Pope John Paul II, **Castel Gandolfo**, on the other side of the lake, has been the summer residence of the popes since 1597. The entrance to the Papal Palace (not open to the public), built by Carlo Maderno under Urban VIII, is on the main square. Opposite are the Church of San Tommaso (1661) and a magnificent fountain, both by Gian Lorenzo Bernini.

Continuing south, **Albano Laziale** is named after Alba Longa, hometown of Romulus and Remus. The remains of the huge military camp built there by Septimius Severus can be seen everywhere – among them is **Il Cisternone**, a third-century cistern that is still in use.

Ariccia is another town of Latin origins. Its medieval centre was rearranged by Bernini, and the lion's share is occupied by **Palazzo Chigi** (Piazza della Repubblica 1, T06-933 0053, palazzochigiariccia.it, guided tours Tue-Fri 1100, 1600, 1730, Sat-Sun 1030,

A detail of Marino's Fountain of the Moors, from which free wine comes out for visitors and locals during the Grape Festival.

It's a fact...

Although *Il Gattopardo* (*The Leopard*), Luchino Visconti's classic 1963 movie, was set in Sicily, most of the interior scenes were shot in Palazzo Chigi in Ariccia, including the famous 45-minute ball sequence with Burt Lancaster and Claudia Cardinale.

Day trips from Rome

1130, 1230 and hourly 1600-1900 in summer and 1500-1800 in winter, €7/4 concession; Cardinal's Rooms Sat-Sun only). Stepping inside is like entering a time machine. Some rooms still feature their original stamped leather wallcoverings, following the Spanish style in vogue in 17th-century Italy. There is also an interesting picture gallery with paintings from the 1600s.

Ariccia is synonymous with Italy's best *porchetta* – roasted suckling pig seasoned with a variety of herbs, including wild fennel. Vans and kiosks selling this local speciality can be found all over the Castelli, often serving the pork in panini to eat on the spot, accompanied by a glass of red wine.

Volcanic **Lake Nemi** is one of the Castelli area's most pleasant spots. The town of **Nemi** itself is worth a visit especially in the summer, when you can taste its famous *fragoline* (wild strawberries). On the slopes of the crater is **Genzano**, with the

beautiful 17th-century **Palazzo Sforza Cesarini**. The town comes to life during the annual Corpus Christi celebrations, when the whole centre is covered with floral carpets (the so-called *Infiorata*), mostly depicting religious themes.

A detail of the fresco cycle by Domenichino inside the Basilica di Santa Maria in Grottaferrata

Frascati, the cathedral.

Listings

Eating
Taverna dello Spuntino €€€€
Via Cicerone 22, Grottaferrata,
T06-945 9366, tavernadellospuntino.com.
Daily 1300-1530, 2000-2300.
The decor is wonderful, with gigantic hams hanging from the ceiling and lush displays of vegetables and flowers in every corner. Popular with Rome's Who's Who (Capitano Totti is a regular), this is the place to sample the area's most traditional dishes, prepared with strictly seasonal ingredients. Homemade pasta is its speciality: try the delicious *gnocchi alle castagne* (chestnut gnocchi).

La Credenza €€€
Via Cola di Rienzo 4, Marino, T06-938 5105.
Mon-Sat 1130-1500, 1930-2200.
Run by husband and wife Maria and Massimo, it mixes the flavours of the Castelli with recipes from the Abruzzo region, where Maria comes from. There is no freezer in the kitchen and no written menu, as everything is prepared exclusively with the freshest ingredients available. Only six tables, so booking is essential.

Le Carceri €€
Via Saurio 24, Genzano di Roma,
T06-939 7691, trattorialecarceri.it.
Thu-Tue 1200-1500, 1930-2400.
For something a bit more unusual, eat inside Genzano's ex-jail. Owner Vincenzo has brilliantly transformed the old prison into a friendly meeting place for foodies. There is a good range of local dishes, portions are huge and prices very reasonable.

Transport
There is a regular train service from Termini to Frascati (30 mins). Several Cotral buses (cotralspa.it for timetables) run from Anagnina metro to many towns of the Castelli, including Grottaferrata, Frascati, Castel Gandolfo and Marino. Frascati's tourist information office is at piazza Marconi 1 (T06-942 0331).

Castelli wine

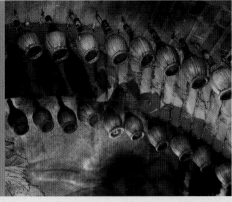

E' mejo er vino/de li Castelli/de questa zozza società ('Castelli wine is better than this dirty society'), runs a popular Roman song, and wine has been produced here for 3000 years. The famous whites are mostly a combination of Malvasia and Trebbiano grapes: Frascati is considered the best, acclaimed by Romans and popes alike. Genzano and Lanuvio produce a full-bodied, velvety white, Colli Lanuvini, and Cannellino is a dessert wine also made in the area. The **Museo Diffuso del Vino** in Monte Porzio Catone (via Vittorio Emanuele II 22, 36 and 46, T06-9434 1027, Fri-Sun 0900-1300, 1500-1900, €2), housed in several old wine cellars, gives an interesting insight into Castelli wine culture.

Contents

Practicalities

Getting there

Air

From UK and Ireland
Flying time from the UK and Ireland is 2-3 hours. **easyJet** depart twice daily from London Gatwick to Ciampino. **Ryanair** fly daily from Liverpool and Dublin to Ciampino. **KLM** and **British Airways** offer (pricier) flights to Fiumicino from regional destinations such as Manchester, Newcastle, Southampton and Aberdeen. Overland travel via train and coach or car is viable, but will take a more leisurely 24 hours (if you're lucky).

From North America
Continental, **American Airlines** and **Delta** fly direct from New York to Fiumicino. **Delta** also flies from Toronto via NY. Other airlines that fly from North America to Rome include: **British Airways**, **KLM**, **Lufthansa**, **Swiss**, **United**, **Air France**.

To search for lower-priced flights to Europe from the US, try **europebyair.com** (T888-387 2479).

From Rest of Europe
Rome is a well-connected city, with daily direct flights to most major European destinations including Paris, Nice, Frankfurt and Berlin. **Air France** alone run six flights per day from CDG to Fiumicino. By rail, overnight sleepers from Paris take 15 hours, travel time from Berlin is 17 hours.

Airport Information
Fiumicino Airport – Leonardo da Vinci, (T06-6595 3640, adr.it), 25 km southwest of the city centre, is the main airport. The **Leonardo Express** (trenitalia. com) rail service connects the airport to the city's central station, Rome Termini, every half an hour from around 0630-2330. It takes 35 minutes and costs €11 (under 12s travel free). Validate your tickets in the yellow machines before boarding. A taxi to or from the city centre costs €45. **Ciampino Airport**, (T06-794941, adr.it), 15 km southeast of the centre, is the smaller airport serving budget airlines. A taxi to the city centre will cost €35. A direct **Terravision** (terravision.eu/rome_ciampino.html) bus service to Termini meets outside the arrivals hall and costs €8 one-way, €14 return. Online booking brings discounts and lets you cut the queues.

Rail

Rome Termini is the central station of Rome, connecting the city with regional and international destinations. You can travel with **Eurostar** (eurostar. com) from London to Paris, before joining an overnight sleeper from Paris Bercy to Rome. The overnight *Palatino* departs at 1900 daily and reaches Rome by 1000 the next morning. Book tickets at **raileurope.com** (T0870-584 8848) searching for trains after 1900. Eurostar starts at £45 return and the Palatino, sharing a six-berth couchette, at £55 return.

Road

London to Rome's 1850 km journey will take 18 hours' driving time. The A1 *autostrade* (motorway) splices Italy vertically – from the north take the exit 'Roma Nord'; from the south, follow 'Roma Est'. Both lead you to Rome's Grande Raccordo Anulare, which loops the city and provides various routes into the centre. **Autostrade** (T055-420 3200, autostrade.it) provides information on motorways in Italy and **Automobile Club Italiana** (T06-49981, aci.it) provides general driving information.

Bus/coach
Eurolines (T0870-580 8080, nationalexpress.co.uk) operate three services per week from London Victoria to Rome, changing in Paris and Milan and lasting around 33 hours. Prices start at £95 return. Coaches arrive and depart in Rome at Stazione Tiburtina.

Getting around

On foot Unless you have Roman moped riding in your genes, walking is the best way to get around Rome. Crossing roads takes a certain amount of bravery. Reticence is never rewarded: watch how the locals do it and you'll soon get the idea. Traffic dodging aside, it's mostly a pleasant city for strolling, with very few large roads and lots of small, cobbled backstreets that weren't designed for cars. Crossing from one side of the centre to the other (Termini to St Peter's, for example) shouldn't take more than an hour, and there's plenty to see en route.

By public transport Rome's public transport network is cheap, and reasonably good, if often chaotic. Until the city's third metro route opens, sometime in the 23rd century, the metro for the most part skirts the city centre. There are a few tram and bus routes which are more useful. The city's public transport website, atac.roma.it has plenty of info in English.

Buses and trams A few particularly useful routes include: the 40 Express from Termini to Piazza Pia, for St Peter's; the H, from Termini to Trastevere via Piazza Venezia and Largo Argentina; and the tiny electric 119, from Piazza del Popolo down via del Corso to piazza Venezia and back via piazza di Spagna. The fast tram 8 connects Largo Argentina with Trastevere station. Night buses run through the night – look for bus stop signs with owls on.

Metro Lines A and B intersect at Termini, the main train and bus station: A is useful for piazza di Spagna, St Peter's and the Vatican; B gets you to the Colosseum and the Caracalla Baths as well as further south to Ostiense and EUR. Trains run 0530-2330; 0030 on Saturday nights.

Tickets Rome has a single ticketing system for its public transport: a €1 ticket allows you to use as many buses and trams as you like for 70 minutes from when you first stamp your ticket, plus one entry to the metro. Buy your undated *biglietto* from a *tabacchi* or news stand and stamp it yourself in the machines on buses or trams the first time you get on. These tickets include EUR and Ostia. There is an all-day ticket available for €4.

Trains For trips out of the city trains are usually the best option. Long distance trains run from Termini, the main station, many also stop at Tiburtina. Trains for Ostia run from Porta San Paolo overground station, next to Piramide metro, those for Tivoli from Tiburtina, and for Viterbo leave from Ostiense (via Trastevere) or Tiburtina.

Taxis Taxis can be a good option, especially if you're trying to get across the city with luggage. You're supposed to get them from taxi ranks but if you're persistent you may be able to flag down a passing one. Allow about €6 or €7 for a 10-minute journey. Taxis (€35 fixed price) are also a good bet for getting to and from Ciampino airport.

Driving The thrills of driving around piazza Venezia can only really be recommended to those for whom bungee-jumping and sky-diving have become dull. If you really need a car, try to avoid driving in the city during busy periods.

Going green

A plane is bound to deliver you to your destination country much faster than a train and – with budget airlines at least – can be the cheaper option. If you have the luxury of time, and the choice of a two-berth couchette, what could be more romantic than lying in crisp white sheets as you speed through lamplit Alpine villages and watching the sun rise over the Italian lakes?

Practicalities
Directory

Customs & immigration

UK and EU citizens do not need a visa, but will need a valid passport to enter Italy. A standard tourist visa for those outside of the EU is valid for up to 90 days.

Disabled travellers

Italy is a bit behind when it comes to catering for disabled travelers; access is sometimes very difficult or ill thought out. Rome is particularly difficult, with many of the city's ancient sites largely inaccessible. Contact an agency before departure for more details such as **Accessible Italy** (aacessibleitaly.com) or **Society for Accessible Travel and Hospitality** (sath.org).

Emergency Numbers

Police T112 (with English-speaking operators) T113 (*carabinieri)*; Ambulance T118; Fire T115; Roadside assistance T116.

Etiquette

Bella figura – projecting a good image – is important to contemporary Romans. Take note of public notices about conduct: sitting on steps or eating and drinking in certain historic areas is not allowed. Covering arms and legs is necessary for admission into some churches, especially St Peter's – in some cases even shorts are not permitted. Punctuality is often an optional luxury in Rome, so be prepared to wait.

Families

Whether it's a run around an amphitheatre or an afternoon in a *gelateria*, families are well accommodated in Rome, and there's plenty to do besides endless museum visits. The family is highly regarded in Italy and *bambini* are indulged. Do note that lone parents or adults accompanying children of a different surname may need evidence before taking children in and out of the country.

Contact your Italian embassy for current details (Italian embassy in London, T020-7312 2200).

Health

Comprehensive travel and medical insurance is strongly recommended for all travel. EU citizens should apply for a free European Health Insurance Card (ehic.org) which offers reduced-cost medical treatment. Late night pharmacies are identified by a large green cross outside. T1100 for addresses of the nearest open pharmacies. The accident and emergency department of a hospital is the pronto soccorso.

Bambino Gesu is a children's hospital, with some English-speaking doctors. Piazza Onofrio 4, T06-68591. Hospital **San Pietro Fatebenefratelli** (via Cassia 600, T06-33581) is one of Rome's best-known hospitals and also has English-speaking doctors.

Insurance

Comprehensive travel and medical insurance is strongly recommended for all travel – the EHIC is not a replacement for insurance. You should check any exclusions, and that your policy covers you for all the activities you want to undertake. Keep details of your insurance documents separately. Emailing yourself with the details is a good way to keep the information safe and accessible. Ensure you have full insurance if hiring a car, and you might need an international insurance certificate if taking your own car (contact your current insurers).

Money

The Italian currency is the Euro. There are ATMs throughout Rome and Lazio that accept major credit and debit cards. To change cash or travellers' cheques, look for a *cambio*. Post offices usually offer better rates, but expect to queue. Many restaurants, shops, museums and art galleries will take major credit cards. Paying directly with debit cards such as Cirrus is less easy in many places, so withdrawing from an ATM and paying cash may be the better option. Keep some cash for toll roads, if you're driving. Banks are usually open Monday-Friday 0830-1330, 1430-1600.

Police

Italian police are subdivided into different but not always very clear-cut categories: the *vigili urbani* are in effect glorified traffic wardens; the *carabinieri*, nominally a branch of the military, deal with public order; and the *polizia* with other crime. If you have a crime to report, ask for the nearest *questura* (police station).

Post

Italian post has a not entirely undeserved reputation for being unreliable, particularly for handling postcards. Overseas post will require *posta prioritaria* (priority mail) and a postcard stamp will cost from €0.60. You can buy *francobolli* (stamps) at post offices and *tabacchi* (look for T signs). The city's most stylish post office is the grand, Fascist-era Testaccio branch.

Safety

The crime rate in Italy is generally low, but rates of petty crime higher. Rome is generally a very safe city, though pickpockets do operate, especially on buses to and from Termini. Take general care when travelling: don't flaunt your valuables, take only what money you need (and don't keep it in the same place): don't take risks you wouldn't at home. Beware of scams and con-artists, and don't expect things to go smoothly if you partake in fake goods. Car break-ins are common, so always remove valuables. Do not make it clear which stop you're getting off at – it gives potential thieves a timeframe to work in. Rome has surprisingly little ethnic diversity for a

European capital, and its status as the capital of the Catholic faith means its gender politics can be old fashioned but, though you may experience both casual racism and sexism, it's unusual for it to feel threatening. A notable exception is found among the city's football fans, who have a reputation for violence against opposing supporters.

Telephone

The code for Rome is 06. You need to use this even when dialling from within the city. The prefix for Italy is +39. You no longer need to drop the initial '0' from area codes when calling from abroad. For directory enquiries call T12.

Time difference

Italy uses Central European Time, GMT+1.

Tipping

Only the more expensive restaurants will necessarily expect a tip, although everywhere will be grateful for one; 10-15% is the norm. A few spare coins with coffee might speed up service. Taxis may add on extra costs for luggage etc but an additional tip is always appreciated. Rounding up prices always goes down well, especially if it means avoiding having to give change – not a favourite Italian habit.

Tourist information

There are tourist information booths around the city, usually well stocked with maps and leaflets, but less useful if you actually want to ask a question. The main office at Via Parigi 5 (T06-0608, en.turismoroma.it) is more useful.

Voltage

Italy functions on a 220V mains supply. Plugs are the standard European two-pin variety.

Language

In hotels and bigger restaurants, you'll usually find English is spoken. The further you go from the tourist centre, however, the more trouble you may have, unless you have at least a smattering of Italian. Along with Italian, people often speak the colourful, regional idiom, called Romanesco. Words are very similar to Italian but they might be pronounced in different ways. Roman dialect has stronger sounds than standard Italian and consonants are very often doubled.

Pronunciation

Stress in spoken Italian usually falls on the penultimate syllable.

Italian has standard sounds: unlike English you can work out how it sounds from how it's written and vice versa.

Vowels

a like 'a' in cat
e like 'e' in vet, or slightly more open, like the 'ai' in air (except after c or g, see consonants below)
i like 'i' in sip (except after c or g, see below)
o like 'o' in fox
u like 'ou' in soup

Consonants

Generally consonants sound the same as in English, though 'e' and 'i' after 'c' or 'g' make them soft (a 'ch' or a 'j' sound) and are silent themselves, whereas 'h' makes them hard (a 'k' or 'g' sound), the opposite to English. So ciao is pronounced 'chaow', but chiesa (church) is pronounced 'kee-ay-sa'.

The combination 'gli' is pronounced like the 'lli' in million, and 'gn' like 'ny' in Tanya.

Basics

thank you   *grazie*
hi/goodbye   *ciao* (informal)
good day (until after lunch/
mid-afternoon)   *buongiorno*
good evening (after lunch)   *buonasera*
goodnight   *buonanotte*
goodbye   *arrivederci*
please   *per favore*
I'm sorry   *mi dispiace*
excuse me   *permesso/scusi*
yes   *si*
no   *no*

Numbers

one	*uno*	17	*diciassette*
two	*due*	18	*diciotto*
three	*tre*	19	*diciannove*
four	*quattro*	20	*venti*
five	*cinque*	21	*ventuno*
six	*sei*	22	*ventidue*
seven	*sette*	30	*trenta*
eight	*otto*	40	*quaranta*
nine	*nove*	50	*cinquanta*
10	*dieci*	60	*sessanta*
11	*undici*	70	*settanta*
12	*dodici*	80	*ottanta*
13	*tredici*	90	*novanta*
14	*quattordici*	100	*cento*
15	*quindici*	200	*due cento*
16	*sedici*	1000	*mille*

Gestures

Italians are famously theatrical and animated in dialogue and use a variety of gestures.

Side of left palm on side of right wrist as right wrist is flicked up   Go away

Hunched shoulders and arms lifted with palms of hands outwards   What am I supposed to do?

Thumb, index and middle finger of hand together, wrist upturned and shaking
What are you doing/what's going on?

Both palms together and moved up and down in front of stomach   Same as above

All fingers of hand squeezed together   To signify a place is packed full of people

Front or side of hand to chin   'Nothing', as in 'I don't understand' or 'I've had enough'

Flicking back of right ear   To signify someone is gay

Index finger in cheek   To signify good food

Questions

how?   *come?*
how much?   *quanto?*
when?   *quando?*
where?   *dove?*
why?   *perché?*
what?   *che cosa?*

Problems

I don't understand   *non capisco*
I don't know   *non lo so*
I don't speak Italian   *non parlo italiano*
How do you say ... (in Italian)?
   come si dice ... (in italiano)?
Is there anyone who speaks English?
   c'è qualcuno che parla inglese?

Shopping

this one/that one *questo/quello*
less *meno*
more *di più*
how much is it/are they? *quanto costa/costano?*
can I have…? *posso avere…?*

Travelling

one ticket for… *un biglietto per…*
single *solo andate*
return *andate ritorno*
does this go to…? *questo va a…?*
airport *aeroporto*
bus stop *fermata*
train *treno*
car *macchina*
taxi *tassi*

Eating & drinking

what do you recommend?
  che cosa mi consegna?
can I have the bill? *posso avere il conto?*
what's this? *cos'è questo?*
is there a menu? *c'è un menù?*
where's the toilet? *dov'è il bagno?*

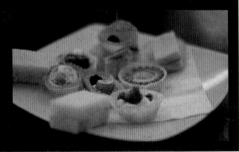

Food & drink

abbacchio alla romana
  milk-fed lamb roman style
acqua frizzante/naturale sparkling/still water
agnello lamb
anguria watermelon
antipasto starter
arancia orange
baccalà salt-cod
birra beer
carciofi artichokes
caffè coffee (ie espresso)
caffè macchiato espresso with a dash
  of foamed milk
carne meat
coda alla vaccinara oxtail
coniglio rabbit
coppa/cono cone/cup
dolce dessert
formaggio cheese
frutti di mare seafood
funghi mushrooms
gelato ice-cream
granita flavoured crushed ice
insalata salad
manzo beef
melanzane aubergine
olio oil
pane bread
peperoncino chilli pepper
peperone pepper (vegetable)
pesce fish
pollo chicken
polpette meatballs
pomodoro tomato
primo first course
rigatoni con la pajata rigatoni with
  unweaned calf intestines
rucola rocket
secondo second course
vino rosso/bianco red/white wine
vitello veal

Time

morning *mattina*
afternoon *pomeriggio*
evening *sera*
night *notte*
soon *presto/fra poco*
later *più tardi*
what time is it? *che ore sono?*
today/tomorrow/yesterday *oggi/domani/ieri*

Days

Monday *lunedi*
Tuesday *martedi*
Wednesday *mercoledi*
Thursday *giovedi*
Friday *venerdi*
Saturday *sabato*
Sunday *domenica*

Conversation

alright *va bene*
right then *allora*
who knows! *bo! / chi sa*
good luck! *in bocca al lupo!* (literally, 'in the mouth of the wolf')
one moment *un attimo*
hello (when answering a phone) *pronto* (literally, 'ready')
let's go! *andiamo!*
enough/stop *basta!*
give up! *dai!*
I like ... *mi piace ...*
how's it going? (well, thanks) *come va?* (bene, grazie)
how are you? *come sta/stai?* (polite/informal)

Hotels

a double/single room
una camera doppia/singola
a double bed *un letto matrimoniale*
bathroom *bagno*
Is there a view? *c'è una bella vista?*
can I see the room? *posso vedere la camera?*
when is breakfast? *a che ora è la colazione?*
can I have the key? *posso avere la chiave?*

Index

Index

credits

Footprint credits

Text editor: Beverley Jollands
Assistant editor: Alice Jell
Picture editor: Kassia Gawronski
Layout & production: Angus Dawson
Maps: Compass Maps Ltd

Managing Director: Andy Riddle
Commercial Director: Patrick Dawson
Publisher: Alan Murphy
Editorial: Sara Chare, Ria Gane,
Jenny Haddington, Felicity Laughton,
Nicola Gibbs
Design: Mytton Williams
Cartography: Sarah Sorenson, Rob Lunn,
Kevin Feeney, Emma Bryers
Sales & marketing: Liz Harper,
Hannah Bonnell
Advertising: Renu Sibal
Business Development: Zoë Jackson
Finance & Administration: Elizabeth Taylor

Print

Manufactured in Italy by EuroGrafica
Pulp from sustainable forests

Footprint Feedback

We try as hard as we can to make each
Footprint guide as up to date as possible
but, of course, things always change.
If you want to let us know about your
experiences – good, bad or ugly – then
don't delay, go to footprintbooks.com
and send in your comments.

Every effort has been made to ensure
that the facts in this guidebook are
accurate. However, travellers should still
obtain advice from consulates, airlines etc
about travel and visa requirements before
travelling. The authors and publishers
cannot accept responsibility for any loss,
injury or inconvenience however caused.

Publishing information

FootprintItalia Rome
1st edition
© Footprint Handbooks Ltd
April 2009

ISBN 978-1-906098-57-5
CIP DATA: A catalogue record for this
book is available from the British Library

® Footprint Handbooks and the Footprint
mark are a registered trademark of
Footprint Handbooks Ltd

Published by Footprint

6 Riverside Court
Lower Bristol Road
Bath BA2 3DZ, UK
T +44 (0)1225 469141
F +44 (0)1225 469461
www.footprintbooks.com

Distributed in North America by

Globe Pequot Press